D0804914

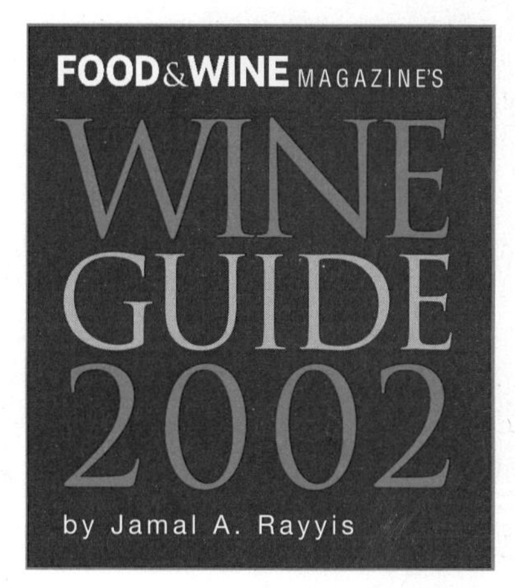
FOOD&WINE MAGAZINE'S
WINE
GUIDE
2002
by Jamal A. Rayyis

Cover photograph **Colin Cooke**

American Express Publishing Corporation
1120 Avenue of the Americas
New York, NY 10036

 ISSN: 1522-001X

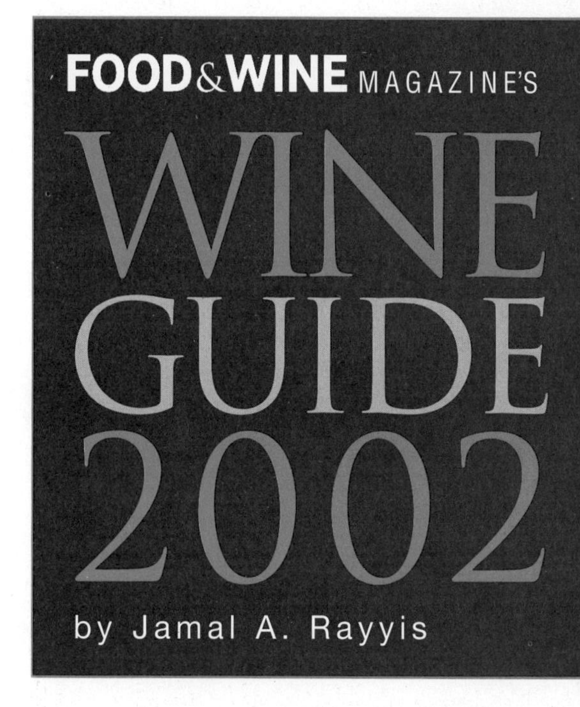

American Express
Publishing Corporation
New York

contents

foreword

by Mario Batali

There has never been a more exciting, rewarding time to be a chef in America. Previously unattainable ingredients and methods are now as close as the local grocery store or the Internet. A renewed appreciation of artisanal food has prompted more and more of us to take an active interest in what's really on the table; this interest naturally extends to the wine we drink. Without insulting the world's prolific producers of the ubiquitous Chardonnay and Merlot, it is safe to say that Americans have become more willing to explore the splendors of the less-known varietals, and equally willing to seek out consistent, informed advice about wine.

The wine experts in my restaurants (affectionately referred to as wine geeks) are trained not only to match wine to food, but also to teach guests a little something along the way. I urge every reader to approach *FOOD & WINE Magazine's Wine Guide 2002* as their own personal sommelier, always at the ready to impart quick and accessible information that will guide you through the exhilarating task of selecting the perfect wine to complement your meal, whether it's a simple plate of pasta with red sauce or, one of my favorites, a luxurious dish of crisp sweetbreads.

Host, *Molto Mario* and *Mario Eats Italy* on the TV Food Network
Co-Owner, Italian Wine Merchants
Chef/Owner, New York City's Babbo, Lupa, and Esca restaurants

introduction

by Jamal A. Rayyis

The world of wine is huge and gets bigger every year. Restaurants and wine shops compete to outdo one another by offering the biggest, most diverse selections possible. Without guidance, even experienced wine lovers can have trouble. You might wonder about wines from the Republic of Georgia, or South Africa's Pinotage, or Washington's Lemberger. Our guide is a map to navigate this sea of wine, giving helpful information as well as recommending specific bottles. As much as possible, we tasted wines blind, that is, with their identities hidden until we made our evaluations. From the thousands of wines tasted, we chose bottles based on these criteria: quality, value, and availability. We give wines from as many makers as possible—including large, national producers—to increase the chances that you'll be able to find the perfect wine for any occasion. But we don't ignore the esoteric—one thing that makes wine fun is discovering bottles from out-of-the-way places. This book isn't a library reference; it is a tool to use in wine shops and restaurants. Carry it with you and choose your wines with confidence.

key to symbols

This guide is different from most: It's up to date. Our recommendations are for the exact wines being released for sale this year. Recommendations include the following symbols:

Type	🍷 / 🍷 / 🍷	red wine / white wine / rosé wine
Quality	★★★★	**Outstanding** Worth a search
	★★★	**Excellent** Top-notch example of its type
	★★	**Very good** Distinctive
	★	**Good** Delicious everyday wine
Price	$$$$	$50 and up
	$$$	$25 to $50
	$$	$12 to $25
	$	$12 or less

guide to grape varieties

Thousands of different grape varieties are made into wine. Some of them are strictly local, while others have become so popular that they're grown almost everywhere that wine is produced. These are called the *international varieties.*

international white varieties

CHARDONNAY

Some of the greatest and some of the most banal wines in the world are Chardonnays. The variety seems to be everywhere wine grapes are grown and made into wines of nearly every style: the elegant, mineral-laden wines of Burgundy; the tropical-fruit- and oak-flavored wines of California; crisp Champagnes; and, in Austria, unctuous, nectarous dessert wines.

CHENIN BLANC

Some of France's greatest wines are made from Chenin Blanc. In the Loire Valley, its high acidity and lush fruit flavors are transformed into full-bodied, long-aging, dry wines, sumptuous dessert wines, and charming sparklers. Chenin Blanc is also honored in South Africa. In the U.S. it is not so respected, though it is made into eminently enjoyable light wines.

RIESLING

Held by many, including us, to be the world's greatest white grape, Riesling makes wines of incredible complexity, with high acidity and a potpourri of aromas and flavors: tropical fruit, apple, and pear along with flowers and minerals. Styles range from bone-dry to nectar-sweet. The best Rieslings come from Alsace, Germany, Austria, and New York State. Many can age for more than a decade.

SAUVIGNON BLANC

An important variety in France, Sauvignon Blanc is one of the two great white grapes of Bordeaux. And it makes even finer wines in the eastern part of the Loire Valley, where it is turned into the lemony, herbaceous wines of Sancerre and Pouilly-Fumé. However, for the last few years, the wine world has been wild about Sauvignon Blancs from New Zealand, which are highly pungent with grapefruit, green pepper, and boxwood flavors. South Africa, California, and Austria also make excellent Sauvignon Blancs.

SEMILLON

Besides Sauvignon Blanc, the other of Bordeaux's most important white grapes is Sémillon. It reaches its pinnacle as the main variety in the region's luxuriously sweet Sauternes. Sémillon is also blended with Sauvignon Blanc to make some great, full-bodied dry wines. It is also big in Australia, where it is frequently paired in blends with Chardonnay, as it is in Washington State.

international red varieties

CABERNET SAUVIGNON

For some wine aficionados, Cabernet Sauvignon is synonymous with red wine. We wouldn't go that far, but it does turn up in most of the world's wine-producing countries. It typically offers flavors like black currant and other berries, cedar, and green bell pepper, all of them smothered with tannin that softens with age. Cabernet excels in France's Bordeaux region and California's Napa Valley.

MERLOT

Once seen only as a grape to blend with Cabernet Sauvignon, Merlot has become one of the world's most popular varietals. It's not hard to understand why, since Merlot is typically easy to drink and full of nice plum and chocolate flavors. Much of the varietal is fairly dull these days, though. At its best, as it is in Bordeaux's Pomerol and in Washington State, Merlot makes some of the world's great wines.

PINOT NOIR

Called the heartbreak grape, Pinot Noir is difficult to grow and difficult to make into wine. But made right, it is as seductive as wine can be, with aromas and flavors like roses and tart fruits complemented by smokiness and earthiness. Burgundy is held up as the ultimate wine made from the variety, but excellent, if different, Pinot Noir comes from New Zealand and the U.S.

SYRAH

Powerful is the first word that comes to mind to describe Syrah. It's typically full-bodied and tannic, with blackberry, pepper, and smoke flavors. The northern Rhône is its domain in France, but California's Central Coast, Washington State, and Australia, where it is generally called Shiraz, also produce great versions.

other popular grapes

CABERNET FRANC

Related to Cabernet Sauvignon, Cabernet Franc is important in France. In Bordeaux, it adds tart-cherry and pepper flavors to blends. In the Loire, it makes light- to medium-bodied wines with tart-cherry, spice, and herb flavors. It's gaining favor in the U.S.

GEWURZTRAMINER

Known for its flamboyant flavors, Gewürztraminer offers honeysuckle and rose, lychee and apricot, mineral and spice. It is especially important in Alsace and parts of Germany. New York State and California also make excellent examples.

MARSANNE

Most at home in the south of France, Marsanne is now finding favor in California, where winemakers prize its honeyed almond flavor and full body. It's also successful in Australia and Switzerland.

MUSCAT

Really a family of white grapes with similar floral, musk, peach, and orange aromas and flavors, Muscat makes excellent dry and sweet wines. It grows in Alsace, the Mediterranean, and California.

NEBBIOLO

If the more than two thousand grape varieties in Italy have a king, it is Nebbiolo. Though grown in a few other places in Italy, as well as California, Nebbiolo shows its glorious black cherry, cedar, tar, and tobacco flavors best in Piedmont, where it is the basis of the noble Barolo and Barbaresco.

PINOT BLANC

Grown in Burgundy, Alsace, Germany, Italy, and California but most important in Austria, where it's called Weissburgunder, Pinot Blanc makes medium-bodied, mild-flavored white wines.

PINOT GRIS

In Italy Pinot Gris is known as Pinot Grigio and is made into light, brisk white wine. Elsewhere it generally produces full-bodied, nutty tasting wines.

SANGIOVESE

The basis of Chianti and Brunello, as well as other wines from all over Italy, Sangiovese is prized for its tart-cherry and leather flavors and its high acidity.

TEMPRANILLO

Grown throughout Spain, Tempranillo is preeminent as Rioja. Wine made from this grape has spice aromas, full, plummy flavor, and medium body.

VIOGNIER

An obscure white grape grown in France's northern Rhône, Viognier seemed on the verge of extinction before it was discovered by California winemakers, who were entranced by its peach, citrus, and floral aromas and flavors. Today it is grown in California's Central Coast region and in many parts of southern France.

ZINFANDEL

California's own great red variety, Zinfandel assumes several forms. It can be a light, quaffable red wine, a full-bodied, tannic wine with blackberry and spice flavors, or even a syrupy Port-style dessert wine. White Zinfandel is a rosé made from red Zinfandel grapes.

shortcut to finding varietals

Whatever your favorite varietal, it's probably made in several countries. Check here to locate recommendations from all the possibilities. You may even find something better than what you usually drink or a version that's just as good and less expensive.

wine style finder

It's white, but will it be too full-bodied to go with trout? What if a recipe suggests you accompany the dish with a full-bodied red like a Barolo from Piedmont, but you don't want to spend the money for that illustrious wine? Here you'll find just what you need and plenty of possibilities in each category—giving you tremendous flexibility in choosing a wine to complement whatever you plan to eat.

country	region	wines
light-bodied, dry white wines		
Argentina		Torrontés, 249
Austria		Grüner Veltliner, 207
California		Chenin Blanc, 31; Sauvignon Blanc, 26
France	*Alsace*	Pinot Blanc, 81; Riesling, 85
	Bordeaux	Entre-Deux-Mers, 95
	Loire Valley	Muscadet, 114
Greece		Roditis, 214
Italy	*Abruzzi*	Trebbiano d'Abruzzo, 167
	Friuli-Venezia Giulia & Trentino-Alto Adige	Pinot Grigio, 147
	Piedmont	Roero Arneis, 145
	Umbria	Orvieto, 167
	The Veneto	Soave, 150
Middle East & Northern Africa		Sauvignon Blanc, 225
Portugal		Bucelas, 189; Vinho Verde, 188
medium-bodied, dry white wines		
Argentina		Chardonnay, 249; Sauvignon Blanc, 249
Australia		Chardonnay, 227; Riesling, 229; Sauvignon Blanc, 230; Semillon, 230
Austria		Grüner Veltliner, 207; Riesling, 206; Weissburgunder, 208
California		Chardonnay, 22; Gewürztraminer, 29; Sauvignon Blanc, 26

country	region	wines
Chile		Chardonnay, 252
Eastern Europe		Chardonnay, 218; Furmint, 218; Sauvignon Blanc, 217
France	*Alsace*	Gewurztraminer, 84; Pinot Gris, 83; Riesling, 85
	Bordeaux	Côtes de Blaye, 95; Bordeaux Blanc, 94; Graves, 94
	Burgundy	Chablis, 99; Côte Chalonnaise, 105; Côte d'Or, 101; Mâconnais, 106
	Loire Valley	Chenin Blanc, 112; Muscadet, 114; Sauvignon Blanc, 115
	The Midi	Languedoc-Roussillon, 123
	Rhône Valley	Côtes-du-Rhône, 134
	Southwest	Côtes de Gascogne, 137
Germany	*Franken*	Müller-Thurgau, 202
	Mosel-Saar-Ruwer	Riesling, 193
	Pfalz	Riesling, 196
	Rheinhessen	Riesling, 200
Greece		Assyrtiko, 214
Italy	*Friuli-Venezia Giulia & Trentino-Alto Adige*	Pinot Grigio, 147; Tocai Friulano, 147
Middle East & Northern Africa		Rkatsiteli, 224
New York State		Chardonnay, 72; Gewürztraminer, 73; Riesling, 72
New Zealand		Chardonnay, 240; Riesling, 241; Sauvignon Blanc, 238
Oregon		Pinot Gris, 60
Portugal		Dão, 189
South Africa		Chardonnay, 256; Chenin Blanc, 257; Sauvignon Blanc, 256
Spain		Rioja, 179; Rueda, 184
Switzerland		Chasselas, 210
Washington State		Chardonnay, 64

country	region	wines

full-bodied, dry white wines

country	region	wines
Australia		Chardonnay, 227; Semillon, 229
Austria		Grüner Veltliner, 207; Riesling, 206; Weissburgunder, 208
California		Chardonnay, 22; Viognier, 30
Chile		Chardonnay, 252
France	*Alsace*	Gewurztraminer, 84; Pinot Gris, 83; Riesling, 85
	Burgundy	Chablis, 99; Côte d'Or, 101; Mâconnais, 106
Germany	*Pfalz*	Riesling, 196; Weissburgunder, 196
	Rheingau	Riesling, 198
	Rheinhessen	Riesling, 200
Greece		Roditis, 214
Italy	*Campania*	Fiano di Avellino, 170; Greco di Tufo, 170
	Piedmont	Chardonnay, 145; Gavi, 145
Middle East & Northern Africa		Chardonnay, 225; Rkatsiteli, 224
New Zealand		Sauvignon Blanc, 238
Portugal		Alentejo, 188; Douro, 188; Vinho Verde, 188
South Africa		Chardonnay, 256; Sauvignon Blanc, 256
Spain		Penedès, 183; Rías Baixas, 184; Rioja, 179
Switzerland		Chasselas, 210
Washington State		Chardonnay, 64

lightly sweet to moderately sweet white wines

country	region	wines
California		Riesling, 30
Germany	*Mosel-Saar-Ruwer*	Riesling, 193
	Rheinhessen	Riesling, 201
South Africa		Chenin Blanc, 257

light-bodied red wines

country	region	wines
France	*Burgundy*	Beaujolais Nouveau, 108
	Loire Valley	Cabernet Franc, 116
Italy	*Tuscany*	Chianti, 156

country	region	wines

medium-bodied red wines

country	region	wines
Argentina		Cabernet Sauvignon, 247
Australia		Shiraz, 231
California		Merlot, 42; Pinot Noir, 45; Syrah, 52
Chile		Cabernet Sauvignon, 251
Eastern Europe		Cabernet Sauvignon, 219
France	*Bordeaux*	Bordeaux Supérieur, 92; Côtes de Bourg, 93; Fronsac, 92; Haut-Médoc, 93; Margaux, 91; Médoc, 92; Pauillac, 91; Pessac-Léognan, 91; Premières Côtes de Bordeaux, 93; St-Estèphe, 92
	Burgundy	Beaujolais, 109; Côte d'Or, 103
	The Midi	Languedoc-Roussillon, 120
	Loire Valley	Cabernet Franc, 116; Sancerre, 117
	Rhône Valley	Côtes-du-Rhône, 133; Côtes-du-Rhône Villages, 133; Crozes-Hermitage, 129; St-Joseph, 129
Greece		Xynomavro, 215
Italy	*Abruzzi*	Montepulciano d'Abruzzo, 166
	Friuli-Venezia Giulia & Trentino-Alto Adige	Refosco, 149
	Piedmont	Dolcetto, 143; Gattinara, 144
	Tuscany	Carmignano, 160; Chianti, 155; Morellino di Scansano, 159; Rosso di Montalcino, 158; Vino Nobile de Montepulciano, 160
Middle East & Northern Africa		Red blends, 222
New York State		Cabernet Franc, 76; Pinot Noir, 76
New Zealand		Pinot Noir, 242
Oregon		Pinot Noir, 62
South Africa		Shiraz, 258; Pinotage, 258
Spain		Priorato, 183; Rioja, 179
Switzerland		Dôle, 211; Merlot, 211
Washington State		Merlot, 67

country	region	wines

full-bodied red wines

country	region	wines
Argentina		Cabernet Sauvignon, 246; Malbec, 246
Australia		Cabernet Sauvignon, 234; red blends, 235; Shiraz, 231
California		Cabernet Sauvignon, 35; Merlot, 42; Pinot Noir, 45; Syrah, 52; Zinfandel, 48
Chile		Cabernet Sauvignon, 254; Carmenère, 251
Eastern Europe		Cabernet Sauvignon, 219; Merlot, 219; Plavac Mali, 219
France	*Bordeaux*	Top Classified Growths *(Crus Classés)*, 91
	Burgundy	Beaujolais, 108; Côte d'Or, 103
	The Midi	Languedoc-Roussillon, 120; Provence, 125
	Rhône Valley	Châteauneuf-du-Pape, 132; Cornas, 128; Côte-Rôtie, 129; Côtes-du-Rhône Villages, 132; Gigondas, 133; Hermitage, 129; Rasteau, 132; St-Joseph, 129; Vacqueyras, 133
	Southwest	Cahors, 136; Côtes de Gascogne, 137; Madiran, 136
Greece		Agiorgitiko, 215
Italy	*Apulia*	Primitivo, 171
	Basilicata	Aglianico del Vulture, 171
	The Marches	Rosso Conero and Rosso Piceno, 166
	Piedmont	Barbaresco, 141; Barbera, 142; Barolo, 141; Dolcetto, 143
	Tuscany	Chianti, 155; Brunello, 157; Other Sangiovese-based wines, 159; Super Tuscans, 161
	The Veneto	Amarone, 152
Middle East & Northern Africa		Cabernet Sauvignon, 222; red blends, 222
Portugal		Douro, 188
South Africa		Merlot, 258; Pinotage, 258
Spain		Navarre, 182; Penedès, 183; Priorato, 182; Ribera del Duero, 180; Rioja, 176
Washington State		Merlot, 67; Cabernet Sauvignon, 67; Syrah, 68

how to handle a wine list

Few things cause diners as much anxiety as the presentation of a wine list. But you can conquer any list with a few easy steps:

Assess the list A good list is diverse or it specializes in a certain region. There should be wines in different price ranges, with a few priced under $30. If you see a Riesling—not popular in the U.S., but an excellent complement to many dishes—the restaurant is probably serious about wine. A poor list might be limited in selection (not necessarily in number: fifty California Chardonnays and a handful of other whites can be trouble), have too many wines from one producer, or fail to list vintages. If the list is poor, order the least expensive thing that you recognize as being reasonably good.

Ask questions A wine list is just a menu. You can ask how tannic the Cabernet is just as you inquire how the salmon is prepared. Very few people can look at a list and know exactly what all the wines taste like at that moment. It's the restaurant's job to explain them to you.

Taste the wine When the bottle arrives, make sure it's exactly what you ordered—the vintage, the producer, the blend or varietal. If not, say so. If the listed wine is out, you might prefer to choose something else. You may be presented with the cork. Ignore it. We've had fine wines with spoiled corks and bad wines with sound corks. Sniff the wine in your glass. If it smells like sulfur, cabbage, or skunk, say that you think the wine might be off and request a few minutes to see if the odors dissipate. If they remain, the wine is probably bad. Another problem: About 5 percent of wines, in all price ranges, are "corked"—the cork was improperly processed, and the wine tastes like musty cork or wet cardboard.

Send a bottle back if necessary If the wine is off, the server should take it away and offer a new bottle. The restaurant gets credit for bad wines anyway. Disliking a wine is not a reason to send a bottle back unless a server described it quite inaccurately, as light and fruity when it's heavy and tannic, for instance.

california

When it comes to wine, California rules. With consistent weather, bright sunshine, ocean-cooled breezes, and a wide variety of terrains, the Golden State dominates the U.S. market. Wine is made in nearly every state, but California vintners account for 96 percent of the country's production and supply 75 percent of bottles purchased in the U.S.

on the label

Overwhelmingly, grape variety takes precedence over region on American wine labels. By California law, a wine labeled by variety must contain at least 75 percent of that grape. Producers often choose especially good quality grapes for wines labeled *reserve* or *proprietor's blend*, but the terms have no legal meaning. *Meritage* refers to blends of traditional Bordeaux varieties. Meritage wines, which can be red or white, are certified by an industry group that enforces strict guidelines, including the rule that the moniker be used only for a winery's best, most expensive wines.

white wines

CHARDONNAY

Countless vintners claim to make Chardonnay, the noble white grape from Burgundy, into wines like those from the fabled French region, but California Chards have a style of their own. Unlike the restrained, lemony, and mineral-tinged Burgundies, California versions tend toward exuberant tropical fruit flavors and more than a hint of smoke and vanilla from oak aging. For

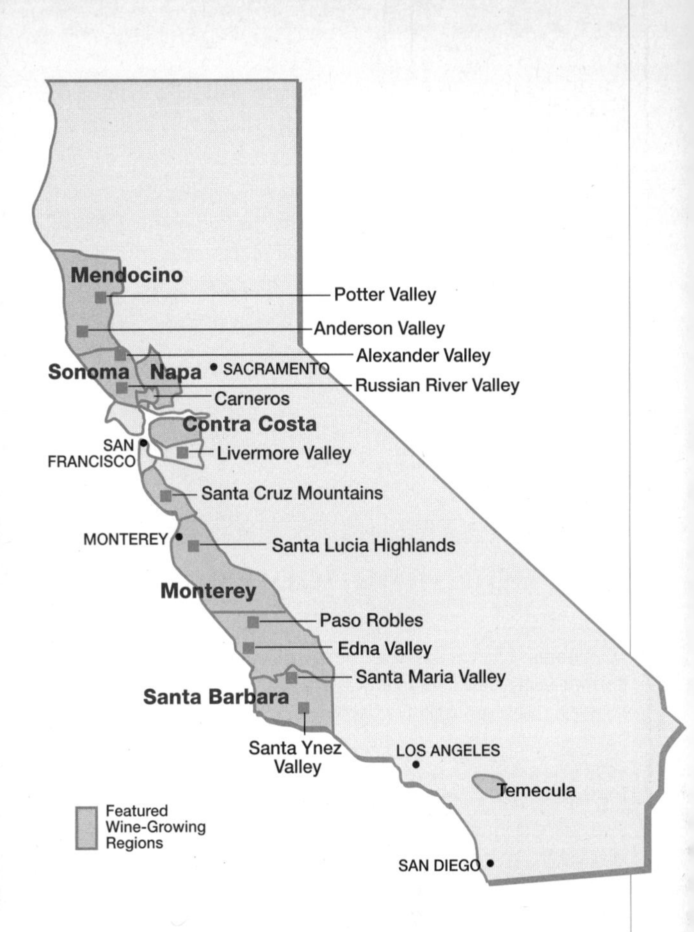

many, this has gone too far. For others, more is still better. Fortunately, among the tens of millions of cases made in the state each year, there is a wide range of styles.

at the table

Because of their assertive flavor, California Chards pose serious matching problems. Subtlety's not in vogue, but many wine-makers are abandoning the big oak crutches and allowing the fruit to stand on its own. Chardonnays that are light and lemony in style go well with lean fish, such as snapper or halibut; medium-bodied wines are good with roast chicken, turkey, or creamy cheeses like Camembert. Save the strong, oaky wines for smoked or grilled salmon or relatively mild-flavored meats like pork or veal, especially when they're served with a fruity sauce.

the bottom line It's hard to find a noteworthy California Chardonnay for under $12. Those that exist tend to taste "manufactured"—not necessarily a bad thing if you're looking for a simple white wine to go with whatever's grilling on the barbecue. Between $12 and $25, things get more interesting. The sky might not yet be the limit at the top end, but some wines are about $75 per bottle, a reflection of their rarity as much as their quality.

what to buy CHARDONNAY

1998	1999	2000
★★★	★★	★★★

recommended wines

1998 Gallo of Sonoma Estate, Northern Sonoma ★★★★ $$$
dry, full-bodied, medium acidity, heavy oak **drink now–10 years**
No holding back here. A big, big Chardonnay, excellent for its style.

1998 Mer Soleil Barrel Fermented, Central Coast ★★★★ $$$
dry, full-bodied, medium acidity, heavy oak **drink now–6 years**
Sure, exuberantly fruity, oaky, buttery Chards are a bit of a cliché, but when they're this good, we can't help but be happy.

1999 Rudd, Russian River Valley ★★★★ $$$
dry, full-bodied, high acidity, medium oak **drink now–10 years**
An incredibly lush wine with delicious peach, pear, orange, and lemon flavors brought out by the acidity.

1999 Far Niente, Napa Valley ★★★ $$$$
dry, medium-bodied, medium acidity, heavy oak **drink now–8 years**
Sumptuous fruit and flowers, with a shake of pepper.

1999 Au Bon Climat Sanford & Benedict Vineyard, Santa Ynez Valley ★★★ $$$
dry, medium-bodied, medium acidity, heavy oak **drink now–6 years**
Toasty oak and fruit flavors with a welcome flinty, mineral edge.

1999 Cakebread Cellars, Napa Valley ★★★ $$$
dry, medium-bodied, medium acidity, medium oak **drink now–6 years**
Nuts and honey mingle with the surprising passion-fruit flavors.

1998 Canepa Gauer Vineyard Adobe III, Alexander Valley ★★★ $$$
dry, medium-bodied, medium acidity, medium oak drink now–8 years
A supremely balanced wine by Helen Turley, the darling of the wine world.

1998 Chateau Montelena, Napa Valley ★★★ $$$
dry, medium-bodied, medium acidity, medium oak drink now–8 years
The winery that beat the best of Burgundy in the famed Paris tasting of 1976 produces another fine Burgundian number with good minerality.

1999 Ferrari-Carano, Alexander Valley ★★★ $$$
dry, medium-bodied, high acidity, medium oak drink now–5 years
Like a yeasty tropical bread with chunks of mango and a squeeze of lime.

1998 Grgich Hills, Napa Valley ★★★ $$$
dry, medium-bodied, high acidity, medium oak drink now–6 years
A beautifully balanced wine full of fruit flavors and striking mineral notes.

1993 Kalin Cuvée LD, Sonoma County ★★★ $$$
dry, full-bodied, medium acidity, medium oak drink now–5 years
Roasted, jammy fruit and vanilla flavors in a rich, golden wine.

1999 Kendall-Jackson Great Estates, Monterey County ★★★ $$$
dry, full-bodied, medium acidity, heavy oak drink now–6 years
An explosion of citrus and creamy mango flavors.

1998 Matanzas Creek Winery, Sonoma Valley ★★★ $$$
dry, full-bodied, medium acidity, medium oak drink now–7 years
A liqueur-like texture. Rich fruit flavors highlighted by vanilla notes.

1999 Sanford Sanford & Benedict Vineyard, Santa Ynez Valley ★★★ $$$
dry, medium-bodied, high acidity, medium oak drink now–6 years
Fruitiness along with excellent acidity make this a winner with food.

1998 Talbott Sleepy Hollow Vineyard, Monterey ★★★ $$$
dry, medium-bodied, high acidity, heavy oak drink now–6 years
The best Sleepy Hollow yet. Big but restrained peach and pineapple flavors.

1999 Babcock Grand Cuvée, Santa Ynez Valley ★★★ $$
dry, medium-bodied, medium acidity, medium oak drink now–6 years
Orange, mango, and pineapple from first sniff to last sip.

1999 Cambria Katherine's, Santa Maria Valley ★★★ $$
dry, full-bodied, medium acidity, medium oak drink now–6 years
So rich we'd swear butter was stirred into this well-made wine.

RAIN, RAIN GO AWAY

In 1998 and 1999, El Niño/La Niña affected some of California's prime winemaking regions by bringing cool summer temperatures and excess rain that led to floods. Overall, wines from these vintages, now coming on the market, are not as full as usual. That said, winemakers have shown their skills in these less than ideal years and have produced some interesting wines. The weather during the 2000 growing season brought some normalcy back to California winemaking, but rains toward the end of the season dampened hopes for a great vintage.

1999 Clos du Bois Calcaire Vineyard, Alexander Valley ★★★ $$
dry, medium-bodied, high acidity, medium oak **drink now–5 years**
A lovely wine with herbal, lemon, pine, and mineral notes.

1999 Cuvaison, Carneros ★★★ $$
dry, full-bodied, high acidity, medium oak **drink now–3 years**
The flavor makes us imagine a spicy pineapple butterscotch pudding. Balanced by mouthwatering acidity. Really good.

1999 Justin Vineyards & Winery Reserve, Paso Robles ★★★ $$
dry, full-bodied, medium acidity, medium oak **drink now–6 years**
A classically big, buttery Chardonnay. Nicely restrained oak.

1999 Mazzocco River Lane, Sonoma County ★★★ $$
dry, light-bodied, high acidity, medium oak **drink now–4 years**
Light, zingy, and full-flavored all at once.

1999 Morro Bay Vineyards, Central Coast ★★★ $$
dry, medium-bodied, medium acidity, medium oak **drink now–6 years**
Very full fruit flavors, with pepper and mineral notes that swoop in at the end.

1998 Navarro Vineyards, Mendocino ★★★ $$
dry, medium-bodied, high acidity, medium oak **drink now–7 years**
Fruit salad minus those pesky little marshmallows. Delicious.

1999 Vita Nova Rancho Viñedo Reserve, Santa Barbara County ★★★ $$
dry, full-bodied, medium acidity, medium oak **drink now–8 years**
Autumn in a bottle, with fresh-pressed apple cider and clovelike scents, dried apricot and lovely orange flavors. Really nice.

1999 Chateau St. Jean, Sonoma County ★★ $$
dry, medium-bodied, medium acidity, medium oak drink now–4 years
Appealing pineapple and lime flavors and vanilla aroma.

1999 Fritz Winery Dutton Ranch, Russian River Valley ★★ $$
dry, full-bodied, high acidity, heavy oak drink now–8 years
Citrus and oak, with some vanilla, mineral, and spice flavors. Great acidity.

1999 Frog's Leap, Napa Valley ★★ $$
dry, medium-bodied, medium acidity, medium oak drink now–3 years
Moderate in everything—entirely reliable, if not wildly exciting.

1999 Hess Collection, Napa Valley ★★ $$
dry, full-bodied, medium acidity, heavy oak drink now–3 years
Loaded with tropical flavors and spicy oak. Buttery texture.

1999 Jekel Vineyards Gravelstone, Monterey ★★ $$
dry, light-bodied, high acidity, medium oak drink now–6 years
As refreshing as green papaya salad dressed with lime vinaigrette.

1999 La Crema, Sonoma Coast ★★ $$
dry, full-bodied, medium acidity, medium oak drink now–5 years
Sumptuous—like lemon mousse with tart, creamy flavor and velvety texture.

1998 Logan, Monterey ★★ $$
dry, medium-bodied, high acidity, medium oak drink now–4 years
Talbott Vineyards' second-label wine does the home team proud.

1998 Robert Mondavi Winery, Carneros ★★ $$
dry, medium-bodied, medium acidity, heavy oak drink now–7 years
Classic California Chardonnay with buttery oak, pineapple, and lemon flavors.

1999 Burgess, Napa Valley ★ $$
dry, medium-bodied, medium acidity, medium oak drink now–2 years
Citrus flavors matched by good acidity.

1999 Kendall-Jackson Camelot Vineyard, Santa Maria Valley ★ $$
dry, full-bodied, high acidity, heavy oak drink now–2 years
A buttery, toasty, pineapple-y cliché of a Chardonnay with a dollop of acidity.

1999 Beringer Founders' Estate, California ★ $
dry, medium-bodied, medium acidity, medium oak drink now
Oak, orange, and pineapple. Nice for the price.

2000 Fetzer Vineyards Sundial, Mendocino ★ $
dry, medium-bodied, high acidity, medium oak drink now
A good, fruity, everyday Chardonnay with excellent acidity.

SAUVIGNON BLANC

Always the bridesmaid in the world of California white wine, Sauvignon Blanc is a grape in search of definition. It has reached its apogee in France's Loire Valley, as well as in New Zealand, but California winemakers seem to be undecided about what to make of it. Many of the state's Sauvignon Blancs are pale and thin, others Chardonnay-esque with heavy oak. This is a shame, since well-made Sauvignon Blanc can be wonderfully aromatic and have flavors of fresh-cut grass, lemon, and melon, along with mouth-tingling acidity. In 1968, Robert Mondavi released an oak-aged Sauvignon Blanc under the moniker Fumé Blanc, which evoked the Loire Valley's famed Pouilly-Fumé. No matter that the styles of wine were very different, Mondavi's sold well, and the name was adopted by other California producers, especially for their cask-aged Sauvignons.

at the table

With its relatively light body, herb and lemon flavors, and good acidity, a fine Sauvignon Blanc is a natural with shellfish and mild-flavored fish like trout or cod. Sauvignon Blanc also works well with simple chicken dishes or pasta in cream sauce. For cheese, think light and fresh—an ash-covered American goat cheese, for instance. Oaky Fumé Blanc requires something more assertive and will make an excellent match with food that's smoky from the grill, especially pork. Also try it with grilled octopus, swordfish, or vegetables.

the bottom line Because it is often, and unfairly, overlooked in favor of Chardonnay, Sauvignon Blanc can be had for a bargain price. Many of the non-oaked bottles sell for between $8 and $14 and are terrific. The oaked wines are more expensive, between $12 and $24, with a few over $30.

recommended wines

1994 Kalin Reserve, Potter Valley ★★★★ $$$
dry, full-bodied, medium acidity, medium oak **drink now–5 years**
By far the oldest California Sauvignon Blanc we tasted this year, as well as the best. We'd compare it to a grand white Bordeaux: Margaux or Haut-Brion.

1998 Grgich Hills Fumé Blanc, Napa Valley ★★★★ $$
dry, medium-bodied, high acidity, light oak **drink now–2 years**
A cornucopia of summer fruit, with melon, fig, peach, and plum flavors.

2000 Blockheadia Ringnosii, Napa Valley ★★★ $$
dry, full-bodied, high acidity, no oak **drink now–2 years**
Here is a wine that goes against the current Sauvignon Blanc vogue by emphasizing tropical fruit rather than the usual grass and gooseberry flavors.

1999 Caymus Vineyards, Napa Valley ★★★ $$
dry, medium-bodied, high acidity, medium oak **drink now–2 years**
Peach, mango, lemon, and oak. Very good acidity.

2000 Dry Creek Vineyard Fumé Blanc, Sonoma County ★★★ $$
dry, light-bodied, high acidity, no oak **drink now**
One of California's most highly regarded producers of Sauvignon Blanc comes through again.

1999 Honig Vineyard Reserve, Napa Valley ★★★ $$
dry, medium-bodied, high acidity, light oak **drink now–2 years**
Lemon, fresh-cut grass, and jalapeños. Very, very good.

1999 Matanzas Creek Winery, Sonoma County ★★★ $$
dry, medium-bodied, high acidity, medium oak **drink now–2 years**
A delicious wine that has everything we want from Sauvignon Blanc: lemon and grass flavors, a touch of smokiness, and very good acidity.

1999 Murphy-Goode Barrel Fermented Reserve Fumé, Alexander Valley ★★★ $$
dry, medium-bodied, high acidity, medium oak **drink now–4 years**
A mélange of citrus, spice, floral, and mineral flavors highlighted by loads of palate-cleansing acidity. A touch of oak adds a bit of smoke.

1999 Navarro Vineyards Cuvée 128, Mendocino ★★★ $$
dry, medium-bodied, high acidity, no oak **drink now**
Vibrant with fruit and chile pepper flavors. Zowie.

1998 Robert Mondavi Winery, Stags Leap District ★★★ $$
dry, medium-bodied, high acidity, medium oak **drink now–3 years**
A unique, lushly flavorful wine from one of California's earliest Sauvignon Blanc innovators.

1999 Sanford, Central Coast ★★★ $$
dry, medium-bodied, high acidity, no oak **drink now**
Excellent grassy, fruity, floral flavors and a really long finish.

2000 Buena Vista, California ★★★ $
dry, medium-bodied, high acidity, no oak **drink now**
Like eating a cool peach in the middle of a fresh-mown lawn.

1999 Duckhorn Vineyards, Napa Valley ★★ $$
dry, full-bodied, high acidity, light oak **drink now–3 years**
Distinct flavors of lemon and minerals along with a nice smokiness.

2000 Ferrari-Carano Fumé Blanc, Sonoma County ★★ $$
dry, medium-bodied, medium acidity, light oak **drink now–3 years**
A rather sumptuous wine with tangy tropical fruit and peach flavors.

2000 Frog's Leap, Napa Valley ★★ $$
dry, medium-bodied, medium acidity, no oak **drink now**
Here's a lemony, rosemary-scented wine, perfect for a simple roast chicken.

2000 Geyser Peak, Sonoma County ★★ $
dry, medium-bodied, high acidity, no oak **drink now**
A straightforward wine. Citrus, just-cut grass, and green pepper flavors.

1999 Jepson, Mendocino County ★★ $
dry, light-bodied, high acidity, no oak **drink now**
Like a light Sancerre, with citrus and melon flavors. Good acidity.

2000 Shenandoah Vineyards of California, Amador County ★★ $
dry, medium-bodied, high acidity, no oak **drink now**
From the Sierra foothills comes a delicious fruity, spicy, floral wine.

1999 Callaway Coastal, California ★ $
dry, light-bodied, high acidity, no oak **drink now**
A good choice for salads. Refreshing.

1999 Meridian Vineyards, California ★ $
dry, medium-bodied, medium acidity, light oak **drink now**
A buttery, citrus-tinged wine with lots of minerality. Drink this one really cold.

other white wines

The California wine industry's history is one of experimentation and of chasing "the next big thing." Now being planted as quickly as possible: white wines from grapes traditionally grown in France's Rhône Valley—such as Viognier (vee-oh-n'yay),

Marsanne, and Roussanne—as well as the Alsace varieties Pinot Blanc and Pinot Gris. California-grown Pinot Blanc may be in vogue because it takes on Chardonnay-like qualities. And while Pinot Gris is often made in the steely Alsace style, it is also made in the more exuberant style of the wildly popular Italian Pinot Grigio (the same grape). The flip side: Grapes can fall from fashion nearly as fast. Gewürztraminer (geh-VAIRTZ-tra-mee-ner), for instance, grows well in California but seems to be on its way out.

at the table

Rhône-style wines usually work exceptionally well with lean white fish, bouillabaisse, and roast Cornish hens. Relatively full in body and flavor, Pinot Blanc and Pinot Gris are great with grilled fish steaks, like swordfish or tuna, and will stand up to pâtés too.

the bottom line Until vineyards reach greater maturity and harvests increase, these "alternative" whites will remain expensive. However, as demand hasn't fully developed, most aren't overly pricey. You can find good quality wines for between $12 and $25. A few rare luxury bottles cost $70 or more. Rieslings (reece-ling), Gewürztraminers, and Chenin Blancs can be found for substantially less, frequently under $15. There are exceptions, of course, but if you pay more for one of these less stylish beauties, you'll generally get a superb bottle of wine.

recommended wines

1993 Kalin Semillon, Livermore Valley ★★★★ $$$
dry, full-bodied, medium acidity, medium oak **drink now–8 years**
Semillon is a bit unusual in California, but is there a better one made in the U.S.? We doubt it.

1999 Caymus Vineyards Conundrum, California ★★★★ $$
dry, full-bodied, high acidity, medium oak **drink now–3 years**
This mélange of white grape varieties is one of our favorite California wines.

1999 Claiborne & Churchill Alsatian Style Dry Gewürztraminer, Central Coast ★★★★ $$
dry, medium-bodied, high acidity, no oak **drink now–8 years**
Great wine—so aromatic and flavorful, it reminds us of a Grand Cru from Alsace.

1999 Equus Viognier, Central Coast ★★★★ $$
dry, full-bodied, medium acidity, medium oak **drink now–8 years**
Viognier from California is often peachy and floral. Here, there are some floral notes, but the smoke, orange, and caramel flavors make it really impressive.

1999 Freemark Abbey Johannisberg Riesling, Napa Valley ★★★★ $
dry, full-bodied, high acidity, no oak **drink now–10 years**
Full-bodied as a dry Rheingau Spätlese. Amazingly, it has the petrol notes a Riesling lover would expect from a fully aged wine.

2000 Au Bon Climat 50% Pinot Blanc, 50% Pinot Gris, Santa Barbara County ★★★ $$
dry, full-bodied, high acidity, medium oak **drink now–2 years**
Racy acidity courses through this citrus- and pear-flavored wine.

1999 Bedford Thompson Gewürztraminer, Santa Barbara County ★★★ $$
dry, full-bodied, high acidity, no oak **drink now–4 years**
Very dry. Honeysuckle, stone, herb, and nut flavors. Excellent.

1999 Etude Pinot Gris, Napa ★★★ $$
dry, medium-bodied, high acidity, no oak **drink now–8 years**
Pure fruit flavors come through: orange, tangerine, grapefruit. Terrific acidity.

2000 Iron Horse Vineyards T bar T Proprietor Grown Viognier, Alexander Valley ★★★ $$
dry, full-bodied, high acidity, no oak **drink now–5 years**
We're always on the lookout for the unusual, and this wine certainly goes beyond the typical Viognier. It stopped us in our tracks.

2000 Jepson Viognier, Mendocino County ★★★ $$
dry, medium-bodied, high acidity, no oak **drink now–3 years**
Lemon and orange. Delicious mango and passion fruit. Very good acidity.

1999 Navarro Vineyards Gewürztraminer, Anderson Valley ★★★ $$
dry, medium-bodied, high acidity, no oak **drink now–8 years**
A quality Gewürz, with an explosion of citrus flavor.

1999 Qupé Alban Vineyard Roussanne, Edna Valley ★★★ $$
dry, full-bodied, medium acidity, medium oak **drink now–6 years**
Like gold in a glass. We love this Roussanne.

1999 R. H. Phillips EXP Viognier, Dunnigan Hills ★★★ $$
dry, full-bodied, high acidity, no oak **drink now–3 years**
A lovely taste in the peach-apricot family. Very good acidity.

IT'S THE BEGONIAS, STUPID

A shipment of ornamental plants from the South may be responsible for the latest woe that has befallen California winemakers—the glassy-winged sharpshooter. The insect carries Pierce's disease, which can kill grapevines in three to five years. Temecula's third-largest winery, Callaway, has lost so many vineyards to Pierce's disease that it now gets most of its grapes from California's Central Coast and has added "coastal" to its name. Bonny Doon has lost all its Santa Cruz Mountains vineyards to the insect, which has now appeared in Napa and Sonoma too.

1999 Treana Winery Mer Soleil Vineyard White, Central Coast ★★★ $$
dry, full-bodied, medium acidity, medium oak **drink now–6 years**
With peachy Viognier and tropical-fruit Marsanne, Treana shows just what the famous Mer Soleil Vineyard can do.

2000 Navarro Vineyards Old Vine Cuvée Chenin Blanc, Mendocino ★★★ $
dry, medium-bodied, high acidity, no oak **drink now–2 years**
Chenin Blanc, which makes some of France's finest wines, often gets short shrift in California. But not here.

1998 Beringer Alluvium Blanc, Knights Valley ★★ $$
dry, full-bodied, medium acidity, medium oak **drink now–4 years**
Sauvignon Blanc and Semillon may be the majority in this blend, but it's the Chardonnay that dominates.

1999 Borgo Buon Natale Primogénito, Santa Maria Valley ★★ $$
dry, medium-bodied, medium acidity, light oak **drink now**
Northern Italy comes to the Central Coast in this blend of Pinot Grigio and Pinot Bianco with Tocai Friulano, which is rarely used in California. Enjoy!

1999 Frog's Leap Leapfrögmilch, Napa Valley ★★ $$
dry, light-bodied, high acidity, no oak **drink now**
Don't let the playful name fool you. Though this is a light-hearted wine, it's not frivolous.

1999 Geyser Peak Riesling, Russian River Valley ★★ $$
dry, full-bodied, high acidity, no oak **drink now–5 years**
A concentrated wine with good balancing acidity.

1999 La Famiglia di Robert Mondavi Pinot Grigio, California ★★ $$
dry, medium-bodied, high acidity, no oak **drink now**
Not as lively on the palate as an Italian Pinot Grigio, this version relies on its fruit appeal. Still, there's plenty of nice tanginess here.

1999 McDowell Marsanne, Mendocino ★★ $$
dry, medium-bodied, medium acidity, light oak **drink now–3 years**
This is a nice wine, with full pineapple and pear flavors that are balanced by fine acidity.

1999 Pepi Arneis, Central Coast ★★ $$
dry, medium-bodied, medium acidity, no oak **drink now–2 years**
Made from the Italian grape variety widely grown in Piedmont. Lots of fruit flavor mixes with palate-cleansing mineral notes.

2000 Qupé Marsanne, Santa Barbara County ★★ $$
dry, full-bodied, medium acidity, light oak **drink now–8 years**
We simply love Marsanne's sumptuous fruit and spice flavors, whether the wine comes from France or California. This one lives up to all our expectations.

2000 Rosenblum Cellars Ripkin Vineyard Viognier, Lodi ★★ $$
off-dry, medium-bodied, high acidity, medium oak **drink now–3 years**
Lovely aroma. Slightly off-dry, with tingly acidity.

2000 Verdad Ibarra-Young Vineyard White Wine, Santa Ynez Valley ★★ $$
dry, full-bodied, medium acidity, light oak **drink now–2 years**
Government bureaucracy keeps Verdad from telling us this is made from northern Spain's Albariño grape. It's a wine any Spaniard would be proud of.

1999 Callaway Coastal Chenin Blanc, California ★★ $
dry, light-bodied, high acidity, no oak **drink now**
Pineapple, lemon, and jalapeño flavors balanced by good acidity.

2000 Dry Creek Vineyard Dry Chenin Blanc, Clarksburg ★★ $
dry, light-bodied, high acidity, no oak **drink now**
A wonderful, refreshing wine with herbal and lemon-lime flavors. Lots of acidity. Very nicely priced.

NV Rosenblum Cellars Vintners Cuvée Blanc III Vin Blanc Extraordinaire, California ★★ $
dry, medium-bodied, medium acidity, no oak **drink now**
A light-hearted wine boasting lemon, peach, and strawberry flavors.

2000 Beringer Johannisberg Riesling, California ★ $
off-dry, medium-bodied, medium acidity, no oak **drink now**
A nice, simple wine. Its slight sweetness is balanced by enough acidity.

1999 Jekel Vineyards Riesling, Monterey County ★ $
dry, medium-bodied, high acidity, no oak **drink now**
Hints of petrol, orange, and mineral scents and flavors immediately give this away as Riesling.

1999 Meridian Vineyards Gewürztraminer, Santa Barbara County ★ $
off-dry, medium-bodied, medium acidity, no oak **drink now**
Some floral notes mixed with lychee, honey, and mineral flavors as well as a touch of botrytis.

rosés

Popular, sweet, uninteresting White Zinfandel has now been joined by more worthy rosés made from Pinot Noir, Grenache, and Cinsault (san-so) grapes.

at the table

Drier than White Zinfandel, with nice fruit flavors and a hint of spice, the Pinot Noir, Grenache, and Cinsault rosés are good not only for summer quaffing, but also with shrimp tacos and other Mexican fare, and with holiday turkeys and hams.

the bottom line You should be able to pick up a decent bottle for about $10.

recommended wines

1998 Beringer Rosé de Saignée, California ★★★★ $$
dry, medium-bodied, high acidity **drink now**
A serious rosé from the world's largest maker of White Zinfandel? Indeed. And it's excellent.

2000 Iron Horse Vineyards Rosato di Sangiovese, Alexander Valley ★★★ $$
dry, medium-bodied, high acidity **drink now**
Complex fruit, spice, and herb flavors that expand with a little time in the glass. Very good acidity.

1999 Makor La Risa de Rosa Carignan Rosé, Redwood Valley ★★ $
dry, medium-bodied, medium acidity **drink now**
The faint fragrances of cherry and rose find bolder expression on the palate. Really nice.

2000 Zaca Mesa Z Gris, Santa Barbara County ★ $
dry, medium-bodied, medium acidity **drink now**
The strawberry and cherry flavors would be nice on their own, but we're intrigued by the hints of orange zest and spices.

red wines

Until about ten years ago, red wines made up only 14 percent of California's production. Interest in reds has picked up considerably, and they are now at 31 percent.

CABERNET SAUVIGNON, CABERNET FRANC, & MERITAGE

The Bordeaux variety Cabernet Sauvignon is king in California. It produces full-bodied, tannic wines that boast a host of flavors ranging from cassis to mint. The best ones age beautifully. If you come across a bottle that's over ten years old, do yourself a favor and try it. A close relation, Cabernet Franc, also from Bordeaux, is smoky and a bit less tannic.

Despite the California penchant for single-grape wines, many vintners have always produced blends, a practice in keeping with traditional Bordeaux winemaking. The best of these bottlings are generally called Meritage (MARE-eh-tij; see On the Label, page 20), and Cabernet Sauvignon often dominates the mix.

at the table

Tannic Cabernet Sauvignon calls for the likes of grilled steaks, rack of lamb, or roasted venison. Vegetarians might try it with grilled vegetable kebabs or a wild mushroom risotto. Cabernet Franc is great with roast loin of lamb. Blends can be used in much the same way; prime rib of beef has no better friend.

the bottom line Interesting Cabernet Sauvignons go for $25 and up—way, way up at the top end, to over $100 a bottle. Blends are about the same. Cabernet Franc can be found for $15 to $50.

what to buy CABERNET SAUVIGNON

1996	1997	1998	1999	2000
★★★	★★★★	★★★	★★	★★★

recommended wines

1997 Burgess Enveiere, Napa Valley ★★★★ $$$$
dry, full-bodied, full tannin, medium acidity **drink in 3–15 years**
One look at the imposing bottle gives you an idea of what to expect. One taste of the deep fruit and violet and lavender flavors says you were right.

1997 Colgin Herb Lamb Vineyard Cabernet Sauvignon, Napa Valley ★★★★ $$$$
dry, full-bodied, full tannin, medium acidity **drink now–15 years**
Loads of fruit and spice aromas and flavors. Excellent.

1997 Dalla Valle Vineyards Cabernet Sauvignon, Napa Valley ★★★★ $$$$
dry, full-bodied, medium tannin, medium acidity **drink now–15 years**
It's all here: beautiful fruit, nut, spice, and floral flavors. One of the finest California Cabernets we have ever tasted.

1996 Heitz Cellar Martha's Vineyard Cabernet Sauvignon, Napa Valley ★★★★ $$$$
dry, full-bodied, medium tannin, medium acidity **drink in 3–12 years**
Heitz has been making some of the best Cabernets in California for more than thirty years, and this one belongs at the top of the heap.

1997 Kathryn Kennedy Cabernet Sauvignon, Santa Cruz Mountains ★★★★ $$$$
dry, full-bodied, full tannin, medium acidity **drink in 5–20 years**
Full fruit and mineral flavors, smoothed out by a kiss of vanilla. A great wine.

1997 Ridge Monte Bello, Santa Cruz Mountains ★★★★ $$$$
dry, full-bodied, full tannin, medium acidity **drink in 3–20 years**
Ridge's Monte Bello consistently dazzles with bold flavor, and in great vintages like 1997, the wine is almost too good for words.

1998 Rudd Jericho Canyon Vineyard Cabernet Sauvignon, Napa Valley ★★★★ $$$$
dry, full-bodied, full tannin, medium acidity **drink in 2–15 years**
Gorgeously balanced flavors: fruits, nuts, herbs, and minerals. Amazing wine.

1997 Beringer Private Reserve Cabernet Sauvignon, Napa Valley ★★★★ $$$
dry, full-bodied, full tannin, medium acidity **drink in 2–15 years**
Cabernet as it should be: cassis and black pepper on the nose; full fruit, tar, tobacco, and big tannin on the palate. A classic.

1998 Franciscan Oakville Estate Magnificat, Napa Valley ★★★★ $$$
dry, full-bodied, full tannin, medium acidity **drink in 2–15 years**
Finally, a top-class wine from a difficult year that costs significantly less than $50. Enjoy the beautifully bold fruit, nut, and vanilla flavors.

1996 Gallo Sonoma Frei Vineyard Cabernet Sauvignon, Dry Creek Valley ★★★★ $$$
dry, full-bodied, full tannin, medium acidity **drink in 2–10 years**
It would be one of California's great Cabernets at any price. For under $30, it's remarkable. Find the space to save this one.

1998 Kathryn Kennedy Lateral, California ★★★★ $$$
dry, full-bodied, medium tannin, medium acidity **drink in 3–10 years**
From a "cult" winery, a smooth wine with fruit, spice, chocolate, and even coconut flavors. Experience what the fuss is about for a relatively modest price.

1997 Cakebread Cellars Benchland Select Cabernet Sauvignon, Napa Valley ★★★ $$$$
dry, full-bodied, medium tannin, medium acidity **drink now–5 years**
Blackberry, vanilla, and chocolate, with good acidity to set it all off.

1997 Frog's Leap Rutherford, Napa Valley ★★★ $$$$
dry, full-bodied, full tannin, medium acidity **drink in 2–10 years**
Like a berry-family reunion, with black pepper and bourbon notes besides.

1998 Long Vineyards Cabernet Sauvignon, Napa Valley ★★★ $$$$
dry, full-bodied, full tannin, medium acidity **drink in 3–12 years**
We love this wine with its decided minerality. Delicious cassis and black pepper flavors, too. Very, very dry.

1997 Nickel & Nickel John C. Sullenger Vineyard Oakville Cabernet Sauvignon, Napa Valley ★★★ $$$$
dry, full-bodied, full tannin, medium acidity **drink now–10 years**
A rich mix of berry, chocolate, and smoky flavors.

WINE PILLS

First, there was the French paradox: Despite higher consumption of saturated fats, the French have lower rates of heart disease than Americans. Then, there were scientific studies showing that the critical factor is the French habit of drinking far more wine than we do, especially red wine. That sent consumption of red wine in the U.S. soaring. So far, so good. Next, concerns about alcohol abuse prompted researchers to isolate the beneficial substances in red wine, polyphenols, and package them in a pill—soon to be in drugstores near you. Some people are skeptical, pointing out that alcohol might facilitate absorption of polyphenols. That's not all it does. A pill is good for people who can't drink wine. But those of us who are able to will probably continue to enjoy the liquid form with its added benefit of promoting relaxation, not to mention the sensual pleasure of taste.

1998 Peju Province Cabernet Sauvignon,
Napa Valley ★★★ $$$$
dry, medium-bodied, medium tannin, high acidity drink in 2–10 years
The wild herbs and finesse evident here make us think of the south of France rather than California. This wine recalibrates our notion of Napa Cab.

1998 Cakebread Cellars Cabernet Sauvignon,
Napa Valley ★★★ $$$
dry, full-bodied, full tannin, high acidity drink in 3–12 years
The cherry, nut, and black pepper flavors appeal. The smooth tannin and Bordeaux-like acidity make things even more interesting.

1998 Chimney Rock Cabernet Sauvignon,
Stags Leap District ★★★ $$$
dry, full-bodied, full tannin, medium acidity drink in 3–12 years
Coconut flavor from aging in American oak barrels really comes through in this wine. It also tastes of baked fruit and has good acidity.

1997 Clos du Bois Briarcrest Vineyard Cabernet Sauvignon,
Alexander Valley ★★★ $$$
dry, full-bodied, medium tannin, medium acidity drink now–10 years
Consistently one of our favorites, Briarcrest impresses us again this year with its lovely cassis, walnut, and violet flavors.

CULT WINES

California has seen its share of cults, but perhaps none has affected so many people as cult wines have. Potions made by an ancient order of alchemists in middle Napa? Sacrifices offered to Dionysus? Not quite. The cult wines are made in small batches and are intensely flavored. Because they're unusual and so few bottles are produced, demand outstrips supply and cultlike followings have developed. Rarely found in shops, the bottles can be procured by getting on the mailing list of one of the wineries (not easy), spending hundreds of dollars a bottle at auction, or shelling out even more at the few high-end restaurants that list them. Are they worth it? The flavors are so concentrated that the experience of sipping one of these wines is sublime. And compared to the prices paid for top Bordeaux made in 30,000-case batches, the expense is not so outrageous. On the other hand, you can forget about matching a cult wine with food; it will completely overwhelm anything on the plate.

Many producers of cult wines release other, quite similar wines in larger quantities for a fraction of the price. Moreover, these are considerably easier to find.

If you covet	**Look for**
Dalla Valle Maya	Dalla Valle Vineyards Cabernet Sauvignon, Napa Valley
Araujo Estate Eisele Vineyard Cabernet Sauvignon	Araujo Estate Cabernet Sauvignon, Napa Valley
Peju Province Reserve Cabernet Sauvignon	Peju Province Cabernet Sauvignon, Napa Valley
Harlan Estate Cabernet Sauvignon	The Maiden Cabernet Sauvignon
Shafer Hillside Select Cabernet Sauvignon	Shafer Stags Leap District Cabernet Sauvignon, Napa Valley
Martinelli Jackass Vineyard Zinfandel	Martinelli Louisa & Giuseppe Zinfandel
Marcassin Chardonnay	Canepa Chardonnay

1999 Cosentino Winery Cabernet Franc, Napa Valley ★★★ $$$
dry, full-bodied, full tannin, medium acidity **drink in 2–10 years**
Where to place a wine so loaded with aromas and flavors? In the cellar for a year or two to sort itself out.

1997 Heitz Cellar Cabernet Sauvignon, Napa Valley ★★★ $$$
dry, medium-bodied, medium tannin, medium acidity **drink in 2–10 years**
We expect nothing less than a classic from Heitz, with its forty years of experience. That's just what we get. Elegantly balanced flavor, tannin, and acidity.

1998 Justin Vineyards & Winery Isosceles, Paso Robles ★★★ $$$
dry, full-bodied, full tannin, medium acidity **drink now–10 years**
Flower power on California's Central Coast. Rose and violet aromas do a sprightly dance with the cherry flavor.

1997 Kendall-Jackson Great Estates Cabernet Sauvignon, Napa Valley ★★★ $$$
dry, full-bodied, full tannin, medium acidity **drink in 2–15 years**
This wine delivers big, bold flavors: blackberry, cassis, cherry, vanilla, and tar.

1998 Lang & Reed Premier Etage Cabernet Franc, Napa Valley ★★★ $$$
dry, full-bodied, medium tannin, high acidity **drink in 1–8 years**
From one of the few Cabernet Franc specialists in California, this wine offers the charms of cherry flavor interwoven with appealing herbal notes.

1998 Napanook, Napa Valley ★★★ $$$
dry, medium-bodied, medium tannin, medium acidity **drink in 2–10 years**
The second-tier wine from Napa's famed Dominus estate; it's one many others would be proud to have as their first.

1997 Robert Mondavi Winery Cabernet Sauvignon, Stags Leap District ★★★ $$$
dry, full-bodied, full tannin, medium acidity **drink in 3–15 years**
Befitting its pedigree, this earthy wine combines a rich mix of flavors.

1996 Rodney Strong Reserve Cabernet Sauvignon, Northern Sonoma ★★★ $$$
dry, full-bodied, medium tannin, medium acidity **drink now–10 years**
Having had five years to smooth out, this big Cab's about ready to go.

1998 Rutherford Hill 24th Anniversary Cabernet Sauvignon, Napa Valley ★★★ $$$
dry, medium-bodied, medium tannin, medium acidity **drink in 2–10 years**
Napa Cabs are sometimes criticized for being so bold in flavor that they're difficult to match with food, but this wine will be great with a number of dishes.

1997 Vita Nova Acronicus, Santa Barbara County ★★★ $$$
dry, full-bodied, medium tannin, high acidity **drink in 2–12 years**
The label evokes Rome, the fruit flavors, Bordeaux, and the herbal notes, Provence. It could come only from California.

1997 William Hill Winery Reserve Cabernet Sauvignon, Napa Valley ★★★ $$$
dry, full-bodied, full tannin, medium acidity **drink in 2–12 years**
Full berry and spice flavors are complemented by the mellow taste of vanilla in this appetite-whetting wine.

1996 York Creek Vineyards Meritage, Spring Mountain District ★★★ $$$
dry, full-bodied, medium tannin, medium acidity **drink now–12 years**
Fritz Maytag owns not only York Creek but Anchor Steam brewery and Maytag blue cheese. He believes in craftsmanship and offers a beautifully crafted wine.

1997 Beringer Cabernet Sauvignon, Knights Valley ★★★ $$
dry, full-bodied, medium tannin, medium acidity **drink in 2–12 years**
A very good wine with fruit and spice as well as lots of vanilla from charry oak.

NV8 Cain Cuvée, Napa Valley ★★★ $$
dry, medium-bodied, medium tannin, medium acidity **drink now–5 years**
Smooth, easy drinking. Loaded with fruit flavors. This is the perfect kind of dress-up or dress-down wine that we love to have handy for any occasion.

1997 Geyser Peak Winemaker's Selection Cabernet Franc, Alexander Valley ★★★ $$
dry, full-bodied, full tannin, medium acidity **drink now–10 years**
As befits the grape, there are lovely cherry flavors matched with herbs and a peppery note. Spicy, vanilla-laden oak aromas linger in the background.

1997 Geyser Peak Winemaker's Selection Malbec, Alexander Valley ★★★ $$
dry, full-bodied, medium tannin, medium acidity **drink now–10 years**
The important, nearly secret ingredient of many great Bordeaux wines, Malbec isn't often bottled on its own in California. This wine makes us wonder why not.

1998 Merryvale Cabernet Sauvignon, Napa Valley ★★★ $$
dry, full-bodied, full tannin, medium acidity **drink in 2–10 years**
Cassis and nuts, along with a certain meatiness that makes us want grilled or smoked food with this wine.

1998 Hess Select Cabernet Sauvignon, California ★★★ $
dry, full-bodied, medium tannin, medium acidity **drink now–5 years**
Rusticity only adds charm to this very good wine at a great price.

1996 Clos du Bois Winemaker's Reserve Cabernet Sauvignon, Alexander Valley ★★ $$$
dry, medium-bodied, medium tannin, medium acidity drink now–8 years
A savory wine full of herbal flavors and spicy notes. Very dry.

1997 Turning Leaf Cabernet Sauvignon, Central Coast ★★ $
dry, full-bodied, full tannin, medium acidity drink now–3 years
If you like your California Cabs big and bold, with black pepper, cassis, and tar, you've got it all here for a good price.

1998 BV Coastal Cabernet Sauvignon, Central/North Coast ★ $$
dry, medium-bodied, medium tannin, medium acidity drink now–3 years
Not a complex wine, but a nice red to have around for everyday drinking.

1998 Beringer Founders' Estate Cabernet Sauvignon, California ★ $
dry, medium-bodied, medium tannin, medium acidity drink now–3 years
It might not be exciting, but you get all the classic Cab flavors for a low price.

MERLOT

Wines made from Merlot, another Bordeaux grape, are similar to those from Cabernet Sauvignon, but they're usually less tannic and more velvety in texture, with plum, chocolate, and violet aromas and tastes. Growers love Merlot because it ripens early, making it less susceptible to unpredictable autumn weather. Restaurateurs love Merlot because it's usually ready to drink upon release, minimizing the need for costly long-term storage. It's hard to believe that fewer than twenty years ago most Merlot was blended into Cabernet and bottles labeled Merlot were rare.

at the table

Merlot is flexible. It goes well with steaks and game, but also with lighter meats like pork or rabbit. Try it with anything grilled, from portobello mushrooms to salmon to chicken to lamb.

the bottom line You'll need to pass the $20 mark for excellent Merlots. Jump to $35 and you'll find some of California's best. The rarest bottles sell for $150.

what to buy MERLOT

1997	1998	1999	2000
★★★	★★★	★★★	★★★

recommended wines

1997 Beringer Vineyards Howell Mountain Bancroft Ranch Private Reserve, Napa Valley ★★★★ $$$$
dry, full-bodied, full tannin, medium acidity **drink now–15 years**
This wine is full of luscious blackberry flavor, plus cocoa, vanilla, and nuts.

1998 Duckhorn Vineyards Estate Grown, Napa Valley ★★★★ $$$$
dry, full-bodied, full tannin, medium acidity **drink in 2–15 years**
The scents and flavors of currants, berries, and vanilla waft through, balanced by slightly bitter chocolate. A wine for the ages.

1997 Matanzas Creek Winery, Sonoma Valley ★★★★ $$$
dry, full-bodied, medium tannin, medium acidity **drink now–15 years**
Though we love experimenting, we also adore the classics. Uncorking this Merlot is like opening the front door on your return from a long trip.

1998 Dashe Cellars, Potter Valley ★★★ $$$
dry, medium-bodied, medium tannin, high acidity **drink in 2–10 years**
This wine embodies the perfect pairing of Californian and French sensibilities that the Dashe Cellars husband-and-wife team brings to winemaking.

1997 Davis Bynum Laureles Estate, Russian River Valley ★★★ $$$
dry, full-bodied, medium tannin, medium acidity **drink now–10 years**
Plum, lavender, and chocolate flavors in a velvet-textured wine.

1997 Dry Creek Vineyard Reserve, Dry Creek Valley ★★★ $$$
dry, full-bodied, full tannin, medium acidity **drink in 2–15 years**
A lush string of fruit and nut flavors. Put it away; patience will be rewarded.

1998 Frog's Leap, Napa Valley ★★★ $$$
dry, medium-bodied, medium tannin, medium acidity **drink now–10 years**
Filled with plum and raspberry flavors accented by chocolate and tobacco.

1998 Robert Mondavi Winery, Carneros ★★★ $$$
dry, full-bodied, medium tannin, medium acidity **drink in 2–10 years**
Fills the mouth with big, bold fruit and spice flavors.

1997 Rodney Strong Estate Bottled, Alexander Valley ★★★ $$$
dry, full-bodied, medium tannin, medium acidity **drink now–10 years**
Good when first opened. An hour of airing yields really delicious flavors.

1998 Shafer, Napa Valley ★★★ $$$
dry, full-bodied, medium tannin, medium acidity **drink in 3–12 years**
Others go for all fruit flavor; Shafer likes to put some earthiness in the mix. Nice.

1998 Clos du Bois Reserve, Alexander Valley ★★★ $$
dry, medium-bodied, medium tannin, medium acidity drink now–8 years
Clos du Bois has long had a reputation for making some of California's most solid Merlots, and this Reserve does the winery proud.

1998 Markham Vineyards, Napa Valley ★★★ $$
dry, full-bodied, medium tannin, medium acidity drink now–6 years
Lovely balance of flavors: plum, violet, and hints of coconut and green pepper.

1998 Rosenblum Cellars Lone Oak Vineyard, Russian River Valley ★★★ $$
dry, medium-bodied, medium tannin, medium acidity drink now–12 years
Fresh berry flavors, along with coconut and vanilla from aging in American oak barrels.

1998 Sterling Vineyards, Napa Valley ★★★ $$
dry, medium-bodied, medium tannin, medium acidity drink now–10 years
As upright as a church vicar, this Merlot provides honest fruit flavors.

1998 Stevenot, Sierra Foothills ★★★ $$
dry, medium-bodied, full tannin, medium acidity drink now–7 years
We love this wine. Fruity, floral, and smoky.

1998 Chateau St. Jean, Sonoma County ★★ $$
dry, full-bodied, full tannin, high acidity drink now–7 years
Fruit, tar, and oak, along with a bit of bitter chocolate. Good acidity.

1999 Coturri Maclise Vineyards, Sonoma Valley ★★ $$
dry, full-bodied, full tannin, high acidity drink in 2–10 years
An intense wine. Not for everyone, but we like it.

1998 Huntington, North Coast ★★ $$
dry, medium-bodied, medium tannin, medium acidity drink now–6 years
Baked tart cherries with a dash of vanilla. Very nice.

1998 Murphy-Goode, Alexander Valley ★★ $$
dry, medium-bodied, medium tannin, medium acidity drink now–8 years
A lovely, fruity wine with the added substance of smoke and cedar flavors.

1998 Castle Rock, California ★★ $
dry, medium-bodied, medium tannin, medium acidity drink now–5 years
The scent of violets and the flavors of plums and spices emerge from this reasonably priced, well-balanced Merlot.

1999 Kendall-Jackson Vintner's Reserve, California ★ $$
dry, medium-bodied, medium tannin, medium acidity drink now–3 years
Strawberry, blackberry, green pepper flavors. Simple but serviceable.

1998 Beringer Founders' Estate, California ★ $
dry, medium-bodied, medium tannin, medium acidity drink now–3 years
Not an inspiring wine, but at the price we have no complaints.

1998 Bogle Vineyards, Central Valley ★ $
dry, medium-bodied, low tannin, medium acidity drink now–3 years
With its full cherry, plum, and vanilla flavors and gentle tannin, this wine reminds us that Bogle continues to make appealing wines at appealing prices.

1999 Michael Sullberg Reserve, California ★ $
dry, medium-bodied, medium tannin, medium acidity drink now–3 years
A straightforward, affordable wine that is true to its grape variety with plum and chocolate flavors.

PINOT NOIR

There's an irony in the world of wine: Grapes grown in warm weather and in the best, most fertile soils usually don't make very good wine. In California, this dictum is most true of Pinot Noir. The noble grape of Burgundy is difficult to grow anywhere, and in California the weather's just too good. Winemakers have found, however, that Pinot Noir does exceptionally well in cooler parts of the state, like Santa Barbara, Sonoma's Russian River Valley, and Carneros. Pinot Noir in California will never be the same as it is in Burgundy, but California Pinots can be delicious, versatile wines in their own right.

at the table

California Pinot Noir is the wine to order when everyone at the table is eating something different. It goes exceptionally well with salmon and tuna but is also good with chicken, duck, and veal or lamb chops.

the bottom line Count on spending in the mid-$20s and into the $30s for most good examples, and up to $70 for especially prestigious bottles. Disappointment reigns at the low end, but we can recommend a couple of Pinots under $12 that are quite good.

what to buy PINOT NOIR

1996	1997	1998	1999	2000
★★	★★★	★★	★★	★★★

recommended wines

1998 Landmark Kastania, Sonoma Coast ★★★★ $$$
dry, medium-bodied, medium tannin, medium acidity drink now–7 years
When we close our eyes and sip this, we almost think it's a Burgundy Grand Cru. This is a wine with aspirations. Excellent.

1998 RSV Four Vineyards Reserve, Carneros ★★★★ $$$
dry, medium-bodied, medium tannin, medium acidity drink now–5 years
An exquisite wine. It has wonderful, beautifully balanced flavors of cherries and chocolate.

1999 Sanford La Rinconada Vineyard, Santa Barbara County ★★★★ $$$
dry, full-bodied, full tannin, medium acidity drink in 2–8 years
A big bruiser of a wine, full-bodied and tannic for a Pinot. We love it.

1999 Au Bon Climat La Bauge Au-dessus, Santa Maria Valley ★★★★ $$
dry, medium-bodied, medium tannin, medium acidity drink now–7 years
Fruit, floral, and spice flavors. Plenty of acidity, lots of finesse.

1998 Navarro Vineyards Méthode à l'Ancienne, Anderson Valley ★★★★ $$
dry, medium-bodied, medium tannin, high acidity drink now–7 years
An Anderson Valley gem. Its fruit and vanilla flavors are accented by smoky and floral notes.

1999 David Bruce, Santa Cruz Mountains ★★★ $$$
dry, full-bodied, medium tannin, medium acidity drink now–8 years
A heavy-bodied, fruit-laden wine with bourbonlike notes.

1999 Davis Bynum Bynum & Moshin Vineyards, Russian River Valley ★★★ $$$
dry, medium-bodied, medium tannin, medium acidity drink in 2–8 years
Full cherry flavor held down to earth with smoky-soil notes.

1999 Iron Horse Vineyards Green Valley, Sonoma County ★★★ $$$
dry, medium-bodied, light tannin, medium acidity drink now–8 years
Delicious. Its light tannin means it goes down exceptionally smoothly.

1998 Kent Rasmussen, Carneros ★★★ $$$
dry, medium-bodied, medium tannin, medium acidity drink now–6 years
This is good now but it will get a lot better with age.

1997 Lafond, Santa Ynez Valley ★★★ $$$
dry, medium-bodied, medium tannin, high acidity drink now–10 years
Wonderfully aromatic. Dried-cherry flavor. Lots of good acidity.

1998 Navarro Vineyards Deep-End Blend, Anderson Valley ★★★ $$$
dry, medium-bodied, medium tannin, medium acidity drink now–7 years
With lavender and vanilla joining the cherry flavor, this is a bit of an oddity, but there's enough tannin and acidity to carry it off. We really like this wine.

1999 Sanford Sanford & Benedict Vineyard, Santa Barbara County ★★★ $$$
dry, full-bodied, medium tannin, medium acidity drink now–8 years
Grapes from Richard Sanford's famed vineyard go into the wines of many producers. With his pick of the crop he makes this substantial, earthy wine.

1999 Cuvaison, Carneros ★★★ $$
dry, medium-bodied, medium tannin, medium acidity drink now–6 years
Fruitiness mixes nicely with oak flavors in this charming but serious wine.

1998 Elke Donnelly Creek Vineyard, Anderson Valley ★★★ $$
dry, medium-bodied, medium tannin, high acidity drink now–6 years
More than a few California winemakers wishfully describe their Pinots as Burgundian. Here's one that might actually qualify.

1998 La Crema, Anderson Valley ★★★ $$
dry, medium-bodied, medium tannin, medium acidity drink now–6 years
A lovely wine full of dried-cherry flavor, with some notes of bitter herbs and a bit of smokiness.

1998 Robert Mondavi Winery, Napa Valley ★★★ $$
dry, medium-bodied, medium tannin, medium acidity drink now–10 years
Cherry and floral flavors balanced by palate-massaging mineral notes.

1998 Rutz Cellars, Russian River Valley ★★★ $$
dry, medium-bodied, medium tannin, medium acidity drink now–8 years
A really delicious wine with cherry, spice, and herb flavors. Velvety texture.

1998 Logan, Monterey ★★ $$
dry, light-bodied, light tannin, medium acidity drink now–6 years
Light as a wisp of smoke, this wine still delivers good dried-cherry flavor.

1999 Ramsay Lot 14, California ★★ $$
dry, light-bodied, light tannin, medium acidity drink now–3 years
Just the thing when you're looking for inexpensive Pinot Noir with straightforward cherry and blueberry flavors.

1999 Beringer Founders' Estate, California ★★ $
dry, medium-bodied, medium tannin, medium acidity drink now–3 years
We really like the dark cherry flavor augmented by minerality and a bit of smokiness. And we love the wine's low price.

1999 Kendall-Jackson Vintner's Reserve, California ★★ $
dry, light-bodied, light tannin, medium acidity drink now–3 years
Vivid tart cherry flavor, accented by a little smokiness. Light and inviting. It's well-priced, too.

1999 David Bruce, Central Coast ★ $$
dry, medium-bodied, medium tannin, medium acidity drink now–5 years
Not as elaborate as some of David Bruce's other Pinots, but with the nice fruit flavors and the low price, we have no complaints.

1998 Morgan, Monterey County ★ $$
dry, medium-bodied, light tannin, high acidity drink now–3 years
A straightforward Pinot Noir. Full cherry flavor and good acidity.

ZINFANDEL

California's own noble variety, Zinfandel, assumes as many guises as a Hollywood actor. It can be a simple charmer; a balanced and sophisticated wine; an intense, thick, high-alcohol Californian that screams for attention and gets it from adoring critics; or even a frivolous starlet of a rosé wine known as White Zinfandel. A fetish currently flourishes for "old-vine" Zins, made from patches of vines that can be up to 100 years of age. Many old-vine wines are indeed special, but so too are some younger ones.

at the table

The simple Zins suit pizza and pasta dishes like lasagna or stuffed cannelloni just fine. Balanced and sophisticated versions work well with rack of lamb or stuffed pork tenderloin. Drink the heavy Zinfandels with beef stews, steaks, or braised lamb shanks.

the bottom line Despite the enthusiasm of Zin-fiends, it's still possible to find reasonably priced bottles. Simple but enjoyable examples can be had for about $15. More elegant versions range from $18 to $35. The multi-medaled stars of the Zinfandel world fetch $30 and more.

what to buy ZINFANDEL

1996	1997	1998	1999	2000
★★★	★★★	★★	★★	★★

recommended wines

1998 Edmeades, Mendocino Ridge ★★★★ $$$
dry, full-bodied, full tannin, medium acidity **drink now–8 years**
One of the finest Zinfandels we have tasted in a long while.

1999 Ridge Geyserville, Sonoma County ★★★★ $$$
dry, full-bodied, full tannin, medium acidity **drink now–15 years**
Winemaker Paul Draper continues his streak of making Zinfandels by which all others must be judged.

1998 Haywood Estate Rocky Terrace, Sonoma Valley ★★★ $$$
dry, full-bodied, full tannin, medium acidity **drink now–8 years**
Full fruit flavors, with a grind of black pepper and a whiff of smoke.

1998 Nickel & Nickel Ponzo Vineyard, Russian River Valley ★★★ $$$
dry, full-bodied, full tannin, medium acidity **drink now–10 years**
A serious wine striving to be the best in the state. It's getting close.

1999 Ridge Lytton Springs, Dry Creek Valley ★★★ $$$
dry, full-bodied, full tannin, medium acidity **drink now–15 years**
Another delicious wine from Ridge. Veritably explodes with fruit, chocolate, and nut flavors.

1999 Turley Duarte, Contra Costa County ★★★ $$$
dry, full-bodied, medium tannin, medium acidity **drink now–10 years**
What do 105-year-old vines do for wine? Here they result in intensely concentrated texture and flavor.

1999 Blockheadia Ringnosii, Napa Valley ★★★ $$
dry, full-bodied, full tannin, medium acidity **drink now–5 years**
The wacky label might make you think this is a less than serious wine. Wrong.

1998 Château Potelle Old Vines, Napa Valley ★★★ $$
dry, full-bodied, medium tannin, medium acidity **drink now–7 years**
The French proprietors of Château Potelle clearly know what they're doing with this Italian/American grape. A terrific wine.

1998 Fife Vineyards Old Vines, Napa Valley ★★★ $$
dry, medium-bodied, medium tannin, medium acidity **drink now**
Lots of strawberry flavor in this nicely balanced wine.

1999 Frog's Leap, Napa Valley ★★★ $$
dry, full-bodied, full tannin, medium acidity **drink in 1–5 years**
This muddle of cherries and berries needs some time to settle down. When it does, it will be very, very good.

1998 Gallo Sonoma Barrelli Creek Vineyard, Alexander Valley ★★★ $$
dry, full-bodied, full tannin, medium acidity **drink now–10 years**
Black is beautiful. Aromas of blackberries, black pepper, smoke, and licorice swirl around the glass, graciously allowing some tangy cherry flavor through.

1998 Grgich Hills, Napa/Sonoma Counties ★★★ $$
dry, medium-bodied, medium tannin, medium acidity **drink now–8 years**
Perfumed with roses and cedar; lovely cherry flavor.

1997 Mazzocco Stone Ranch, Alexander Valley ★★★ $$
dry, full-bodied, full tannin, high acidity **drink now–8 years**
With its complex flavor and generous acidity, this Zin pays homage to its southern Italian roots.

1998 Robert Mondavi Winery, Napa Valley ★★★ $$
dry, medium-bodied, medium tannin, medium acidity **drink now–8 years**
Cherry, cranberry, and pepper flavors, with some floral notes and good acidity.

1998 Rodney Strong Knotty Vines, Northern Sonoma ★★★ $$
dry, full-bodied, full tannin, medium acidity **drink now–8 years**
Bold cherry and berry flavors, with bitter-herb grace notes at the end.

1999 Rosenblum Cellars Oakley Vineyards, San Francisco Bay ★★★ $$
dry, full-bodied, medium tannin, medium acidity **drink now–6 years**
There's a lot of fruitiness, to be sure, but it's the unexpected, provocative flavors of Chinese five-spice powder that really capture our attention.

1998 Clos du Bois, Sonoma County ★★ $$
dry, medium-bodied, medium tannin, medium acidity **drink now–4 years**
The blackberry and spice flavors tell us to try this with barbecue.

1999 De Loach Estate Bottled, Russian River Valley ★★ $$
dry, full-bodied, full tannin, medium acidity **drink now–8 years**
Zinfandel gives cherry flavor; 5 percent Petite Sirah adds earthy notes.

1999 Fritz Winery Old Vine, Dry Creek Valley ★★ $$
dry, full-bodied, medium tannin, high acidity **drink now–6 years**
Sixty- to eighty-year-old vines produce intense fruit with unusual flavors. Slightly buttery and nutty.

1997 Gallo Sonoma Frei Ranch Vineyard, Dry Creek Valley ★★ $$
dry, full-bodied, full tannin, medium acidity **drink now–10 years**
The baked cherry and smoky flavors really come through.

1998 Hendry Block 7, Napa Valley ★★ $$
dry, medium-bodied, medium tannin, high acidity **drink now–6 years**
Berry and spice flavors, plus some earthiness and good acidity.

1999 Jessie's Grove Vintner's Choice Old Vine, Lodi ★★ $$
dry, full-bodied, full tannin, high acidity **drink now–5 years**
A peppery wine with berry and cherry flavors balanced by good acidity and an appealing earthiness.

1997 Martini & Prati Riserva di Famiglia Old Vine, Russian River Valley ★★ $$
dry, medium-bodied, full tannin, high acidity **drink now–3 years**
A wine that shows off its Italian heritage with cherry, strawberry, and herb flavors brought out by astringent acidity. Very good with food.

1998 Rancho Zabaco Sonoma Heritage Vines, Sonoma County ★★ $$
dry, full-bodied, full tannin, medium acidity **drink now–5 years**
Luscious berry and black cherry flavors explode in this concentrated wine with a long, long blackberry finish.

1999 Sobon Estate Fiddletown, Sierra Foothills ★★ $$
dry, medium-bodied, medium tannin, medium acidity **drink now–5 years**
Berries, cherries, and spice balanced by good acidity and earthy notes.

1998 Vigil Mohr-Fry Ranch Old Vine, Lodi ★★ $$
dry, full-bodied, full tannin, medium acidity **drink now–5 years**
Berries, cherries, black pepper, and herbs. Nice.

1998 Castle Rock, Paso Robles ★★ $
dry, medium-bodied, medium tannin, medium acidity **drink now–2 years**
Sometimes we just want a Zin that's gentle and fruity. Here 'tis.

NV Rosenblum Cellars Vintners Cuvée XXII, California ★★ $
dry, medium-bodied, medium tannin, medium acidity **drink now–1 year**
The price says it's a simple wine; the juicy berry and peach flavors tell us it's a bit more.

1998 Turning Leaf Coastal Reserve, North Coast ★ $
dry, medium-bodied, low tannin, medium acidity **drink now–2 years**
Sure, it's simple, but with a bit of nuttiness adding to its fruit flavors, this wine is a fine, inexpensive choice.

ITALIAN & RHONE VARIETALS

It didn't escape the notice of California's Italian immigrant winemakers that the state's climate was similar to that of their Mediterranean motherland. As early as 1860, they started planting Italian grapes. The 1990s brought renewed interest in Italian varieties, like Barbera, Dolcetto, and Sangiovese, and acreage has increased tremendously. Though often rich in flavor, Cal-Itals, as they're sometimes called, tend to lack the refreshing acidity so typical of Italian wines.

Perhaps the greatest shift in the California red profile is the increased prominence of Rhône varieties: Syrah, Petite Sirah, Mourvèdre, Grenache, and Carignan. In the 1980s, an eclectic coterie of vintners, dubbed the Rhône Rangers, became convinced that since California's climate was close to that of France's Rhône Valley, the state's best wines could be made from Rhône grapes. The theory has been borne out by outstanding wines that are often second to none in the state.

at the table

Barbera (bar-BEAR-ah), Dolcetto (dohl-CHET-oh), and inexpensive Sangiovese (san-joh-VAY-zeh) tend to be simple, so think accordingly: spaghetti with marinara or red clam sauce, hamburgers, and meatloaf. Finer Sangioveses are worthy of wild mushroom tarts. Use Mourvèdre (moor-VEDr) and Grenache (greh-nah'sh) as you would the simpler Italians. Syrah is perfect with osso buco, lamb stew, or braised oxtails. You'll need rich red meat like prime beef or braised lamb shanks to tame the tannic Petite Sirah.

the bottom line Single varietals can be found for $9 to $12. Better Barberas and Grenaches are available for $16 to $22. Very good Sangioveses cost $18 to $35. Simple Rhône blends offer some of the state's best values, at $9 to $12. Syrahs range from $15 to $30, Petite Sirahs $20 to $25.

what to buy SYRAH

1996	1997	1998	1999	2000
★★★★	★★★	★★★	★★	★★★

recommended wines

1999 Beckmen Vineyards Cuvée Le Bec, Santa Barbara County ★★★★ $$$
dry, full-bodied, full tannin, medium acidity **drink now–10 years**
This mix of Grenache, Mourvèdre, and Syrah is among the finest blends of Rhône grapes we have ever sampled, those from the Rhône Valley included.

1998 Dalla Valle Vineyards Pietre Rosse, Napa Valley ★★★★ $$$
dry, full-bodied, medium tannin, high acidity **drink now–8 years**
There's a lot of heart in this wine made with Tuscan varieties in a smoky, spicy southern Italian style.

1999 Edmunds St. John Wylie-Fenaughty Syrah, El Dorado County ★★★★ $$$
dry, full-bodied, full tannin, medium acidity **drink in 2–10 years**
The label says "produced with intuition & blind luck." We doubt the latter. A beautiful expression of *terroir*.

1999 Eleven Oaks Sangiovese, Santa Barbara County ★★★★ $$$
dry, full-bodied, medium tannin, medium acidity **drink in 2–10 years**
Flavorful fruitiness and pepperiness, with mineral notes.

1998 Geyser Peak Reserve Shiraz, Sonoma County ★★★★ $$$
dry, full-bodied, full tannin, medium acidity **drink now–7 years**
A superior example of the big, brash, bold style of Shiraz, full of blackberry and cherry, herb, coffee, burnt sugar, and sweet tobacco flavors.

1999 Babcock Black Label Cuvée Syrah, Santa Barbara County ★★★ $$$
dry, full-bodied, medium tannin, medium acidity **drink now–10 years**
A beautiful wine with fruit, herb, and nut flavors and an appealing smokiness.

1996 Foppiano Centennial Harvest Petite Sirah, Russian River Valley ★★★ $$$
dry, full-bodied, full tannin, medium acidity **drink in 2–8 years**
Berries, burnt sugar, and a distinct taste of bourbon make this a wine worth waiting for.

1998 Foxen Morehouse Vineyard Syrah, Santa Ynez Valley ★★★ $$$
dry, full-bodied, full tannin, medium acidity drink now–7 years
A summer cookout in a bottle: Smoke, roasted meat and herbs, plum and black cherry salad for dessert, and a bit of tobacco for afterward.

1999 H. Coturri & Sons Crane Vineyards L'Art de Vivre Syrah, Sonoma Valley ★★★ $$$
dry, full-bodied, medium tannin, high acidity drink now–8 years
The Coturri style of fermenting very ripe grapes with wild yeasts sometimes makes wines that are almost Port-like. This one, though, is dry and delicious.

1999 Palmina Vino da Tavola della Costa Centrale, Central Coast ★★★ $$$
dry, full-bodied, full tannin, high acidity drink now–10 years
A wonderful, Italian-inspired wine. Deliciously spicy.

1998 Pepi Colline di Sassi, Napa Valley ★★★ $$$
dry, full-bodied, full tannin, high acidity drink now–8 years
A tasty Napa/Super-Tuscan blend of Sangiovese, Cabernet Sauvignon, and Merlot. Wonderful cherry, vanilla, black pepper, and smoke flavors.

1998 Tablas Creek Vineyard Rouge, Paso Robles ★★★ $$$
dry, full-bodied, medium tannin, medium acidity drink now–10 years
The southern Rhône comes to California. A beautiful wine with berries, herbs, and a great stony quality.

1998 Treana Red Proprietary Blend, Central Coast ★★★ $$$
dry, full-bodied, medium tannin, medium acidity drink now–10 years
Bordeaux and the Rhône Valley meet in California to fine effect in this wine made from Cabernet Sauvignon, Merlot, Syrah, Petite Sirah, and Mourvèdre.

1999 Beckmen Vineyards Syrah, Santa Barbara County ★★★ $$
dry, full-bodied, full tannin, medium acidity drink now–10 years
Herbes de Provence plus blackberry and cedar flavors add up to an entirely delicious wine.

1998 Bedford Thompson Syrah, Santa Barbara County ★★★ $$
dry, full-bodied, full tannin, medium acidity drink in 2–10 years
A great-tasting, smoky wine with concentrated roasted cherry flavor and hints of tar and black pepper.

1998 Bricco Buon Natale Riserva Barbera, Santa Maria Valley ★★★ $$
dry, full-bodied, medium tannin, medium acidity drink now–6 years
Earthy and bitter-green flavors add to the fruitiness of this beguiling wine. A long finish makes us like it even more.

1998 Chameleon Cellars Nettare, Napa Valley ★★★ $$
dry, full-bodied, full tannin, medium acidity **drink in 1–6 years**
Equal parts Syrah, Sangiovese, Dolcetto, Charbono, and Merlot. Positively luscious.

1998 Equus Syrah, Paso Robles ★★★ $$
dry, full-bodied, medium tannin, high acidity **drink now–8 years**
Black cherry, chocolate, and vanilla flavors bring to mind the classic Black Forest cake. Very good acidity.

1998 Iron Horse Vineyards T bar T Sangiovese, Alexander Valley ★★★ $$
dry, medium-bodied, medium tannin, high acidity **drink now–8 years**
California Sangiovese often has either a lot of fruit flavors without the variety's distinctive acidity or plenty of acidity but not much fruit. Here, you get both.

VINEYARD DESIGNATIONS

The current craze among California vintners is vineyard-specific wines. The idea is that grapes from a particular place take on certain characteristics, and this is frequently true in Europe. In California, however, some vineyards, like Santa Barbara's Bien Nacido, can cover several hundred acres, and the state's geological instability means soil types can vary tremendously within even a few square yards. For small, consistent vineyards, the mineral content of the soil and the exposure to the sun will, of course, result in grapes with their own distinct taste. Just be a bit skeptical.

1998 Long Vineyards Seghesio Vineyards Sangiovese, Sonoma County ★★★ $$
dry, full-bodied, medium tannin, medium acidity **drink now–8 years**
A heavy-duty Sangiovese showing what the California sun can do with this grape. Black cherry and brown sugar flavors. Almost thick.

1997 Markham Vineyards Petite Sirah, Napa Valley ★★★ $$
dry, full-bodied, full tannin, medium acidity **drink now–10 years**
A rum toddy of a wine with big berry flavors, burnt sugar, tar, vanilla, and, of course, nuances of dark rum. Delicious.

1999 Qupé Los Olivos Cuvée, Santa Barbara County ★★★ $$
dry, full-bodied, full tannin, medium acidity **drink in 2–10 years**
A fine blend of Syrah, Mourvèdre, and Grenache by one of California's most prominent proponents of Rhône-style wines.

1999 Sobon Estate Grenache,
Shenandoah Valley ★★★ $$
dry, full-bodied, full tannin, high acidity **drink in 1–8 years**
One of the Shenandoah Valley's best. Full of cherry, rose, and lots of black pepper flavors. Very, very good.

1999 Sobon Estate Primitivo,
Shenandoah Valley ★★★ $$
dry, full-bodied, medium tannin, medium acidity **drink now–5 years**
DNA tests say Primitivo is the same as Zinfandel, but the Sobons, who grow the two side-by-side, are skeptical. We're just happy for this fine wine.

1998 Chameleon Cellars Sangiovese, North Coast ★★ $$
dry, medium-bodied, medium tannin, high acidity **drink now–5 years**
With full cherry flavor and good acidity, this is a good, straightforward example of what California can do with Italy's favorite grape.

1998 Chatom Vineyards Syrah, Calaveras County ★★ $$
dry, medium-bodied, medium tannin, medium acidity **drink now–6 years**
Deep cherry flavor and smoky tannin make for delicious drinking anytime.

1999 David Bruce Petite Syrah, Central Coast ★★ $$
dry, full-bodied, full tannin, high acidity **drink in 2–10 years**
Black cherry flavor combines with tart pomegranate and floral notes. Nice minerality adds further complexity.

1999 Geyser Peak Shiraz, Sonoma County ★★ $$
dry, full-bodied, full tannin, medium acidity **drink now–3 years**
A California Shiraz made in the Australian, fruit-forward style, with loads of blackberry and vanilla and some smoky qualities.

1999 Jaffurs Wine Cellars Syrah,
Santa Barbara County ★★ $$
dry, medium-bodied, medium tannin, medium acidity **drink in 2–8 years**
Blended with a little Viognier, à la Côte Rôtie, this wine has all the smoky and cherrylike elements one expects from Syrah, plus floral notes.

1998 La Famiglia di Robert Mondavi Sangiovese, California ★★ $$
dry, medium-bodied, medium tannin, high acidity **drink now–4 years**
Mondavi's Italian heritage emerges in the cherry and herbal flavors and the sharp acidity.

1998 Peju Province Provence, California ★★ $$
dry, light-bodied, light tannin, high acidity **drink now**
An easy-drinking wine that's more than a simple quaffer. Hints of red cherry, smoke, and herbs. Very good acidity.

1999 Pepi Barbera, North Coast ★★ $$
dry, full-bodied, medium tannin, medium acidity **drink now–4 years**
This rich-bodied, blackberry- and tar-tinged wine is the slightest bit sweet, just right for barbecue or spaghetti with meat sauce.

1999 Qupé Bien Nacido Reserve Syrah, Santa Barbara County ★★ $$
dry, full-bodied, medium tannin, medium acidity **drink in 2–6 years**
We love black-as-ink Syrahs like this, full of smoke, berry, and anise flavors.

1999 R. H. Phillips EXP Syrah, Dunnigan Hills ★★ $$
dry, full-bodied, full tannin, medium acidity **drink now–3 years**
A nice Syrah with berry, chocolate, herbs, black pepper, and smoke flavors.

1998 Santa Barbara Winery Syrah, Santa Ynez Valley ★★ $$
dry, medium-bodied, full tannin, medium acidity **drink now–5 years**
Earthy and floral at the same time. And it works well.

1999 Zaca Mesa Z Cuvée, Santa Barbara County ★★ $$
dry, medium-bodied, medium tannin, medium acidity **drink now–2 years**
A unique blend with Rhône grapes offering a load of flavors. We love it.

1998 Castle Rock Syrah, California ★★ $
dry, medium-bodied, medium tannin, medium acidity **drink now–2 years**
Fruity with a touch of smoke. Elegant restraint—and cheap.

1999 Laurel Glen REDS, California ★★ $
dry, full-bodied, medium tannin, medium acidity **drink now–2 years**
Exuberant berry, tamarind, and smoke flavors. Very good.

1999 Beaulieu Vineyard Beauzeaux, Napa Valley ★ $$
dry, medium-bodied, light tannin, medium acidity **drink now–2 years**
A circus of blackberries, cherries, and raspberries in an easy-drinking wine.

1998 Hess Select Syrah, California ★ $$
dry, full-bodied, full tannin, medium acidity **drink now**
There's better Syrah out there, but at this price, not much can compare.

1999 Ca' del Solo Big House Red, Santa Cruz ★ $
dry, medium-bodied, medium tannin, medium acidity **drink now**
Simple black cherry flavor and a little spice make a good quaffer.

THERE ARE OTHER STATES?

California so dominates the U.S. wine industry that even New York, Washington, and Oregon have to fight to get into the picture. And forty-two other states have wine industries. Many of their wines are well worth trying. Some producers to look for:

Connecticut Chamard Vineyards

Idaho Ste. Chapelle Winery

Maryland Elk Run

Massachusetts Westport Rivers

Michigan Château Grand Traverse, L. Mawby

Missouri Mt. Pleasant Winery, St. James Winery, Stone Hill Winery

New Mexico Gruet Winery

North Carolina Westbend Vineyards

Pennsylvania Chaddsford Winery

Rhode Island Sakonnet Vineyards

Texas Alamosa Wine Cellars, Llano Estacado

Virginia Barboursville Vineyards, Chrysalis Vineyards, Horton Cellars, Linden Vineyards

pacific northwest

Specialization is the name of the game in the Northwest. As opposed to California, where vintners grow everything, Oregon and Washington winemakers focus on varieties that do especially well in their climates. So, in Oregon it's Pinot Gris and Pinot Noir; in Washington, the white grapes Chardonnay, Sauvignon Blanc, and Semillon and the red Merlot and Cabernet Sauvignon.

oregon

Oregon's primarily small wineries have gained big-time notice in the last couple of decades, mainly for doing what their California counterparts cannot: producing world-class Pinot Noirs comparable to those produced in the Burgundy region of France. The Willamette Valley is the most famous area. Also important are the Umpqua, Rogue, Columbia, and Walla Walla Valleys.

on the label

Like California, Oregon generally uses varietal labels; the wine must be made of at least 90 percent of the particular grape, with the exception of Cabernet Sauvignon, which must contain a minimum of 75 percent of that grape. Vineyard designations are permitted as long as 95 percent of the grapes originated at the specific vineyard. Regional labeling has its own set of rules. To get around these complicated regulations, many wineries have come up with proprietary names for blends of their own choosing—for example, Sokol Blosser's "Evolution."

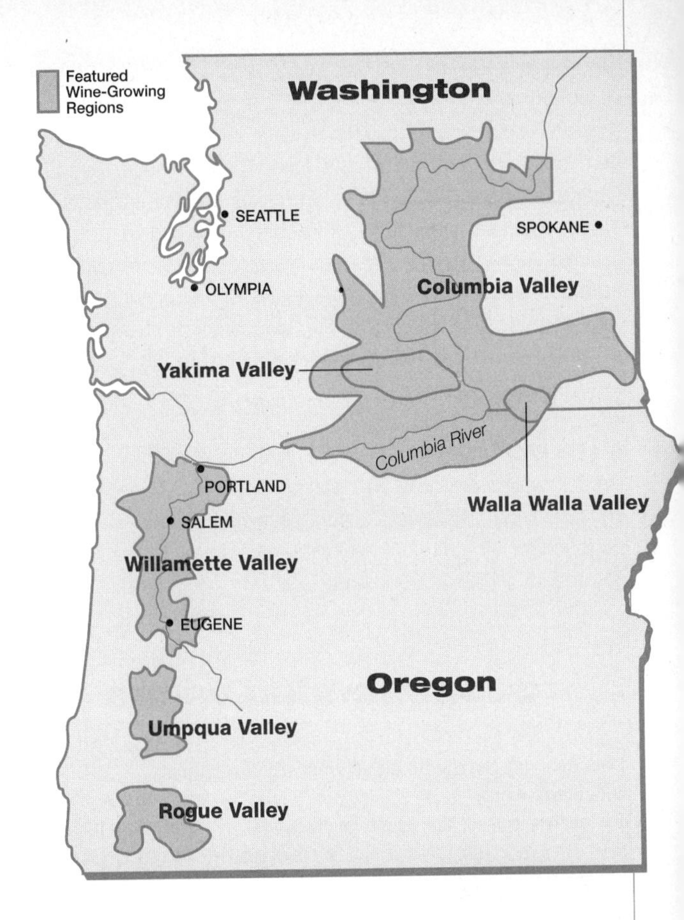

white wines

The Alsace varieties—the hugely successful Pinot Gris as well as Pinot Blanc, Riesling (reece-ling), and Gewürztraminer (geh-VAIRTZ-tra-mee-ner)—are planted in the state, as are Burgundian Chardonnay and the Loire Valley's Sauvignon Blanc. You'll also find German Müller-Thurgau, a variety that seems to do better in Oregon than in its homeland.

at the table

Oregon's white wines are higher in acidity than California's and therefore go better with many foods. Also, since these wines can be highly aromatic, many are able to stand up not only to fish and fowl, but also to mild meats like veal or pork. They're great with spicy foods, too (think Thai fish soup and Indian tandoori chicken). Drink Pinot Gris with lean fish, shellfish, smoked ham, or slightly aged goat cheese. Oregon Chardonnay and Pinot Blanc are good accompaniments to salmon, goose, pheasant, or rabbit. Light-bodied but full-flavored Gewürztraminer and Riesling go beautifully with delicate trout and also with somewhat heartier fish, like monkfish. Serve mellow, fruity Müller-Thurgau with light sandwiches and chilled summer vegetable soups and other luncheon fare or on its own as an aperitif.

the bottom line Considering their high quality, Oregon whites are quite well priced. Good Pinot Gris will cost you $12 to $20; Riesling, Gewürztraminer, and Pinot Blanc can be found for $8 to $15. The Chardonnay range is broad—from $12 to $35. Müller-Thurgau is under $10.

recommended wines

1999 Domaine Serene Côte Sud Vineyard Chardonnay, Willamette Valley ★★★★ $$$
dry, medium-bodied, high acidity, medium oak **drink now–10 years**
Quite simply a brilliant wine with the flavors of peaches, lemons, and tangerines and thrilling minerality. Very good acidity.

1999 Amity Vineyard Oregon Dry Riesling, Willamette Valley ★★★ $$
dry, medium-bodied, high acidity, no oak **drink now–5 years**
Amity does Alsace, with the classic petrol scents of Riesling, plus peach, pear, and almond flavors. Very good wine.

1999 Cristom Pinot Gris, Oregon/Washington ★★★ $$
dry, medium-bodied, high acidity, no oak **drink now–5 years**
This wine has a concentration of flavors that would make an Alsace winemaker proud.

1999 Ken Wright Cellars Freedom Hill Vineyard Pinot Blanc, Willamette Valley ★★★ $$
dry, full-bodied, high acidity, no oak **drink now–3 years**
Racy acidity gives vigor; floral aromas provide charm; notes of pear and yeast provide flavor and depth.

1999 Henry Estate Dry Gewürztraminer, Umpqua Valley ★★★ $
dry, medium-bodied, medium acidity, no oak **drink now–2 years**
Flavor so fresh you'd think it was squeezed directly from a lime. Nice grass and mineral notes.

1999 Montinore Vineyards Pinot Gris, Willamette Valley ★★★ $
dry, medium-bodied, high acidity, no oak **drink now–3 years**
A lovely example of what Oregon Pinot Gris can be. Nice lemon and pear flavors with hints of almond.

GREAT VINTAGES

Harvests in 1998, 1999, and 2000 proved to be among the best in Northwest winemaking history. With wines from all three vintages now on the market, consumers can see how good wines from the region can be.

1999 Adelsheim Vineyard Chardonnay, Oregon ★★ $$
dry, medium-bodied, high acidity, medium oak **drink now–8 years**
Well-balanced and subtle lemon, vanilla, and oak.

1999 Adelsheim Vineyard Pinot Gris, Oregon ★★ $$
dry, medium-bodied, high acidity, no oak **drink now–3 years**
Brisk grapefruit and mineral flavors provide the perfect antidote for dull-white-wine fatigue.

1998 Foris Vineyards Winery Pinot Gris, Rogue Valley ★★ $$
dry, medium-bodied, medium acidity, no oak **drink now–3 years**
A luau of tropical flavors—including pineapple, mango, and kiwi.

NV Sokol Blosser 5th Edition Evolution, Oregon/Washington ★★ $$
off-dry, medium-bodied, high acidity, no oak **drink now**
This blend of nine different grape varieties offers terrific fruit flavors and good acidity to balance that touch of sweetness.

1999 Chateau Benoit Müller-Thurgau, Willamette Valley ★★ $
dry, medium-bodied, high acidity, no oak **drink now**
Usually a dullard in its native Germany, Müller-Thurgau steps lively in the Beaver state. Refreshingly fruity.

red wines

PINOT NOIR

Oregon's Pinot Noir is its most celebrated varietal. The state's Pinots are on a par with French Burgundies, which, of course, are made from the same grape.

at the table

Pinot Noir is one of the most flexible wines in the world. Oregon Pinot is an excellent choice for those times when one person has ordered steak and another, fish. When you're not looking for compromise, try a bottle alongside a duck breast with a tart cherry sauce.

the bottom line Pinot Noir can be a tricky grape to grow, and you pay for the trouble. Expect to top $20 to get a really good one. Many excellent bottles are more than $40.

what to buy PINOT NOIR

1996	1997	1998	1999	2000
★★★	★★	★★★	★★★★	★★★★

recommended wines

1998 Cristom Reserve, Willamette Valley ★★★★ $$$
dry, full-bodied, medium tannin, high acidity **drink now–15 years**
Cherry and raspberry flavors, with hints of chile pepper for excitement and a smooth leatherlike quality for depth.

1999 Archery Summit Premier Cuvée, Oregon ★★★ $$$
dry, medium-bodied, medium tannin, high acidity **drink now–12 years**
Raspberry and cherry with stony and smoky flavors. Wow.

1999 Bethel Heights Vineyard Freedom Hill Vineyard, Willamette Valley ★★★ $$$
dry, medium-bodied, medium tannin, high acidity **drink now–8 years**
The aroma of toasty almond pastry and the flavors of strawberry and rhubarb remind us of a just-baked pie.

1998 Chelaham Rion Reserve, Willamette Valley ★★★ $$$
dry, full-bodied, medium tannin, high acidity **drink now–10 years**
Nice smoky oak and tobacco plus loads of acidity echo Burgundy's Corton.

1998 Cooper Mountain Vineyards Estate Reserve, Willamette Valley ★★★ $$$
dry, medium-bodied, full tannin, medium acidity **drink now–5 years**
An honest Pinot, with a cherry flavor and a touch of smoke.

1999 Domaine Serene Yamhill Cuvée, Yamhill County ★★★ $$$
dry, medium-bodied, medium tannin, high acidity **drink now–12 years**
A country-gentleman sort of wine, elegant but earthy, with the intense flavor of wild raspberries and hints of sage.

1998 Erath Vineyards Reserve, Willamette Valley ★★★ $$$
dry, medium-bodied, medium tannin, medium acidity **drink now–8 years**
Good cherry and strawberry flavors joined by an appealing nuttiness.

1998 Sokol Blosser, Yamhill Valley ★★★ $$$
dry, medium-bodied, medium tannin, high acidity **drink now–8 years**
Hints of cherry and raspberry flavors, with smokiness for complexity and good acidity for balance.

NV Wallace Brook Cellars, Oregon ★★ $$
dry, light-bodied, light tannin, medium acidity **drink now**
From the second label of the famed Adelsheim winery, this light wine offers real pleasure at a low price.

washington state

The largest wine regions in Washington are in the arid desert valleys east of the Cascade Range. Though it may not be immediately obvious, the area's dry, hot summers and bitter winters are as ideal for grapes as they are for apples. The Columbia Valley is the state's biggest wine region; the Yakima and Walla Walla Valleys are subregions.

on the label

As in California and Oregon, labeling by variety is most common.

LATITUDINAL POSTURING

In the late 1970s and early 1980s, a nascent Washington wine industry promoted itself in an odd ad campaign. It suggested that since the state is at the same latitude as Bordeaux, its wines would naturally be as fine. In fact, if this were true, Maine would be a great wine state, and Nova Scotia and Mongolia would be full of up-and-coming vintners. Now Washington produces many world-class wines, and absurd assertions are a thing of the past.

white wines

CHARDONNAY

Washington's Chardonnays can offer relief for those weary of too much oakiness and butteriness. This doesn't mean that you can't find the California style in Washington Chardonnays; certainly a few winemakers provide it. Generally, though, the flavor profile includes apple and pineapple, with a touch of minerality.

at the table

Lean-bodied and high in acidity, typical Washington Chardonnay does well with a lot of light dishes. Try it with white fish, like cod or catfish. Fuller-bodied versions can stand up to a rich risotto or grilled salmon.

the bottom line Even as the state's most expensive white, Washington Chard rarely costs more than $25 a bottle.

recommended wines

1999 Columbia Winery Otis Vineyard Block 6, Yakima Valley ★★★ $$$
dry, full-bodied, high acidity, medium oak **drink now–8 years**
Columbia Winery's many Chards are good across the board, but this, with just a touch of oak, clearly stands out.

1999 L'Ecole No 41, Columbia Valley ★★★ $$
dry, medium-bodied, medium acidity, medium oak **drink now–8 years**
Buttery, but with finesse. A nice mate for lobster.

1999 Hogue Vineyard Selection, Columbia Valley ★★ $$
dry, full-bodied, medium acidity, heavy oak **drink now–4 years**
Not too complex. Still, this Chard has all the right citrus and tropical fruit flavors—and lots of oak.

1999 Covey Run, Columbia Valley ★ $
dry, medium-bodied, high acidity, light oak **drink now**
A refreshing, peachy summer sipper with very good acidity.

RAPID EXPANSION

Growth of the wine industry in the Northwest has been phenomenal. In the last three years, the number of wineries in Washington has almost doubled, increasing from 96 to 170. In Oregon, it's up from 127 to 165.

SAUVIGNON BLANC & SEMILLON

Due to their complementary qualities, tart Sauvignon Blanc and unctuous Semillon (SEH-mee-yohn) are frequently paired in blends. These two grapes also regularly go it alone as single varietals. Grassy, lemony Sauvignon Blanc can have the refreshing effect of sipping lemonade in the middle of a just-cut lawn on a warm summer day. Semillon grown in Washington often has enough acidity to bring out its subtle nut and orange flavors. The varietal is among the state's most appealing wines.

at the table

Refreshingly tart Sauvignon Blanc is just the thing for raw oysters or for mild white fish, like trout, sea bass, or red snapper. Semillon has a bit more body and does well with seared sea scallops, smoked fish, garlicky roast chicken, or pan-seared pork chops. Blends of the two are right for richer dishes, such as fettucine Alfredo or lobster served with melted butter.

the bottom line You shouldn't have to pay more than $15 to get a fine bottle of Sauvignon Blanc or Semillon. Good Sauvignons can even be found for as low as $9. Blends of the two will cost you about the same.

recommended wines

2000 Chateau Ste. Michelle Horse Heaven Vineyard Sauvignon Blanc, Columbia Valley ★★★ $$
dry, medium-bodied, high acidity, light oak **drink now–2 years**
Fresh, zingy fruit flavors like green apples and citrus.

1999 L'Ecole No 41 "Barrel-Fermented" Semillon, Columbia Valley ★★ $$
dry, full-bodied, medium acidity, medium oak **drink now–6 years**
Looking to wean your friends off Chardonnay? This combines familiar Chard flavors with those typical of good Semillon.

1999 Hogue Fumé Blanc, Columbia Valley ★★ $
dry, medium-bodied, medium acidity, light oak **drink in 2 years**
Citrus flavors with a bit of oak, like a yellow ribbon tied 'round the old oak tree.

red wines

at the table

Full-bodied and full-flavored, most Washington reds require big food. Think hearty braised meats (oxtails, lamb shanks, short ribs), roast leg of lamb, or wild mushroom ragù over pasta or polenta. Lighter reds like those made from the Lemberger grape are great for barbecued anything.

the bottom line Washington reds come in all price ranges, though it's unusual to see one over $50. Big wineries (three companies control 50 percent of the state's production) offer a reasonable selection of wines under $15, but for really good quality, spend a little bit more, $18 to $30. Good Syrah will definitely run about $30. At $10 to $12, Lemberger makes an interesting alternative to Beaujolais Nouveau.

MERLOT & CABERNET SAUVIGNON

A few top California Merlots might match or beat the best from Washington. But the average quality of Merlot from Washington is the highest in the country and possibly, excluding the Pomerol region of Bordeaux, in the world. Washington Merlots are full-bodied but generally have less power than those from California. They also tend to be better balanced, with higher acidity. Cabernet Sauvignons are frequently powerful and impressive, more similar to those from Bordeaux than those from California.

what to buy MERLOT & CABERNET SAUVIGNON

1996	1997	1998	1999	2000
★★★	★★★	★★★	★★★	★★★

recommended wines

1999 Woodward Canyon Merlot, Columbia Valley ★★★★ $$$
dry, full-bodied, medium tannin, medium acidity drink now–12 years
This supreme balancing act between fruitiness and minerality shows how well Washington understands Merlot.

1997 Columbia Winery Red Willow Vineyard Milestone Merlot, Yakima Valley ★★★ $$$
dry, full-bodied, full tannin, high acidity drink now–10 years
Plum and spice flavors made even more interesting by a touch of cedar.

1998 DiStefano Cabernet Sauvignon, Columbia Valley ★★★ $$$
dry, full-bodied, medium tannin, medium acidity drink now–8 years
This Cab takes us straight to the Médoc, albeit with an American accent.

1997 Powers Parallel 46, Columbia Valley ★★★ $$$
dry, full-bodied, full tannin, medium acidity drink in 2–12 years
A truckload of cherry flavor with a spot of bourbon adding interest.

1998 Gordon Brothers Cabernet Sauvignon, Columbia Valley ★★★ $$
dry, medium-bodied, medium tannin, medium acidity drink now–8 years
A French female winemaker adds a touch of je ne sais quoi to a luscious, fruity wine.

1998 Columbia Crest Reserve Merlot, Columbia Valley ★★ $$$
dry, medium-bodied, medium tannin, medium acidity **drink now–8 years**
Fruit flavors combine nicely with those from oak aging.

1998 Northstar Merlot, Columbia Valley ★★ $$$
dry, full-bodied, medium tannin, medium acidity **drink now–5 years**
All the velvety texture and plummy flavor we like in an easy-drinking Merlot.

1998 Chateau Ste. Michelle Canoe Ridge Estate Vineyards Merlot, Columbia Valley ★★ $$
dry, medium-bodied, medium tannin, high acidity **drink now–8 years**
Finesse from the cellars of the Pacific Northwest's vinous behemoth. Very dry.

1998 Powers Merlot, Columbia Valley ★ $
dry, medium-bodied, medium tannin, medium acidity **drink now–5 years**
A juicy wine filled with the flavors of plums and apples.

other red wines

Something of an oddity in the U.S., Lemberger (better known in Austria as Blaufränkisch) produces a simple, fruity wine in Washington. Significantly more complex and increasingly popular are Syrah and Cabernet Franc. Syrah is more Rhône-like in Washington than it is in California, with blackberry, smoke, and leather aromas. Cabernet Franc is often blended into other varieties, but it also makes good, spicy wine on its own.

recommended wines

1998 Columbia Crest Reserve Syrah, Columbia Valley ★★★ $$$
dry, full-bodied, medium tannin, medium acidity **drink now–8 years**
Plum and berry aromas with a hint of smokiness lead to tart cherry flavor in this thick, satisfying wine.

1998 Columbia Red Willow Vineyard Syrah, Yakima Valley ★★★ $$$
dry, full-bodied, full tannin, medium acidity **drink in 3–15 years**
Perhaps the most serious Syrah we've encountered from Washington. We'd let this age at least a few years.

1998 Columbia Winery Syrah, Yakima Valley ★★★ $$
dry, full-bodied, full tannin, medium acidity **drink now–8 years**
While the Red Willow Syrah (above) ages, enjoy this lovely though simpler sibling from the same winery.

1997 Hogue Genesis Blue Franc Lemberger, Yakima Valley ★★★ $$
dry, full-bodied, medium tannin, medium acidity **drink now–3 years**
Most Lemberger is a rather simple affair, but fortified with a little Syrah and a touch of Cab, this one belongs at the adults' table.

2000 Glen Fiona Bacchus Vineyard Syrah, Columbia Valley ★★ $$
dry, medium-bodied, medium tannin, medium acidity **drink now–4 years**
A dark berry punch of a wine with mineral flavors that say this isn't for kids.

1999 Kiona Lemberger, Yakima Valley ★★ $$
dry, medium-bodied, light tannin, medium acidity **drink now–3 years**
Need a change? Here's a Lemberger with a bit more to it than the norm.

1997 Preston Cabernet Franc, Columbia Valley ★★ $$
dry, medium-bodied, medium tannin, medium acidity **drink now–5 years**
A wine with the smoke, cherry, black pepper, and tar flavors so characteristic of Cabernet Franc.

1999 Hedges Cellars Red, Columbia Valley ★★ $
dry, medium-bodied, medium tannin, medium acidity **drink now–5 years**
An unusual blend of Bordeaux varieties and Syrah yields a very nice wine.

new york state

Often forgotten, even by New Yorkers themselves, the Empire State is in fact the second largest wine producer in the country. And at the moment, New York may be the most dynamic wine-growing state in the union, with the focus of excitement on Long Island. Its Gulf Stream-moderated climate nurtures French grape varieties, and waves of visitors from nearby New York City provide an eager market.

BUFFALO
Lake Erie
Lake Erie

grapes & styles

Upstate wineries, particularly around Lake Erie, the Finger Lakes, and the Hudson Valley, make the bulk of the state's wine. A lot of it is undistinguished, made from hardy indigenous grapes.

Crosses between native and European grapes frequently lack the complexity of European varieties but make some charming off-dry wines. The best examples, such as Seyval Blanc (say-vahl blahn) and Vidal Blanc (vee-dahl blahn), can be reminiscent of Riesling, Pinot Blanc, or a mild Sauvignon Blanc.

Viticulturists seek out just the right microclimates for the noble varieties to thrive. Rieslings (reece-ling) from the Finger Lakes are the finest of their type in the U.S. Pinot Noir also enjoys some success in the area, as does Chardonnay, particularly for sparkling wine. Though most Hudson Valley wines are made from hybrids, international varieties have done well in some parts of the region. On Long Island, the word is Bordeaux (Cabernet Franc, in particular) for reds, Burgundy (Chardonnay) for whites. All make good, flavorful wines that are more French in style than Californian.

on the label

New York follows the American standard of varietal labeling. A few winemakers use proprietary names for blends, like Cupola, the Bordeaux-style bottling from Bedell Cellars.

white & rosé wines

at the table

Dry New York Riesling is a natural with freshwater fish, like pike. It's also perfect with crab cakes and at clam bakes. Dry, aromatic Gewürztraminers (geh-VAIRTZ-tra-mee-ner) go with spiced Asian dishes like chicken with Szechuan garlic sauce and hot-and-sour shrimp. Pair lighter Long Island Chardonnays with seared tuna or grilled swordfish, oakier ones with lobster or scallops. Hybrids like Seyval or Vidal Blanc can be wonderful as aperitifs. Sip rosé as an apertif, too, or with a luncheon salad.

the bottom line With the exception of a few Long Island Chardonnays, New York whites are a bargain; most prices remain well under $20. Top-quality Rieslings will run you no more than $14; Gewürztraminers cost about $20. Hybrids go for under $10. For Chardonnay, prices hover in the $12 to $20 range, but some of the oaked Long Island wines might set you back $25. Though rosés are inexpensive, $8 to $12, you'll often get better quality at the same price from rosés from the south of France.

what to buy WHITE & ROSE WINES

1998	1999	2000
★★★	★★★	★★★

recommended wines

1997 Hermann J. Wiemer Reserve Johannisberg Riesling, Finger Lakes ★★★★ $$
dry, full-bodied, high acidity, no oak **drink now–8 years**
This is simply the finest American Riesling we have ever tasted.

1997 Hermann J. Wiemer Chardonnay, Finger Lakes ★★★★ $
dry, medium-bodied, medium acidity, light oak **drink now–5 years**
Beautiful aroma, beautiful taste, with a touch of pepperiness and minerality to set it off.

2000 Dr. Konstantin Frank Vinifera Wine Cellars Rkatsiteli, Finger Lakes ★★★ $$
dry, medium-bodied, high acidity, no oak **drink now–3 years**
Rkats-what? The fourth most widely grown white grape in the world—mainly in the former Soviet Union—is made by a master vintner into a fine wine.

1998 Schneider Chardonnay, North Fork ★★★ $$
dry, medium-bodied, medium acidity, light oak **drink now–5 years**
Schneider makes some of the most interesting wines in New York. Some exotic flavor typifies his wine, and this jasmine-touched example is no exception.

1999 Standing Stone Vineyards Reserve Chardonnay, Finger Lakes ★★★ $$
dry, medium-bodied, high acidity, light oak **drink now–7 years**
Loads of fruit flavor in this one, along with some minerality. And the acidity makes it all sing.

2000 Dr. Konstantin Frank Vinifera Wine Cellars Semi-Dry Johannisberg Riesling, Finger Lakes ★★★ $
off-dry, medium-bodied, high acidity, no oak **drink now–8 years**
A lovely potpourri of fruit and flowers, with lots of minerality thrown in.

1999 Fox Run Vineyards Semi-Dry Riesling, Finger Lakes ★★★ $
off-dry, full-bodied, high acidity, no oak **drink now–5 years**
A candidate for the Green Party, this Riesling reminds us of herbs and pine trees. There's lemon zest and some mineral flavors, too.

GETTING AROUND THE BLUE LAWS

Strange but true: In New York City—the city that never sleeps—bars don't close until 4 A.M., but by state law it is illegal to buy a bottle of wine on Sunday, except in restaurants and bars. Because this restriction proved onerous to New York wineries, who derive much of their income from sales to weekend visitors, the state legislature exempted winery tasting rooms from the prohibition. The law did not specify that a winery could have only one tasting room, that it had to be at the winery, or that only the winery's wines could be sold. So Susan Wine (yes, that's her real name), owner of the Hudson Valley's Rivendell Winery, decided that New York City really needed a tasting room. She opened Vintage New York, where you can not only taste but buy any day of the week.

1998 Hermann J. Wiemer Chardonnay, Finger Lakes ★★★ $
dry, medium-bodied, medium acidity, light oak **drink now**
Riesling specialist Wiemer brings out all the typical Chard tropical fruit flavors, but manages to get in a few Riesling-like petrol notes as well.

1998 Lenz Gewürztraminer, North Fork ★★★ $
dry, medium-bodied, high acidity, no oak **drink now–2 years**
The flavors explode on the tongue. Tastes like flowers and herbs generously spritzed with lime.

2000 Wölffer Rosé, The Hamptons ★★★ $
dry, medium-bodied, high acidity **drink now**
Wonderful fruit flavors, to be sure, but also floral and mineral notes.

1999 Corey Creek Vineyards Reserve Chardonnay, North Fork ★★ $$
dry, medium-bodied, medium acidity, medium oak drink now–2 years
Flowers, fruit, and nuts. Oak, too, and good acidity to balance it all.

2000 Galluccio Estate Vineyards Gristina Rosé of Cabernet Sauvignon, North Fork ★★ $$
dry, medium-bodied, medium acidity drink now
Except for its pink color, there's nothing frivolous about this very good wine made from Cabernet Sauvignon.

1998 Lieb Family Cellars Pinot Blanc, North Fork ★★ $$
dry, full-bodied, medium acidity, no oak drink now–2 years
The fruit-touched-by-vanilla flavor here should keep you happy.

2000 Macari Vineyards Sauvignon Blanc, North Fork ★★ $$
dry, medium-bodied, high acidity, no oak drink now–1 year
Good tropical fruit flavors are accentuated by the acidity.

1999 Standing Stone Vineyards Chardonnay, Finger Lakes ★★ $$
dry, medium-bodied, medium acidity, light oak drink now–5 years
Here's a fruit basket of flavors, with a touch of vanilla. Mineral notes add an appealing edge.

1999 Standing Stone Vineyards Gewürztraminer, Finger Lakes ★★ $$
dry, medium-bodied, high acidity, no oak drink now–5 years
Tinged with floral and mineral flavors as a Gewürz should be, this wine also has lush fruit flavors. Very good.

2000 Dr. Konstantin Frank Vinifera Wine Cellars Dry Johannisberg Riesling, Finger Lakes ★★ $
dry, medium-bodied, high acidity, no oak drink now–4 years
Good acidity balances the hints of sweetness in this otherwise dry, fruity, and herbal wine.

1999 Fox Run Vineyards Dry Riesling, Finger Lakes ★★ $
dry, light-bodied, high acidity, no oak drink now–3 years
A nice, dry Riesling at a great price. What's not to like?

1999 Hermann J. Wiemer Dry Johannisberg Riesling, Finger Lakes ★★ $
dry, medium-bodied, medium acidity, no oak drink now–4 years
We don't know whether or not it takes a German to produce a German-style Riesling in New York, but Wiemer certainly makes a distinctive one.

2000 Salmon Run Johannisberg Riesling, Finger Lakes 🍷 ★★ $
dry, medium-bodied, medium acidity, no oak **drink now**
The blue bottle makes us think gimmick. The lovely wine inside just makes us think delicious.

2000 Paumanok Riesling Dry Table Wine, North Fork 🍷 ★ $$
dry, medium-bodied, high acidity, no oak **drink now**
This is a relatively simple wine, but it delivers lovely fruit flavors and the crisp acidity to balance them.

1999 Peconic Bay Winery Rosé of Merlot, North Fork 🍷 ★ $$
dry, medium-bodied, medium acidity **drink now**
While California marketers push sweet-and-a-bit-stupid White Merlot on the masses, folks on Long Island are making a rosé worth drinking.

1999 Clinton Vineyards Seyval Blanc, Hudson Valley 🍷 ★ $
dry, medium-bodied, medium acidity, no oak **drink now**
One of the best hybrids we've tasted, with citrus and pear flavors combined with a nice grassiness and lots of palate-tingling minerality.

2000 Laurel Lake Vineyards Estate Bottled Lake Rosé Cabernet Sauvignon, North Fork 🍷 ★ $
off-dry, medium-bodied, medium acidity **drink now**
A cheerful rosé with cherry flavor accented by a smidgen of spice.

red wines

at the table

Long Island's finest reds can stand up to the standard array of red meat: New York strip, anyone? They are also a fine match for strong-flavored game, like venison. Pinot Noir is perfect with fruit-sauced duck, pork with prunes, or cassoulet.

the bottom line Long Island wines used to be criticized for being overpriced. Quality has risen tremendously in the last few years, and prices had, until recently, remained stable. However, fame, as well as investors who want to see more returns for their money, have pushed prices up. Expect to pay $16 to $20 for most wines, though proprietary blends can be as high as $35. Finger Lakes Pinot Noirs are a tremendous bargain, with few costing more than $12.

what to buy RED WINES

1996	1997	1998	1999	2000
★★★	★★★	★★★★	★★	★★

recommended wines

1999 Fox Run Vineyards Reserve Pinot Noir, Finger Lakes ★★★★ $$
dry, medium-bodied, medium tannin, medium acidity **drink now**
The wonderful concentration of flavors puts this among the finest U.S. Pinots.

1998 Bedell Cellars Cupola, North Fork ★★★ $$$
dry, full-bodied, medium tannin, medium acidity **drink in 1–8 years**
A hodgepodge of earthy, smoky, fruity, spicy, even vegetal flavors. But it works—well.

1997 Palmer Select Reserve Red, North Fork ★★★ $$$
dry, full-bodied, medium tannin, medium acidity **drink now–6 years**
Almost like walking into a humidor, with the wonderful scent of moist tobacco. A mélange of berries, too. Very good.

1998 Dr. Konstantin Frank Vinifera Wine Cellars Cabernet Sauvignon, Finger Lakes ★★★ $$
dry, medium-bodied, full tannin, medium acidity **drink now–10 years**
Terrific Cab. So much for the notion that Riesling's the area's only great wine.

1999 Hermann J. Wiemer Old Vines Pinot Noir, Finger Lakes ★★★ $$
dry, medium-bodied, medium tannin, high acidity **drink now–5 years**
Seems there's something to the idea that old vines produce exceptional fruit. A fine, fine wine.

1998 Paumanok Cabernet Franc, North Fork ★★★ $$
dry, medium-bodied, full tannin, medium acidity **drink in 1–8 years**
Wonderfully fruity and herbal. Mouth-puckering tannin.

1998 Pellegrini Vineyards Cabernet Franc, North Fork ★★★ $$
dry, medium-bodied, full tannin, medium acidity **drink now–8 years**
Chocolaty flavor with hints of black cherry and coffee.

1998 Schneider Cabernet Franc, North Fork ★★★ $$
dry, medium-bodied, medium tannin, high acidity **drink now–10 years**
Bright fruit flavor made even snappier by the good acidity.

O CANADA/VIVA MEXICO

You'd expect Canada to be too cold to make good wine and Mexico too hot. Wrong and wrong. Both countries have microclimates in which the weather is less extreme than in the rest of the nation. At the top of the wine heap in Canada are dessert wines (see page 285) and dry whites, with Riesling and Pinot Blanc the best of all. Among reds, Cabernet Franc and Pinot Noir do well. Mexico produces some Chardonnay and Sauvignon Blanc, but the best wine comes from red varieties like Syrah, Petite Sirah, Tempranillo, Cabernet Sauvignon, and Zinfandel. Wines from both countries are slowly but steadily entering the U.S. market. Look for bottles from these wineries:

Canada Burrowing Owl Vineyard, Cave Spring Cellars, Henry of Pelham, Inniskillin, La Frenz, Pelee Island Winery, Quail's Gate

Mexico Château Camou, L.A. Cetto, Monte Xanic

1999 Standing Stone Vineyards Glen Eldridge Merlot, Finger Lakes ★★★ $$
dry, medium-bodied, medium tannin, medium acidity drink now–8 years
A very good wine from one of New York's most consistent producers.

1998 Hargrave Pinot Noir, North Fork ★★ $$$
dry, medium-bodied, medium tannin, medium acidity drink now–6 years
A spicy, berry-cherry wine. Piquant.

1998 Peconic Bay Winery Cabernet Franc, North Fork ★★ $$
dry, medium-bodied, medium tannin, medium acidity drink now–6 years
An herbal circus. Fruity, too. Interesting.

1999 Potato Barn Red, North Fork ★★ $$
dry, medium-bodied, medium tannin, medium acidity drink now–2 years
We didn't expect much when we pulled the cork but found lots of flavor and good dusty tannin.

NV Dr. Konstantin Frank Vinifera Wine Cellars Fleur de Pinot Noir, Finger Lakes ★ $$
dry, light-bodied, light tannin, medium acidity drink now
Beaujolais style. A nice, simple quaffer.

france

Charles de Gaulle once said of France, "How can you govern a country with 246 different kinds of cheese?" He might have made his point even more strongly had he referred to wine. To date, France has fourteen officially designated wine regions, making an estimated 62,000 types of wine from countless varieties of grapes. The classic wines from Bordeaux, Burgundy, Champagne, and the Rhône are the models on which others around the world are based.

grapes & styles

Unlike most California winemakers, who aim for strong flavors from a single variety of grape, French vintners generally take a more subtle approach. A key concept in France is ***terroir.*** Loosely translated as soil, *terroir* more accurately includes not only the mineral content of the soil and its hydrologic attributes, but also climate, topography, the amount of exposure a vineyard has to the sun, and even such details as scents of aromatic plants growing nearby. A wine reflects its *terroir,* the place from which it came.

on the label

Traditionally, French labels mention the place where a wine comes from rather than the variety or varieties of grapes used to make it. (Wines of Alsace are a major exception.) Still, within regions it is traditional to use certain varieties. Red Burgundy, for instance, is almost invariably made from Pinot Noir. Over the years, it became apparent in each area that particular grapes, and certain vinification techniques, made better wines than others. To ensure set levels of quality, standards were established that codified the different varieties of grapes and techniques

allowed in each region. This system of standards is called Appellation d'Origine Contrôlée (AOC or AC), as is its top category. The hierarchy of AC designations, from highest to lowest, is:

Appellation d'Origine Contrôlée In order to qualify for this designation, a wine must be made in accordance with strict rules concerning geography, grape varieties, harvest size (harvests that are too big are assumed to yield fruit that is too dilute to make excellent wine), vinification techniques, and the amount of alcohol in the wine. These standards vary from region to region, and for subregions within an appellation, stricter standards apply. The requirements for a wine labeled Médoc, a subregion of Bordeaux, are more restrictive than for those labeled simply Bordeaux. And the rules that govern labeling a wine Pauillac, an area within the Médoc, are even more stringent. Generally speaking, the smaller the geographic area named on the label, the more esteemed the wine. Most French wine imported into the U.S. bears an AC label.

Vin Délimité de Qualité Supérieure Despite the fact that the name sounds better, VDQS wines are less prestigious than AC wines. Frequently, the VDQS label is a sort of vinous purgatory, and the wine is eventually promoted to the pearly gates of AC status. VDQS wines make up less than 1 percent of those produced in France.

Vin de Pays Vin de Pays, or country wine, is a broad category guaranteeing that a wine comes from a specific region and meets certain standards. Many innovative winemakers use this designation to experiment with grape varieties and vinification techniques that would be prohibited under AC regulations.

Vin de Table The lowest category, Vin de Table bottlings are usually of no better than jug-wine quality. However, a handful of Vin de Table wines are exceptionally good, made by innovative winemakers who can't be bothered trying to qualify even for Vin de Pays recognition.

alsace

Alsace has a unique place in France. Bordering Germany, it was part of that country twice in the twentieth century. A large number of its residents bear German names, several of its most famous dishes are Germanic, and many of its wines are made from German grapes.

grapes & styles

Over 90 percent of Alsace wine is white. The wines see little time, if any, in new oak. Fruit flavors dominate and are perfectly balanced by high acidity. The Riesling, Gewurztraminer, Muscat, and Pinot Gris age beautifully for a decade or more.

on the label

Wines from Alsace tend to be labeled varietally. About fifty vineyards in Alsace have been designated as superior to others and can bear the designation Grand Cru. Some firms use the name of the vineyard along with the grape variety and leave off the term Grand Cru. Though special terms like Réserve Personelle and Cuvée Particulière are generally applied responsibly to wines of especially good quality, they have no legal meaning. Edelzwicker, sometimes called Gentil, is a simple blend. A few top makers bottle more sophisticated blends and name them for the vineyard from which the grapes came.

what to buy ALSACE

1995	1996	1997	1998	1999	2000
★★★	★★★	★★★	★★	★★★	★★★

PINOT BLANC

The simplest of varietally labeled Alsace wines, Pinot Blanc is generally light-bodied, with nutty and lemony flavors. Unlike many Alsace varietals, this one doesn't age well, but it's honest and enjoyable.

at the table

Since Pinot Blanc is simple, serve it with straightforward dishes, such as roast chicken or herb-crusted turkey breast, baked fish, or a summery pasta tossed with chopped fresh tomatoes, basil, and olive oil.

the bottom line Pinot Blanc can be picked up for a pittance. Bottles from big producers can be found for around $10. A few dollars extra will get you a more complex wine.

recommended wines

1999 Domaine Marc Kreydenweiss Kritt Les Charmes ★★★ $$
off-dry, medium-bodied, high acidity, no oak **drink now–5 years**
Kreydenweiss's labors to restore the earth via the practice of *biodynamie* are rewarded in this fabulous wine with lush earthy and fresh fruit flavors.

1999 Domaine Weinbach Réserve Clos des Capucins ★★ $$
off-dry, medium-bodied, medium acidity, no oak **drink now–2 years**
Weinbach is responsible for some of Alsace's finest and most expensive wines. Here's an opportunity to enjoy their art at an affordable price.

1999 Josmeyer ★★ $$
dry, medium-bodied, medium acidity, no oak **drink now–3 years**
There's an almost beeswax texture to this wine, which allows the lush tropical flavors to wash down smoothly.

1999 Domaine Armand Hurst ★★ $
dry, full-bodied, high acidity, no oak **drink now–3 years**
A wine so intense you'd think it were pear liqueur—except that it's dry.

1998 Preiss-Henny ★★ $
dry, full-bodied, medium acidity, no oak **drink now**
We could happily smell this marzipan- and orange-scented nectar for days. An interesting wine from an old-fashioned producer.

1999 Albert Seltz Réserve ★ $
dry, medium-bodied, medium acidity, no oak **drink now**
Seltz isn't among the ranks of Alsace's best producers, but this wine is just what Pinot Blanc should be—and you can't beat the price.

1999 Paul Blanck ★ $
dry, medium-bodied, high acidity, no oak **drink now**
A perfect, palate-puckering wine, flowery and as tart as a green apple.

1998 Trimbach ★ $
dry, light-bodied, medium acidity, no oak **drink now**
Nice and citrusy. Simple, but a good casual wine.

PINOT GRIS

Also known as Tokay Pinot Gris or Tokay d'Alsace, Pinot Gris is relatively full-bodied and definitely full-flavored, with a nutty, smoky personality.

at the table

Pour Pinot Gris at tables laden with Alsatian specialties, such as sausages, pork, duck, or all of them combined with sauerkraut in *choucroute garni.* Pinot Gris is a winner with roast goose, too. The flexibility of this varietal is such that it will also go with lighter fare, like fish or the local onion tart.

the bottom line Not much Pinot Gris is produced in Alsace, so prices are a little high. Good bottles can be found for around $16, with prices going up to $85. Wines in the mid-$20s offer very good value.

recommended wines

1997 Haag Grand Cru Zinnkoepfle Cuvée Théo ★★★ $$$$
off-dry, full-bodied, medium acidity, no oak **drink now–5 years**
Full aromas of marzipan and baked fruit match the wine's voluptuous body.

1998 Josmeyer ★★★ $$
dry, full-bodied, high acidity, no oak **drink now–5 years**
Bronze-hued and lush with baked fruit, toasted nut, and spice flavors.

1998 Trimbach Réserve ★★★ $$
off-dry, medium-bodied, medium acidity, no oak **drink now–5 years**
Long one of our favorites, this offers the complex flavor found in more expensive wines.

1998 Dopff & Irion ★★ $$
dry, medium-bodied, medium acidity, no oak **drink now–2 years**
Comfortable, not too complicated, but a bit of spice makes it interesting.

1998 Haag Vallée Noble ★★ $$
dry, medium-bodied, medium acidity, no oak **drink now–2 years**
Flavors so lively that sipping the wine is like biting into a caramel apple.

1999 Léon Beyer ★★ $$
dry, medium-bodied, medium acidity, no oak **drink now–2 years**
Supposedly a simple, fruity wine, but this has a more serious earthy quality, too.

1999 Paul Ginglinger Cuvée des Prélats ★★ $$
dry, full-bodied, high acidity, no oak **drink now–5 years**
Mineral flavors so pronounced that it's as if the grapes grew straight through the cracks of a giant piece of granite.

GEWURZTRAMINER

Some people think that Gewurztraminer (geh-VAIRTZ-tra-MEE-ner) offers too much of everything: too much aroma, too much body, too much flavor of fruit, mineral, and spice (*gewürz* is German for "spiced"). But it's a favorite with us. Styles range from medium- to full-bodied.

at the table

Flavorful Gewurztraminer can stand up to pungent or spicy foods. It's a classic companion to ripe Alsatian Muenster cheese sprinkled with cumin. It works as well with hearty vegetarian dishes that contain sweet potatoes or winter squash, and with Indian dishes like chicken *tikka masala* or *aloo gobhi* (spicy potatoes and cauliflower).

the bottom line Basic Gewurztraminers can be found for about $13. Each step up—from bottles in the $18 to $23 range to those around $30 to those over $50—will bring an improvement in quality, making wine from each price category a good value.

recommended wines

1999 Domaine Albert Mann Grand Cru Steingrubler ★★★ $$$
off-dry, full-bodied, medium acidity, no oak **drink now–5 years**
Stuffed with all the classic Gewurz flavors, here's a wine that shows that Albert Mann is one of Alsace's great—and underappreciated—winemakers.

1998 Trimbach ★★★ $$
off-dry, medium-bodied, high acidity, no oak **drink now**
All the typical spice and floral characteristics, plus unusual tropical fruit flavors.

1999 Albert Seltz Réserve ★ $$
dry, medium-bodied, medium acidity, no oak **drink now**
A bit of flowers, spice, and citrus from Seltz.

RIESLING

Alsace produces exceptional Rieslings (reece-ling)—dry, medium-bodied but powerful wines that are beautifully aromatic and full of the flavors of citrus zest, ripe peaches, and minerals.

at the table

Alsace Riesling is one of the world's most flexible wines. It goes as well with grilled fish as it does with game birds or even wild boar. It has the acidity to cut through cream-based sauces and the flavor to stand up to spicy Southeast Asian dishes like Hanoi-style fried fish from Vietnam or curries from Thailand.

the bottom line It's hard to find a better value than Alsace Riesling. Those for $12 are very good; those going for around $25, sublime; those for more, otherworldly.

recommended wines

1999 Domaine Weinbach
Grand Cru Schlossberg Ste-Cathérine ★★★★ $$$$
off-dry, full-bodied, high acidity, no oak **drink now–20 years**
A titan of a wine, grand in quality and scale. This is what Grand Cru is about.

1998 Clos St-Landelin Grand Cru Vorbourg ★★★★ $$$
off-dry, full-bodied, high acidity, no oak **drink now–20 years**
Simply a wonderful wine—an unctuous mouthful with laser-sharp acidity to cut through the slight sweetness.

1995 Léon Beyer Comtes d'Eguisheim ★★★ $$$
dry, full-bodied, high acidity, no oak **drink now–10 years**
Wow. A powerful wine possessing all the Riesling qualities we love.

1999 Domaine Ostertag Vignoble d'Epfig ★★★ $$
dry, medium-bodied, medium acidity, no oak **drink now–3 years**
André Ostertag, one of Alsace's most dynamic and innovative producers, offers a wine that has classic structure but unusual flavors for a Riesling.

1998 Haag Vallée Noble ★★★ $$
off-dry, full-bodied, medium acidity, no oak **drink now–2 years**
More fruit flavor than typical Riesling petrol notes. A palate-pleaser.

1998 Josmeyer ★★★ $$
dry, medium-bodied, medium acidity, no oak **drink now–5 years**
A typically lively and especially good Riesling at a nice price.

1998 Paul Ginglinger Grand Cru Pfersigberg ★★★ $$
dry, full-bodied, high acidity, no oak **drink now–10 years**
Once we realized how little this Grand Cru costs, we happily indulged.

1998 Trimbach ★★ $$$
dry, medium-bodied, high acidity, no oak **drink now–3 years**
A classic Alsatian Riesling from one of the region's best producers.

1997 Albert Seltz Brandluft ★★ $$
dry, medium-bodied, medium acidity, no oak **drink now**
A Riesling of moderation that hums all of the varietal's tunes, without breaking out into roaring song. Nice.

1998 Domaine Marcel Deiss Beblenheim ★★ $$
dry, medium-bodied, medium acidity, no oak **drink now–5 years**
As pleasant as a garden tea party, with flowers, honey, and a squeeze of lemon. Lovely.

1997 Dopff & Irion Domaine du Château de Riquewihr Les Murailles ★★ $$
dry, medium-bodied, high acidity, no oak — **drink now–10 years**
Not for the faint of heart. Still, we're big fans of the deep mineral flavors matched with notes of nuts and honey in this very dry wine.

1999 Paul Ginglinger Cuvée Drei Exa ★★ $$
dry, full-bodied, medium acidity, no oak — **drink now–5 years**
A very nice wine, aromatic with the scents of citrus blossoms and lime flavor that seems to grow with each sip.

1998 Hugel ★ $$
dry, light-bodied, high acidity, no oak — **drink now**
Possibly the best-selling Alsace Riesling in the U.S., with good reason.

1998 Dopff & Irion  ★ $
dry, light-bodied, high acidity, no oak — **drink now**
A good, basic Riesling that lets the food it accompanies take center stage.

OTHER WHITE WINES

Muscat, Sylvaner, and Chasselas turn up on Alsace wine labels, but these varietals can be hard to find. Muscat typically has an abundance of honeysuckle and citrus flavors. Chasselas is usually simple and light-bodied. Sylvaner has a bit more to it—fuller body and higher acidity. Charming though they might be, neither Chasselas nor Sylvaner command very high prices, and they're frequently put into simple blends. Pinot Auxerrois, widely planted in Alsace, usually appears in blends, or in undistinguished bottles labeled (legally) Pinot Blanc. Wines called Auxerrois can be terrific with nutty and smoky flavors.

recommended wines

1995 Josmeyer Herrenweg Pinot Auxerrois ★★★★ $$
dry, full-bodied, high acidity, no oak — **drink now–10 years**
Twenty-five-year-old vines and centuries-old barrels make a stunning wine.

1997 Domaine Marcel Deiss Burg ★★★ $$$
off-dry, full-bodied, high acidity, no oak — **drink now–5 years**
Edelzwicker wines are usually pleasant, if pedestrian. Not this one. A delicious melange of fruit, honeysuckle, and mineral flavors with a drizzle of caramel.

1999 Domaine Armand Hurst Grand Cru Muscat ★★★ $$
dry, full-bodied, high acidity, no oak **drink now–10 years**
Typically floral Muscat notes times ten. Excellent.

1999 Domaine Weinbach Réserve Sylvaner ★★ $$
dry, medium-bodied, high acidity, no oak **drink now–2 years**
This spicy Sylvaner from a top Alsace producer shows just what the grape can do.

1999 Hugel Gentil ★ $
off-dry, light-bodied, medium acidity, no oak **drink now**
Very easy drinkin'.

RECOMMENDED PRODUCERS
Domaine Weinbach (especially anything with the names Ste-Cathérine, Laurence, or Furstentum on the label), Domaine Zind-Humbrecht, Trimbach (Pinot Gris Réserve, Gewurztraminer Cuvée des Seigneurs de Ribeaupierre, Rieslings Cuvée Frédéric Emile and Clos Ste-Hune), Josmeyer (especially Pinot Auxerrois "H" Vieilles Vignes, Riesling Brand, and Gewurztraminer Hengst)

bordeaux

For many, Bordeaux is the quintessential French wine. It is elegant, yet has substance. The region inspires winemakers around the world, providing the model for whites and reds grown in all continents except Antarctica. Imitators don't often succeed. Fortunately, with the tremendous amount of wine produced in Bordeaux—nearly 700 million bottles a year—there's enough to go around.

grapes & styles
Bordeaux is a land of blends. Red wine, which accounts for 70 percent of Bordeaux production, must be made from one or more of five grape varieties: Cabernet Sauvignon, Merlot, Cabernet Franc, Malbec, and Petit Verdot. The first three are by far the most used. White wine comes second in the region overall, but is highly regarded. Whites in Bordeaux must be made with Sauvignon Blanc, Sémillon, Muscadelle, or any mixture of the three.

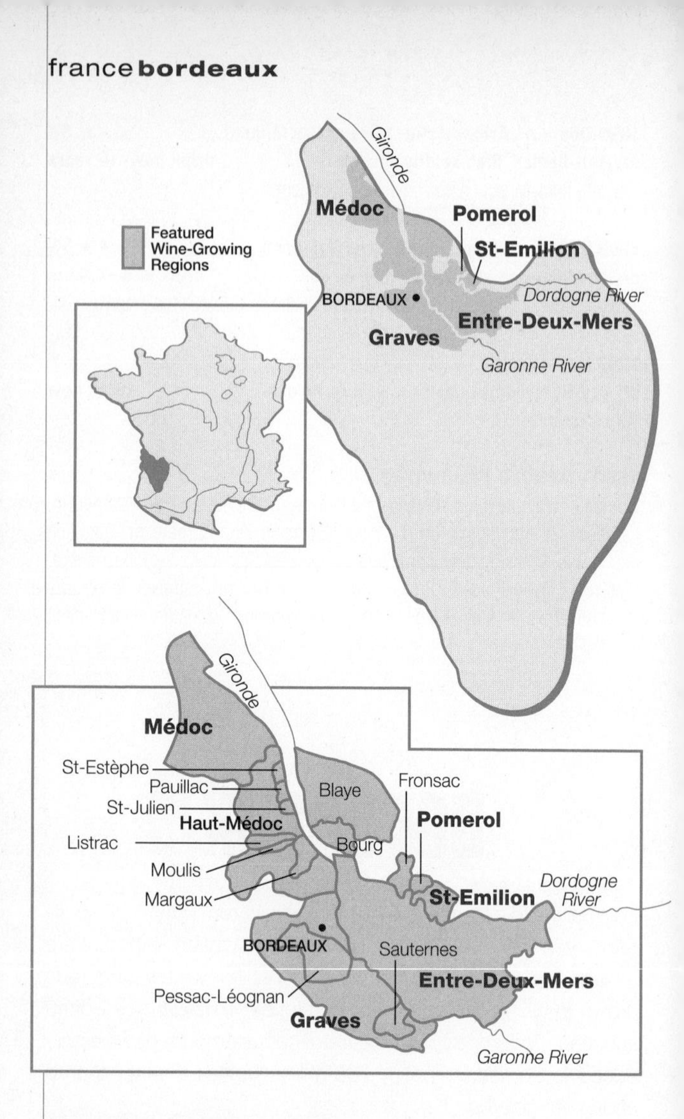

the lay of the land

Bordeaux is divided into three parts: the Left Bank, on the west side of the Gironde estuary and Garonne River; the Right Bank, on the east side of the estuary and the Dordogne River; and Entre-Deux-Mers, between the two rivers. The northern Left Bank is the Médoc, the most prestigious part of which is the Haut-Médoc. Within the Haut-Médoc are several famous villages, such as St-Julien, St-Estèphe, Margaux, and Pauillac. Graves, in the southern Left Bank, contains the prestigious subregion Pessac-Léognan. Pomerol and St-Emilion are the most famous parts of the Right Bank.

on the label

Bordeaux's Cru Classé (classified growth) system ranks individual wineries (called châteaux) and provides a guide to relative quality and price, though certainly not an infallible one. For the wines of the Left Bank, rankings established in 1855 for the best wines are still in place, despite fluctuations in the quality of the wine from different châteaux. Nevertheless, Left Bank wines with the top rating of Premier Cru are still reliably superlative. In 1955, the quality châteaux in St-Emilion on the Right Bank were ranked, and standings are revised every ten years. The great wines of Pomerol remain unclassified, as do the generally simple wines of Entre-Deux-Mers.

red wines

at the table

Red Bordeaux practically demands meat. The wine's strong character and acidity cry out for rack of lamb, filet mignon with a rich sauce, grilled strip steak, or a beef rib roast. Succulent, slow-roasted pork butt also makes an excellent accompaniment. You might not think of Bordeaux and sweetbreads, but that's another great match. For vegetarians, smoked and grilled tofu will stand up to red Bordeaux, but be sure to char it well. Or you can serve Bordeaux with a chunk of Roquefort, which will also provide the fat and flavor needed to tame this tannic wine.

the bottom line Bordeaux is dear in both senses of the word: It's beloved and it's costly. New releases from top-ranked châteaux start at over $150, and for bottles from some stylish micro-wineries (so-called "garage wines"), you can double that figure. The 1999 and 2000 vintages are being heralded as great, so prices in the top category won't be coming down anytime soon. Excellent, less highly ranked wines can be found for a fraction of the cost—$40 to $60. It's still rather a lot. More reasonable are the thousands of Bordeaux wines from less famous appellations. A few from Moulis and Listrac approach the ranked wines in quality. So too can several from Fronsac, Premières Côtes de Blaye, and Côtes de Bourg.

what to buy BORDEAUX RIGHT BANK

1990	1991	1992	1993	1994	1995
★★★★	no stars	★	★★	★★★	★★★

1996	1997	1998	1999	2000
★★★★	★★	★★★★	★★★	★★★★

what to buy BORDEAUX LEFT BANK, EXCLUDING GRAVES

1990	1991	1992	1993	1994	1995
★★★★	★	★	★★	★★★	★★★★

1996	1997	1998	1999	2000
★★★★	★★	★★★	★★★	★★★★

what to buy RED GRAVES

1990	1991	1992	1993	1994	1995
★★★★	★	★	★★★	★★★	★★★

1996	1997	1998	1999	2000
★★★	★★★	★★	★★	★★★★

HIGH PRICES TO COME

The 2000 vintage is reputed to be one of the finest in Bordeaux for several years. The millennium year also has symbolic cachet for collectors. So prices were expected to be significantly higher than those of the preceding year. Sure enough, the announced prices of the 2000s (which haven't even been bottled yet) are more than double those of the 1999s. The anticipated cost to consumers eager for a bottle of 2000 Château Latour when it's released in 2003, for instance, will be well over $300. Nevertheless, all the Premier Cru châteaux and a few other elite châteaux have already sold out the millennium vintage—not bad money, since most of these châteaux produce 240,000 to 360,000 bottles annually.

recommended wines

1998 Château Léoville-Las Cases Grand Vin de Léoville du Marquis de Las Cases, St-Julien ★★★★ $$$$
dry, full-bodied, full tannin, high acidity **drink in 10–20 years**
This prestigious wine from the village of St-Julien proudly displays its pedigree with multiple layers of flavor and a long finish. The wonderful flavors just go on and on and on.

1998 Alter Ego de Palmer, Margaux ★★★★ $$$
dry, full-bodied, medium tannin, medium acidity **drink in 3–15 years**
This second wine of the great Château Palmer offers superb quality—and great value, too.

1998 Blason d'Issan, Margaux ★★★ $$$
dry, medium-bodied, medium tannin, high acidity **drink in 3–10 years**
Other wines of Bordeaux impress us, but when we want to be charmed, we look to this from Château d'Issan.

1998 Carruades de Lafite, Pauillac ★★★ $$$
dry, full-bodied, full tannin, medium acidity **drink in 5–15 years**
With all this flavor, it's amazing that this wine is close to one-tenth the cost of its parent Château Lafite. A fine second-label wine.

1998 Château Chasse-Spleen, Moulis-en-Médoc ★★★ $$$
dry, full-bodied, medium tannin, medium acidity **drink in 3–10 years**
This is a Cru Bourgeois that's a big, babbling brook of berry flavors with a tide of vanilla besides.

1998 Château Lagrange, Pomerol ★★★ $$$
dry, full-bodied, medium tannin, medium acidity **drink in 3–15 years**
Thirty-year-old Merlot vines provide wonderfully rich black-cherry and plum flavors that are soft as velvet in the mouth.

1998 Château Lagrange, St-Julien ★★★ $$$
dry, full-bodied, medium tannin, high acidity **drink in 5–15 years**
Why does one classified wine sell for so much less than another? Enjoy the mysteries of the market with this lovely wine.

1998 Château Mirebeau, Pessac-Léognan ★★★ $$$
dry, medium-bodied, medium tannin, medium acidity **drink in 2–15 years**
In a land where a château's age is measured in centuries, it's thrilling to see something from a new estate that's as good as this.

1998 Château St-Georges, St-Georges-St-Emilion ★★★ $$$
dry, full-bodied, full tannin, medium acidity **drink in 3–10 years**
Like an overstuffed closet, this wine's many aromas and flavors tumble out the minute it's opened.

1998 Château Sociando-Mallet, Haut-Médoc ★★★ $$$
dry, full-bodied, full tannin, medium acidity **drink in 5–10 years**
Comparable in quality to a classified wine. Impressive.

1998 Château Fourcas Hosten, Listrac-Médoc ★★★ $$
dry, full-bodied, full tannin, high acidity **drink in 5–10 years**
The intensity of the fruit flavors makes us think of California; the dry, dry finish brings us back to Bordeaux.

1998 Château Greysac Cru Bourgeois, Médoc ★★★ $$
dry, medium-bodied, medium tannin, medium acidity **drink in 3–10 years**
Floral and earthy flavors combined with the full, fruity taste of cassis. Lovely.

1997 Château Pichon Longueville Comtesse de Lalande Réserve de la Comtesse, Pauillac ★★★ $$
dry, medium-bodied, medium tannin, medium acidity **drink in 5–12 years**
Others can pay four times as much for Château Pichon Longueville. We'll take this marginally less fine second-label wine.

1998 Château De La Tour, Bordeaux Supérieur ★★★ $
dry, medium-bodied, medium tannin, high acidity **drink now–5 years**
Bordeaux, a land of unsung bargains? With wines like this, we have to say yes.

2000 Château Penin Clairet, Bordeaux ★★★ $
dry, medium-bodied, light tannin, high acidity **drink now**
A charming example of wine made from Clairet, a light red grape. Rare to find these rosé-like Bordeaux in the U.S.

1998 Château de Carles, Fronsac ★★ $$
dry, medium-bodied, medium tannin, medium acidity **drink in 3–8 years**
More spicy fruit flavor than Bordeaux costing twice the price. Buy some now and put it away.

1997 Château Frank Phélan, St-Estèphe ★★ $$
dry, medium-bodied, medium tannin, medium acidity **drink now–7 years**
This second-label wine of Château Phélan Ségur, a Cru Bourgeois that deserves a higher rank, offers lovely drinking without long aging.

1998 Château La Cardonne Cru Bourgeois, Médoc ★★ $$
dry, medium-bodied, medium tannin, high acidity **drink in 2–5 years**
For years a favorite among the affordable Bordeaux, this pleases yet again.

1997 Château Larose-Trintaudon Cru Bourgeois, Haut-Médoc ★★ $$
dry, medium-bodied, medium tannin, medium acidity **drink in 2–5 years**
A reasonably priced wine that comes close to the big boys.

1998 Château Les Ricards, Premières Côtes de Blaye ★★ $$
dry, full-bodied, full tannin, medium acidity **drink in 3–8 years**
Thirty-five-year-old vines and low grape yields make a wine full of wonderfully concentrated fruit flavors and hints of cedar.

1998 Château Puy-Blanquet Grand Cru, St-Emilion ★★ $$
dry, full-bodied, medium tannin, medium acidity **drink now–8 years**
There's a lot of depth to this Grand Cru, but it's friendly enough to have with dinner tonight.

1998 Moulin de Duhart, Pauillac ★★ $$
dry, full-bodied, full tannin, medium acidity **drink in 3–10 years**
The second-tier wine of Château Duhart-Milon. Very good.

1997 Château des Graves, Bordeaux Supérieur ★★ $
dry, medium-bodied, light tannin, medium acidity **drink now–3 years**
Though this wine is full of fine mineral flavors, it has an easy-to-drink fruitiness as well.

1998 Château Guiraud-Cheval Blanc, Côtes de Bourg ★★ $
dry, medium-bodied, full tannin, medium acidity **drink now–3 years**
Don't be fooled by the low price. This is a very good wine, full of rich berry and cassis flavors.

1999 Château Saint-Sulpice, Bordeaux ★★ $
dry, light-bodied, medium tannin, high acidity **drink now**
A wine to remind us that most Bordeaux is everyday wine. This one can make every day a bit more pleasant.

1996 Château du Queyron, Premières Côtes de Bordeaux ★ $
dry, medium-bodied, medium tannin, high acidity **drink now**
An elegant, appealing wine at a low price.

1999 Château Haut Maginet, Bordeaux ★ $
dry, medium-bodied, light tannin, medium acidity **drink now–2 years**
A simple wine with juicy fruit flavors and a little spice.

1999 Lafleur Chévalier, Bordeaux ★ $
dry, medium-bodied, medium tannin, medium acidity **drink now**
This is simple, sure, but it has some nice berry flavors and it tastes just like Bordeaux should.

white wines

In addition to the simple, light whites from Entre-Deux-Mers, there are serious white Bordeaux, most notably those from Graves (grahv). These typically medium-bodied wines are full of character, reflecting the gravel-based soil in which the grapes are cultivated.

at the table

There used to be a French advertising slogan, "entre deux huitres, Entre-Deux-Mers" (between two oysters, Between-Two-Seas), emphasizing the perfect pairing of oysters or other raw shellfish with Entre-Deux-Mers wines. Match them with salads or lean fish as well. More complex whites, such as those from Graves, can accompany a range of possibilities, from light fish to somewhat heavier fare: scallops and lobster; oily, full-flavored fish, like salmon, tuna, or mackerel; and poultry with cream sauce.

the bottom line Demand isn't generally high for white Bordeaux, so values are great. A lot of Entre-Deux-Mers is under $10. Most good Graves will cost just $10 to $15. Rare Graves wines from top producers can be expensive—over $50—but look for bottles priced in the low $20s for equally good drinking.

recommended wines

1998 Château Carbonnieux, Pessac-Léognan ★★★★ $$$
dry, full-bodied, medium acidity, light oak **drink now–8 years**
One of our favorite Grand Cru Classé whites from France, with a beautiful balance of luscious flavors, tropical fruit, mineral, and oak.

1999 Les Arums de Lagrange, Bordeaux ★★★ $$
dry, full-bodied, medium acidity, light oak **drink now–8 years**
So full of fruit flavors that it seems off-dry at first. A second sip reveals herbal notes and gives a much drier impression.

1996 Château Rahoul, Graves ★★ $$$
dry, medium-bodied, medium acidity, medium oak **drink now**
An unusual Graves with caramel and earth flavors as well as lemon. Interesting.

1999 Château Valoux, Pessac-Léognan ★★ $$
dry, light-bodied, medium acidity, light oak **drink now–3 years**
The grapes draw a palate-stimulating steeliness from the gravelly soil, adding interest to the citrus flavor of this wine.

2000 Château Bonnet, Entre-Deux-Mers ★★ $
dry, medium-bodied, high acidity, no oak **drink now**
In a sea (or two) of mediocre whites coming from Entre-Deux-Mers, this crowd-pleaser stands out with zippy, refreshing peach and grass flavors.

1998 Château La Rose Bellevue, Côtes de Blaye ★★ $
dry, medium-bodied, medium acidity, light oak **drink now**
Here's an ideal summer sipper. It has refreshing citrus, tropical fruit, and melon flavors.

1999 Château Terres Douces, Bordeaux ★ $
dry, light-bodied, high acidity, light oak **drink now**
Cheap and cheerful, with a touch of lime flavor and excellent acidity. Good with raw shellfish.

1999 Sauvignon des Tourelles, Bordeaux ★ $
dry, light-bodied, high acidity, no oak **drink now**
A lemon-lime, green-grass quencher.

Let's be up-front about this: Burgundy is confusing. It's a bureaucratic puzzle complicated further by the fact that companies, rather than individual winemakers, are the traditional driving force in the region. Whereas in Bordeaux there is a relatively clear-cut system of classifying châteaux (individual wineries), in Burgundy it's the vineyards that are ranked—and each one can be split among dozens of people, some of whom own only a few rows of vines. Therefore, grapes harvested from a single ranked vineyard can find their way into the wines of dozens of different companies. But working through the confusion is well worthwhile. At its best, the wine of Burgundy is simply the finest in the world.

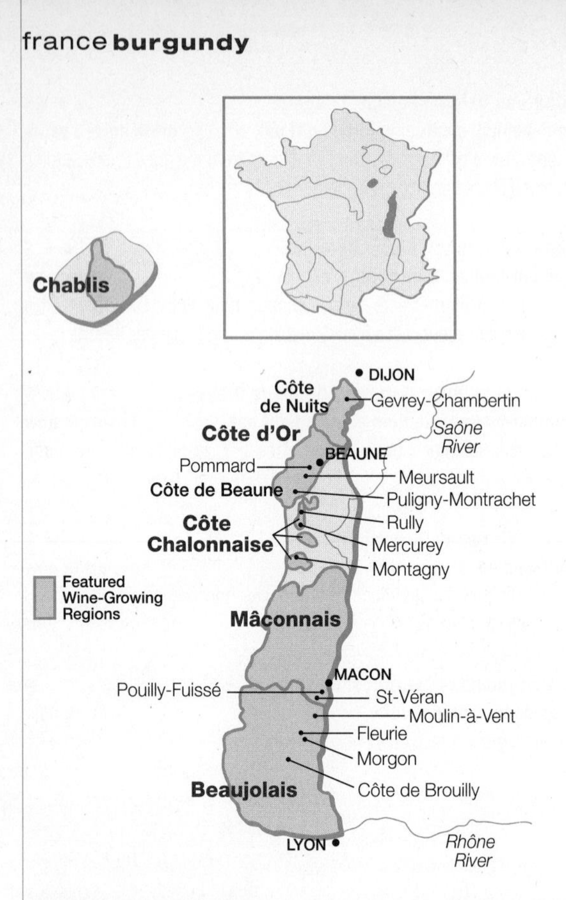

lay of the land

Burgundy is divided into five districts, from north to south: Chablis is white wine country, the Côte d'Or and the Côte Chalonnaise produce both red and white, the Mâconnais white, and Beaujolais primarily red.

grapes & styles

The grapes of Burgundy are incredibly easy to master. Everywhere except for Beaujolais, it's Pinot Noir for reds, Chardonnay for whites. Another white grape, Aligoté, is also used in the region, but wines made from it are not often seen in the U.S. Pinot Blanc is present, too, but minimally. In Beaujolais, the Gamay grape is used for reds. Unlike many Chardonnays from California, Burgundian whites exude finesse; they're rarely overbearing in their oakiness. Reds can be light- to full-bodied, with most falling in between. They have medium tannin.

on the label

Though in reality understanding Burgundy wines may be difficult, the basis of the Burgundian Appellation Contrôlée system is similar to that used all over France, moving from the general to the more specific, and is entirely logical:

Regional Any wine produced in Burgundy (Bourgogne) from designated grape varieties grown in the region. Sometimes the grape variety will also appear on the label, such as Bourgogne-Pinot Noir.

Subregion/District Wine produced from designated grapes grown in one of the named districts—Chablis, for instance. Subregion names with the word *villages* appended, like Chablis-Villages, are even better.

Village Wine made from grapes grown within the boundaries of a particular village and labeled with its name, like Volnay.

Premier Cru Wine made from grapes grown in vineyards that have been recognized as excellent. Of roughly 4,000 vineyards in Burgundy, fewer than 600 have Premier Cru status. Wines that are a blend of grapes from different Premier Cru vineyards can append the village name to the designation Premier Cru. Wines from grapes grown in a single Premier Cru vineyard are even more prestigious and are allowed to add the name of the vineyard rather than that of the village, as in Corbettes Premier Cru. It should be noted that though Premier Cru is secondary to Grand Cru in Burgundy, in Bordeaux, the terms are reversed, with Premier Cru the superior designation.

Grand Cru Fewer than forty vineyards in Burgundy have been granted the distinction Grand Cru. Wines from these vineyards are usually the finest of the region and often require several years of aging for their potential to emerge. The reputations of these vineyards are so great that often Grand Cru won't even appear on the label. The vineyard name, such as Montrachet or Chambertin, says it all. If the names don't ring Grand Cru in your ears, their prices certainly will.

Caution: Several villages that have a Grand Cru vineyard within their borders have, in their pride, appended its name to their own. For example, the village of Gevrey became Gevrey-Chambertin. Wine labeled Gevrey-Chambertin is often excellent, but it isn't Chambertin. It's a Village wine, not a Grand Cru.

at the table

White Burgundies have higher acidity than Californian or Australian Chardonnays and are therefore more food-friendly. Chablis's mineral flavors match the brininess of oysters perfectly. Pair a simple Mâconnais white with grilled chicken. Premier or Grand Cru wines are right for whole white fish roasted with herbs and are also powerful enough for salmon or pork loin.

Reds offer great flexibility. Light-bodied wines can be served with most fish, heavier ones with red meat and game. The largest category, medium-bodied, is an excellent choice when people have ordered different dishes in a restaurant. As for Beaujolais, the simplest are good with burgers or pizza. The more complex do well with bistro dishes: roast chicken, *boeuf bourguignon,* lamb stew.

the bottom line The total production of Burgundy is relatively small: one-tenth that of Bordeaux. And yet Burgundy prices are often lower than those asked for Bordeaux. A simple but enjoyable Mâconnais can be found for around $10. Many Bourgogne Blancs go for $14, and a few Village wines sell for under $20. Frequently overlooked, quality wines from the Chalonnaise, including some Premier Crus but not those from Mercurey, can be had for between $15 and $25. Premier and Grand Cru whites from the more famous areas start at $35 and can skyrocket from there. Among reds, simple Bourgogne wines are available for around $16. More substantial wines start at $40. The simplest Beaujolais is cheap, $6, and superior bottlings can be found for under $20.

chablis

Light- to medium-bodied and very dry, Chablis whites are some of the best on earth. Unlike most Chardonnays, those of Chablis traditionally see little oak, and so the taste of the grapes and the *terroir* (see page 78) come through clearly. The region's cool climate keeps acidity levels high, and Chablis has a steely edge from the region's chalky-limestone soil. The most typical fruit flavor is that of lemon; sometimes there's a taste of pear as well.

what to buy CHABLIS

1996	1997	1998	1999	2000
★★★★	★★★	★★★	★★★	★★

recommended wines

1999 Christian Moreau Père & Fils Grand Cru Les Clos ★★★★ $$$$
dry, full-bodied, medium acidity, medium oak **drink now–10 years**
Mysteriously, tropical fruit flavors show up in this wine from the mineral-laden soils of Chablis. Exceptional.

1998 Domaine William Fèvre Grand Cru Les Preuses ★★★★ $$$$
dry, full-bodied, medium acidity, light oak **drink now–10 years**
An excellent Grand Cru that lives up to its designation with complex flavors.

1998 Jean-Marc Brocard Premier Cru Montée de Tonnerre ★★★★ $$
dry, medium-bodied, high acidity, no oak **drink now–10 years**
A superb wine combining fruit flavors with excellent minerality.

1998 Domaine Laroche Premier Cru Les Vaillons Vieilles Vignes ★★★ $$$
dry, full-bodied, medium acidity, medium oak **drink now–8 years**
The wisdom of age shows; the old vines that produce the grapes in this wine seem to have absorbed all that the soil offers.

1999 Jean-Pierre Grossot Premier Cru Fourneaux ★★★ $$$
dry, medium-bodied, medium acidity, light oak **drink now–6 years**
So buttery, you'd think its maker was California dreamin'. But it's enlivened by the lemon and mineral flavors of home.

1999 Verget Terroir de Chablis ★★★ $$
dry, medium-bodied, medium acidity, no oak **drink now–3 years**
Any of the wines of Jean-Marie Guffens (the man behind Verget) are well worth drinking. This one is no exception.

1998 Prosper Maufoux Premier Cru Mont de Milieu ★★ $$$
dry, medium-bodied, medium acidity, medium oak **drink now–6 years**
Good, typical lemon and mineral flavors pour out of this wine.

1999 Christian Moreau Père & Fils ★★ $$
dry, medium-bodied, high acidity, no oak **drink now–2 years**
A great wine to complement any raw shellfish.

1999 Olivier Leflaive ★★ $$
dry, full-bodied, medium acidity, no oak **drink now–3 years**
As if the steely mineral and lemon flavors weren't enough, the low price from a fine producer makes us like this even more.

RECOMMENDED PRODUCERS
Billaud-Simon, Jean-Marc Brocard, La Chablisienne, Jean Dauvissat, René et Vincent Dauvissat, William Fèvre, Jean-Pierre Grossot, Domaine Laroche, Olivier Leflaive, Christian Moreau Père & Fils, Jean-Marie Raveneau, Verget, Domaine du Chardonnay

OAK BARRELS

Just as the variety of grape, where the grapes are grown, and how they're vinified affect the taste of wine, so too does the type of oak used to make barrels, the size of the barrels, and their age. French oak, currently the most coveted oak in the world, imparts subtle spice and vanilla flavors. Much more assertive in flavor, American oak contributes stronger spice and vanilla flavors along with its telltale taste of coconut. American oak barrels are favored in the U.S., throughout Spain, and in Australia, where they complement hearty grapes like Shiraz. Slovenian oak, quite popular in Italy, has a strength somewhere between American and French. Wine aged in small barrels gets more oak taste because it has more exposure to the wood than it does in large barrels. The older a barrel is, the less effect it has. After three years of use, a barrel has given all its flavor to wine, and its effect is negligible.

côte d'or

The world's finest Chardonnays and Pinot Noirs come from the Côte d'Or—bar none. Famous red-wine producing villages in the subregion Côte de Nuits include Flagey-Echezeaux, Gevrey-Chambertin, Morey-St-Denis, and St-Aubin. The Côte de Beaune is renowned for its medium-bodied whites. Among the most important village names are Meursault (muhr-so) and Puligny-Montrachet (poo-lee-n'yee mohn-rah-shay). Excellent red wines are also made in the district, most famously the powerful Pommard and the silky Volnay, but also Aloxe-Corton and Beaune. Chassagne-Montrachet and Santenay are known for both reds and whites. In both Côte de Nuits and Côte d'Or, the finest wines are named after their vineyards—for example, Montrachet or Romanée-Conti.

what to buy COTE D'OR WHITE WINES

1997	1998	1999	2000
★★★	★★★	★★★	★★★

recommended white wines

1999 Domaine Jacques Prieur Clos de Mazeray Monopole, Meursault ★★★★ $$$$
dry, full-bodied, high acidity, medium oak **drink now–10 years**
One of Meursault's best producers makes one of Meursault's best wines from one of Meursault's best vineyards. Luscious.

1999 Domaine Jacques Prieur Grand Cru, Montrachet ★★★★ $$$$
dry, full-bodied, medium acidity, heavy oak **drink in 3–15 years**
Simply a great wine—loads of flavor, yet so well balanced that it's elegant.

1999 Henri Clerc Grand Cru, Chevalier-Montrachet ★★★★ $$$$
dry, full-bodied, medium acidity, medium oak **drink in 2–10 years**
A Grand Cru that deserves its designation. Lots of citrus and a grind of fresh pepper.

1999 Jean-Marc Boillot Premier Cru Champ-Gain, Puligny-Montrachet ★★★★ $$$$
dry, full-bodied, medium acidity, medium oak **drink in 3–12 years**
A superb wine from one of Burgundy's best vintners. The fruit flavors mingle perfectly with the oak and smoky minerality.

1999 Roger Belland Premier Cru Les Champs Gains, Puligny-Montrachet ★★★ $$$$
dry, medium-bodied, high acidity, light oak **drink now–10 years**
Limestone-rich soil and a lot of exposure to the sun bring us this terrific wine high in spice, mineral, and fruit flavors.

1999 Bernard Moreau Premier Cru Morgeot, Chassagne-Montrachet ★★★ $$$
dry, full-bodied, high acidity, medium oak **drink in 2–10 years**
An oaky, smoky, intensely orange- and lemon-flavored wine that needs a couple of years to settle down. Oh, but when it does...

1999 Domaine Chandon de Briailles Premier Cru Ile des Vergelesses, Pernand-Vergelesses ★★★ $$$
dry, medium-bodied, medium acidity, medium oak **drink now–10 years**
Here's a wonderful wine with a floral scent, fruit and mineral flavors, and a silky texture.

1999 Domaine Hubert Lamy Premier Cru Les Frionnes, St-Aubin ★★★ $$$
dry, full-bodied, medium acidity, heavy oak **drink in 2–10 years**
Lots of oak, but lots of pineapple, smoke, and mineral flavors, too. This is an excellent wine.

1999 Olivier Leflaive, Puligny-Montrachet ★★★ $$$
dry, medium-bodied, medium acidity, light oak **drink now–7 years**
Burgundy's too far north for olive trees, but somehow this wine picked up notes of olive oil to go with its smoke and lemon.

1999 Jean Pierre Diconne, Auxey-Duresses ★★★ $$
dry, medium-bodied, medium acidity, light oak **drink now–8 years**
Another white from a mostly red land; another success with tropical fruit flavors checked by a jolt of minerals.

1999 Olivier Leflaive Les Sétilles, Bourgogne ★★★ $$
dry, medium-bodied, medium acidity, light oak **drink now–5 years**
Leflaive must have mixed up the barrels for this one; it's a far better wine than its basic Bourgogne label (and price) indicate.

1999 Antonin Rodet, Meursault ★★ $$$
dry, full-bodied, medium acidity, medium oak **drink now–5 years**
Appealing orange and clove flavors sharpened by flinty notes.

1999 Domaine Giboulot Les Pierres Blanches, Côte de Beaune ★★ $$$
dry, medium-bodied, medium acidity, light oak **drink now–8 years**
Applying biodynamic agricultural techniques and using wild yeasts, Giboulot offers all-natural wines full of flavor.

1999 Henri Clerc Chaume Gaufriot, Beaune ★★ $$$
dry, full-bodied, medium acidity, medium oak **drink now–5 years**
This vineyard isn't designated, but its wines are definitely Premier Cru quality.

1998 Domaine Geantet-Pansiot, Bourgogne ★★ $$
dry, medium-bodied, medium acidity, heavy oak **drink now–6 years**
There's a bit too much toasty oak for our taste, but with the nice spice and citrus flavors and low price, we're not complaining.

RECOMMENDED PRODUCERS
Jean-Marc Boillot, Henri Clerc, Marc Colin, Domaine des Comtes Lafon, Domaine Michel Colin-Deléger, Château Génot-Boulanger, Domaine Leflaive, Olivier Leflaive, Verget, Domaine Ramonet, Domaine Guy Bocard, Antonin Rodet, Etienne Sauzet

what to buy COTE D'OR RED WINES

1997	1998	1999	2000
★★★	★★★	★★★	★

recommended red wines

1999 Robert Arnoux Grand Cru, Echezeaux ★★★★ $$$$
dry, full-bodied, full tannin, medium acidity **drink in 5–15 years**
An exceptional, highly perfumed wine with rich fruit and spice flavors.

1998 Joseph Voillot Premier Cru Les Rugiens, Pommard ★★★ $$$$
dry, full-bodied, medium tannin, medium acidity **drink in 2–10 years**
A classic Pommard, with strawberry flavor and herbal notes.

1998 Vincent Girardin Grand Cru, Corton-Perrières ★★★ $$$$
dry, full-bodied, full tannin, medium acidity **drink in 3–15 years**
So dense that if we didn't know better we'd swear this was Cornas (from the Rhône) rather than Corton. Smoky and meaty.

1999 Henri Perrot-Minot, Gevrey-Chambertin ★★★ $$$
dry, medium-bodied, medium tannin, medium acidity **drink now–5 years**
Not many Gevrey-Chambertins live up to the last half of their name, but this comes close.

1999 Jean-Marc Bouley Premier Cru Les Reversées, Beaune ★★★ $$$
dry, medium-bodied, medium tannin, medium acidity **drink now–5 years**
Straightforward fruit, spice, and smoke flavors.

1999 Joseph Voillot Premier Cru Les Frémiets, Volnay ★★★ $$$
dry, full-bodied, medium tannin, medium acidity **drink in 2–10 years**
Rich fruit and mineral flavors and, unusual for wine from Frémiets, full-bodied.

1999 Olivier Leflaive Premier Cru, Monthélie ★★★ $$$
dry, medium-bodied, medium tannin, medium acidity drink now–8 years
A delicious wine with berry flavors.

1998 Château de Gevrey-Chambertin, Gevrey-Chambertin ★★★ $$
dry, medium-bodied, medium tannin, medium acidity drink now–8 years
Wonderful, deep raspberry flavor.

1999 Jean-Claude Belland, Santenay ★★★ $$
dry, medium-bodied, medium tannin, medium acidity drink now–6 years
Lip-smacking cherry, chocolate, and anise flavors from start to finish; all for a fair price.

1999 Nicolas Potel Maison Dieu Vieilles Vignes, Bourgogne ★★★ $$
dry, medium-bodied, medium tannin, medium acidity drink now–8 years
Really intense for a simple Bourgogne. A bargain.

1999 Château Génot-Boulanger Premier Cru Clos du Chapitre, Aloxe-Corton ★★ $$$
dry, medium-bodied, medium tannin, medium acidity drink now–7 years
It isn't Corton, but it's good value, with more accessible flavors when young than its illustrious neighbor.

1998 Vincent Girardin Premier Cru Clos des Ormes, Morey-St-Denis ★★ $$$
dry, medium-bodied, full tannin, medium acidity drink in 2–10 years
A smoky wine with red fruit flavors and cedarlike aromas.

1999 Château de Maltroye, Chassagne-Montrachet ★★ $$
dry, medium-bodied, medium tannin, medium acidity drink now–5 years
This is a different sort of red Burgundy—loaded with mineral flavors carried by ripe fruit.

1999 Robert Arnoux Pinot Fin, Bourgogne ★★ $$
dry, medium-bodied, medium tannin, medium acidity drink now–5 years
When we want the taste of good Burgundy without paying a Burgundian price, we reach for this.

RECOMMENDED PRODUCERS

Robert Arnoux, Jean-Claude Belland, Domaine Sylvain Cathiard, Domaine Dujac, Camille Giroud, Château Génot-Boulanger, Louis Jadot, Nicolas Potel, Gaston et Pierre Ravaut, Antonin Rodet, Domaine de la Romanée-Conti, Domaine Armand Rousseau, Domaine de l'Arlot, Olivier Leflaive, Henri Perrot-Minot, Domaine Jean Boillot, Domaine des Lambray, Joseph Voillot

côte chalonnaise

Just because you aren't a star doesn't mean you can't act. The Côte Chalonnaise is less celebrated than the Côte d'Or, but it produces a lot of very good wine, much of it, red and white, with Premier Cru status. And because the Côte Chalonnaise lacks flash, its wines are more reasonably priced than those from the Côte d'Or. Look for reds from Givry, Mercurey, and Rully; whites from Montagny and Rully.

recommended wines

1999 Jean-Marc Boillot Premier Cru La Pucelle, Rully ★★★★ $$$
dry, full-bodied, medium acidity, medium oak **drink now–10 years**
From one of the greatest producers in Burgundy: an absolutely luscious wine.

1999 Domaine Ragot Premier Cru La Grande Berge, Givry ★★★★ $$
dry, full-bodied, full tannin, medium acidity **drink now–10 years**
Rich berry flavor and a compelling earthiness. Great.

1999 Antonin Rodet Château de Rully, Rully ★★★ $$
dry, medium-bodied, medium acidity, light oak **drink now–8 years**
Intensely aromatic. This could pass for a great Chenin Blanc from the Loire.

1999 Domaine Emile Juillot Premier Cru Les Combins, Mercurey ★★★ $$
dry, medium-bodied, medium tannin, medium acidity **drink now–8 years**
A mineral-studded wine with blackberry and cherry flavors.

1999 François Raquillet Premier Cru Les Peuillets, Mercurey ★★★ $$
dry, full-bodied, medium tannin, medium acidity **drink now–8 years**
This wine is thick with concentrated berry and spice flavors.

1999 Château Génot-Boulanger Les Bacs, Mercurey ★★ $$
dry, medium-bodied, medium acidity, medium oak **drink now–8 years**
A charming wine with citrus flavors, a bit of oak, and a creamy texture.

1999 Jacques Dury La Chaume, Rully ★★ $$
dry, medium-bodied, medium acidity, light oak **drink now–6 years**
An earthy white with mineral and almond notes and appealing lemon flavors.

1999 Michel Picard Château de Davenay Premier Cru, Montagny 🍷 ★★ $$
dry, full-bodied, high acidity, medium oak **drink now–6 years**
Nice citrus and floral flavors here.

RECOMMENDED PRODUCERS
Jean-Marc Boillot, Jacques Dury, Domaine Jean-Marc Joblot, Faiveley, Michel Juillot, Louis Latour, Antonin Rodet, A & P de Villaine, Château Génot-Boulanger

mâconnais

Not so long ago, many saw the Mâconnais as the simpleton of the cultured Burgundy family. Most of its inexpensive wines were fine for quaffing in cafés, but rarely suitable company for a fine repast. Things have changed. Sloppy viticulture favoring quantity over quality has been replaced by better techniques. Mâcon now produces white wine with good acidity and mineral flavors. Pouilly-Fuissé (poo-yee fwee-say) is the best-known appellation in the Mâconnais, and, accordingly, the most expensive. The wines of St-Véran are often just as good and a little cheaper. Look for wines labeled Mâcon Villages, or Mâcon plus the name of a village, for the best value. Mâcon-Viré or Mâcon-Lugny are particularly good.

what to buy MACONNAIS

1997	1998	1999	2000
★★★	★★★	★★★★	★★

recommended wines

1999 Château Fuissé, Pouilly-Fuissé ★★★ $$$
dry, full-bodied, medium acidity, light oak **drink now–5 years**
True orange flavors are joined by a bit of spice.

1999 Château Fuissé Vieilles Vignes, Pouilly-Fuissé ★★★ $$$
dry, full-bodied, medium acidity, light oak **drink now–5 years**
Old vines show their stuff with generous marzipan flavor along with citrus and minerals. Very good.

1999 Château de Beauregard, Pouilly-Fuissé ★★★ $$
dry, full-bodied, medium acidity, medium oak **drink now–5 years**
A fruit cocktail of concentrated apple, orange, and pear flavors complemented by good minerality.

1999 Domaine de Roally, Mâcon-Villages ★★★ $$
dry, full-bodied, medium acidity, medium oak **drink now–4 years**
Loaded with luscious fruit flavors and good acidity.

1999 Domaine des Deux Roches Les Terres Noirs, St-Véran ★★★ $$
dry, full-bodied, medium acidity, heavy oak **drink now–6 years**
Whether it's the black earth of its name or some sort of black magic, this organically grown wine is sumptuous.

1999 Domaine St-Denis, Mâcon-Chardonnay ★★★ $$
dry, medium-bodied, medium acidity, no oak **drink now–5 years**
The tropical fruit flavors might lull you to sleep—if it weren't for the jolt of acidity at the end.

1999 Louis Jadot, Pouilly-Fuissé ★★★ $$
dry, medium-bodied, medium acidity, medium oak **drink now–5 years**
A caramel-tinged wine with spicy fruit flavors and herb and mineral notes.

1998 Domaine les Combelières, Viré-Clessé ★★ $$
dry, medium-bodied, medium acidity, light oak **drink now–3 years**
Lots of tasty lemon in this wine from an often overlooked area of Burgundy. Some floral and stony characteristics, too.

1999 J.J. Vincent Propriété Marie-Antoinette Vincent, Pouilly-Fuissé ★★ $$
dry, medium-bodied, medium acidity, light oak **drink now–2 years**
This wine delivers consistently year after year. Citrus and floral flavors with cleansing minerality.

1999 Michel Picard, Pouilly-Fuissé ★★ $$
dry, full-bodied, medium acidity, medium oak **drink now–2 years**
A creamy-textured wine that carries exotic spice flavors.

1999 Mâcon-Lugny Les Charmes Chardonnay, Mâcon-Lugny ★★ $
dry, medium-bodied, medium acidity, no oak **drink now**
Lovely fruit flavors in a charming wine.

RECOMMENDED PRODUCERS

Domaine André Bonhomme, Domaine des Deux Roches, J.A. Ferret, Domaine Guillemot-Michel, Domaine Louis Jadot, Château Fuissé, Domaine de Roally, Domaine Thomas, Jean Touzot, Verget, J.J. Vincent

beaujolais

"If it's Beaujolais, it's okay." This is typical advice to people who are inexperienced at ordering wine. Light-bodied, fruity, and low in tannin, simple Beaujolais is fine for many dishes. But a lot of Beaujolais is heavier, more complex, and more tannic. Because many Americans aren't aware of them, the more sophisticated wines from the area can be an absolute bargain.

on the label

There are four categories of Beaujolais that you're likely to find in shops:

Beaujolais Nouveau One of the most heavily marketed wines in the U.S. today, this wine is released each year on the third Thursday of November. Made only a few weeks earlier, Beaujolais Nouveau is as simple as wine gets—and it's always inexpensive. Only the more expensive ones (still cheap) are worth buying.

Beaujolais Also simple stuff, plain Beaujolais has a bit more to it than most Beaujolais Nouveau, and much of it isn't bad for light-bodied wine.

Beaujolais-Villages Made with more care than its less serious siblings, Beaujolais-Villages comes from grapes grown in one of thirty-nine select villages in the region. The taste of many of the wines reflects the granite-laced hills from which they come.

Cru Beaujolais At the top of the hierarchy sit the wines of the ten best villages in the region. These often have medium body, bold berry flavors, and noticeable tannin. The Crus are: Brouilly, Chénas, Chiroubles, Côte de Brouilly, Fleurie, Juliénas, Morgon, Moulin-à-Vent, Régnié, and St-Amour.

recommended wines

1999 Louis Jadot Château de Poncié, Fleurie ★★★★ $$
dry, full-bodied, medium tannin, medium acidity **drink now–8 years**
We really love this wine. It reminds us of just-baked cherry pie with a homemade, butter-rich crust.

1999 Domaine des Grands Fers Clos des Grands Fers, Fleurie ★★★ $$
dry, full-bodied, full tannin, medium acidity **drink now–6 years**
Concentrated, flavorful wine from a plot of 100-year-old vines.

1999 Jacky Janodet Fins Graves, Chénas ★★★ $$
dry, full-bodied, medium tannin, medium acidity **drink now–8 years**
A taste of this spicy, smoky, strawberry-saturated wine will forever erase the idea that Beaujolais is just for simple sipping.

1998 Château de Beauregard, Fleurie ★★ $$
dry, medium-bodied, medium tannin, medium acidity **drink now–5 years**
Typically Fleurie: balanced fruitiness, minerality, and acidity, never too much of this or too little of that.

1999 Domaine du Granit, Moulin-à-Vent ★★ $$
dry, medium-bodied, medium tannin, medium acidity **drink now–5 years**
Granite is the basis of this wine, full of mineral but also raspberry flavors. Granit's spectacular Vieilles Vignes is also worth a search.

2000 Jean-Jacques Béréziat, Côte de Brouilly ★★ $$
dry, full-bodied, medium tannin, medium acidity **drink now–5 years**
No mirrors (though a bit of smoke) in this wine. Just honest, concentrated cherry flavor.

2000 Georges Duboeuf Château de Javernand, Chiroubles ★★ $
dry, full-bodied, medium tannin, medium acidity **drink now–3 years**
A serious wine. This is about as far as Duboeuf normally goes from his ubiquitous Beaujolais Nouveau—though others go much farther.

1999 Louis Jadot Château de Bellevue, Morgon ★★ $
dry, full-bodied, full tannin, medium acidity **drink now–7 years**
Displays Morgon's tendency to make the heaviest Beaujolais. Full body and lots of blackberry flavor with hints of spice.

1999 Château de La Chaize, Brouilly ★ $
dry, medium-bodied, medium tannin, high acidity **drink now–4 years**
Nice berry and earth flavors.

2000 Georges Duboeuf Château de Varennes, Beaujolais-Villages ★ $
dry, medium-bodied, medium tannin, medium acidity **drink now–2 years**
Relax and enjoy the straightforward cherry and vanilla flavors.

RECOMMENDED PRODUCERS

Guy Breton, Château de Juliénas, Clos de la Roilette, Domaine Berrod, Georges Duboeuf, Jacky Janodet, Jean-Paul Thevenet, Joël Rochette, Kermit Lynch, Louis Jadot, Paul Janin

loire valley

If not the largest wine region, the Loire Valley is certainly the longest, stretching some 250 miles alongside the Loire River from the center of France to the Atlantic Ocean. Because it's so long, the region includes many microclimates and soil types and therefore produces a great diversity of wines. Yet with the exception of the well-known Sancerre and Pouilly-Fumé, Loire wines are underappreciated in the U.S. The Loire Valley producers make some of the best wines in France—and, luckily for us, the prices are low.

grapes & styles

Five grapes dominate the Loire Valley: at the eastern end, Sauvignon Blanc for whites and Pinot Noir for reds; in the center, Chenin Blanc for whites and, for reds, Cabernet Franc; and in the delta opening to the Atlantic, the white Muscadet, also called Melon de Bourgogne.

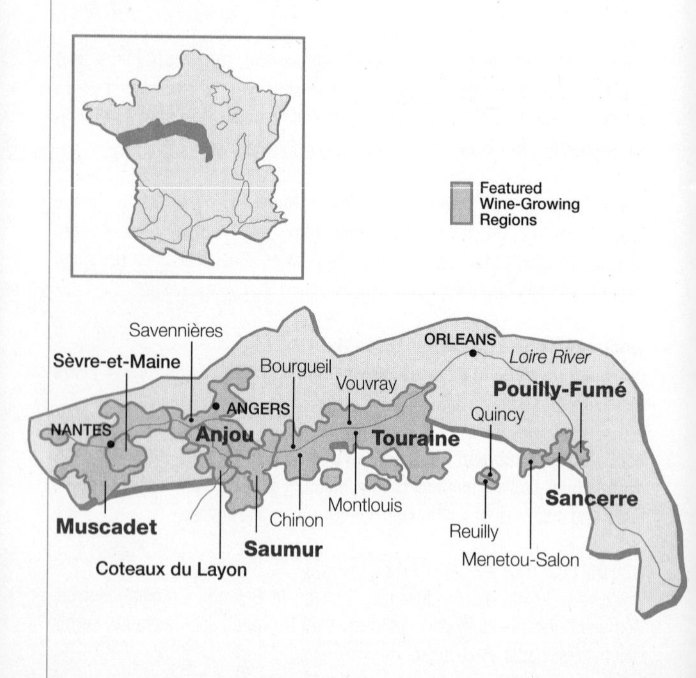

on the label

Loire Valley wines are labeled according to appellation. As in Burgundy, traditions are so well established that the name of the place indicates what's in the bottle (see Grapes & Styles and map, facing page). In a few cases where the wine is made from a grape variety different from the norm, the variety will be appended to the region's name, for example Anjou-Gamay.

white wines

CHENIN BLANC

One of the world's most underappreciated grape varieties, Chenin Blanc makes some of our favorite wines, with flavors that can be flowery, nutty, honeyed, mineral, or all of these combined in one. It flourishes from Anjou to Saumur to the Touraine. The wines of Savennières in the Anjou are positively thrilling. Though most can be enjoyed young, many are meant for aging. The town of Vouvray in the Touraine is the most famous appellation. With some exceptions, we find most Vouvray a bit dull. The same is true of neighboring Montlouis.

at the table

Chenin from the Anjou, particularly Savennières, has enough presence to match a pork roast, but try it also with oily fish, like salmon, tuna, or sardines. Less distinguished Chenin Blanc is a natural with sautéed fish. Off-dry versions work well with Chinese food and other Asian cuisines.

the bottom line Outstanding Chenin Blanc from Savennières, which has to be ranked among the top whites in the world, sells for $14 to $19, though a few incredible bottles can be $28 to $50. Good Vouvray runs $12 to the mid-$20s. Montlouis provides amazing bargains, with its better bottles starting at $9.

what to buy DRY CHENIN BLANC

1996	1997	1998	1999	2000
★★★★	★★★	★★★	★★	★★

recommended wines

1996 Domaine des Baumard, Savennières ★★★★ $$
dry, full-bodied, medium acidity, medium oak **drink now–10 years**
Incredibly intense tropical fruit aromas, then nut and mineral flavors.

1997 Domaine des Baumard Trie Spéciale, Savennières ★★★★ $$
dry, full-bodied, high acidity, medium oak **drink now–15 years**
One of the great wines of France. Filled with fruit, floral, and nut flavors. Excellent now; exceptional later.

1998 Nicolas Joly Château de la Roche-aux-Moines Becherelle, Savennières ★★★ $$$
dry, full-bodied, medium acidity, medium oak **drink now–10 years**
A crescendo of fruit, herbs, spices, and minerals.

1998 Château de Fesles "B" de Fesles, Anjou ★★★ $$
dry, medium-bodied, high acidity, light oak **drink now–5 years**
So true are the essences of cassis and pomegranate that if you closed your eyes, you'd think you were drinking a light red wine.

1999 Château d'Epiré Cuvée Spéciale, Savennières ★★★ $$
dry, medium-bodied, medium acidity, light oak **drink now–6 years**
A favorite. It's refreshing now and will evolve into golden ambrosia with age.

2000 Domaine Bourillons-d'Orléans Coulée d'Argent Vieilles Vignes, Vouvray Sec ★★★ $$
dry, full-bodied, medium acidity, light oak **drink now–5 years**
Apples and spice and everything nice from one of Vouvray's finest producers.

1999 Domaine du Closel Clos du Papillon, Savennières ★★★ $$
dry, medium-bodied, medium acidity, medium oak **drink now–10 years**
Wonderfully complex flavors: fruit, nuts, stone, honey, and flowers.

2000 Domaine Le Peu de la Moriette, Vouvray ★★★ $$
off-dry, medium-bodied, medium acidity, light oak **drink now–6 years**
Really lovely fruit flavors in this just slightly sweet wine.

1999 Thierry Nerisson, Vouvray Sec ★★★ $$
dry, medium-bodied, medium acidity, light oak **drink now–8 years**
A great wine made by Nerisson, one of France's top sommeliers.

1998 Thierry Nerisson, Saumur-Champigny ★★ $$
dry, medium-bodied, medium acidity, light oak **drink now–5 years**
Judging by this wine, biodynamic techniques are more than moonstruck fantasy.

MOONSTRUCK

Biodynamics (*biodynamie* in French), organic agriculture with astrological and homeopathic twists, is sweeping France as an antidote to the ills of modern, chemical-dependent agronomy. More than simply eschewing chemical fertilizers and pesticides, practitioners of biodynamics view the earth (and soil) as an organism, living in symbiosis with the air and cosmos. Since humans affect the earth, they are responsible for seeing that it is continuously nurtured. Moreover, the positions of the moon, sun, and stars are believed to affect different aspects of plant growth. Biodynamic farmers schedule their activities according to the positions of the cosmos, the season, and the time of day. Skeptical? Well, many of France's greatest winemakers believe in it, the most vocal proponent being Nicolas Joly, owner of Savennières' Coulée de Serrant. Other advocates include Burgundy's Domaine Leflaive, Alsace's Domaines Kreydenweiss and Ostertag, and the Rhône's M. Chapoutier. California's Robert Sinskey has also gone biodynamic, as have all of wine-giant Fetzer's operations.

MUSCADET

The top Muscadets (mus-cah-day) are labeled *sur lie* (on lees). This means the wine was aged with the yeasty sediment that's left after fermentation, thereby developing a greater complexity of flavor. A slight *pétillance,* or sparkle, is typical. The appellation Muscadet de Sèvre-et-Maine produces the best wines.

at the table

High in acidity and often slightly yeasty, Muscadet is a wine made for shellfish, especially the excellent oysters that come from the nearby estuary leading to the Atlantic Ocean. It's also a great accompaniment to simply prepared fish, whether lean or oily.

the bottom line Good Muscadet can be found for under $10. In general, it's best the year it's released; avoid "bargains" more than two years old, though a few are fine for three.

recommended wines

1999 Château de la Ragotière Premier Cru du Château Sélection Vieilles Vignes Muscadet sur Lie, Sèvre-et-Maine ★★★ $$
dry, medium-bodied, medium acidity, no oak **drink now**
Though this wine has all of Muscadet's famed minerality, the citrus flavors make it more than a simple raw-oyster wine.

2000 Domaine Les Hautes Noëlles Muscadet sur Lie, Côtes de Grandlieu ★★★ $
dry, medium-bodied, medium acidity, no oak **drink now**
The best Muscadet we've ever had? Could be. We certainly love the full fruit and steely mineral flavors.

1999 Clos de Beauregard Muscadet sur Lie, Sèvre-et-Maine ★★ $
dry, light-bodied, high acidity, no oak **drink now**
Tastes like an ocean breeze blowing through an apple orchard; a real pleasure.

SAUVIGNON BLANC

Grassy is the description most often applied to Sauvignon Blanc. It also has lemon and gooseberry flavors and refreshing acidity. Those from Sancerre offer straightforward pleasure with few surprises. The Pouilly-Fumé (poo-yee foo-may) version is a bit heavier, with more minerality. Its name (*fumé* means "smoked") comes as much from the frequent presence of fog in its vineyards as from the supposedly smoky qualities the wine acquires from the flinty soil. The appellations Quincy (can-see), Menetou-Salon, and Reuilly (ruh-yee) make Sauvignon Blancs that are often lighter in body with more floral elements than those of their better-known neighbors.

at the table

Sauvignon Blanc is an excellent accompaniment to vegetables, fish or shellfish, and chicken. Traditional pairings in the region are Sancerre with the local chèvre and Pouilly-Fumé with crayfish. Serve lighter Sauvignons with salads or crudités.

the bottom line Because of their popularity in restaurants around the world, Sancerre and Pouilly-Fumé are often overpriced, starting around $15, climbing to $50 for the rarest and best; $24 will get you something really good. Wines from the less-known regions can be found for $16 to $24.

recommended wines

1999 Château de Maupas, Menetou-Salon ★★★ $$
dry, medium-bodied, medium acidity, light oak **drink now–3 years**
When you're tired of margaritas, try this refresher. Lots of lime flavor with touches of mango and a cuminlike spiciness.

1999 Alphonse Mellot Domaine la Mousière, Sancerre ★★ $$
dry, medium-bodied, medium acidity, no oak **drink now–2 years**
The heir of one of Sancerre's oldest families breaks the mold with this sumptuous wine with ripe peach and stone flavors.

1999 Pascal Jolibet, Pouilly-Fumé ★★ $$
dry, medium-bodied, high acidity, light oak **drink now–2 years**
A wine to liven the senses with the slightest bit of sparkle and a hint of pineapple flavor almost never seen in Pouilly-Fumé.

2000 Domaine Henri Beurdin, Reuilly ★★ $
dry, medium-bodied, medium acidity, no oak **drink now–2 years**
Sauvignon Blanc takes a creamy turn in this wine of mellow apple and pear flavors, with a tingle of pepper.

2000 Domaine Augis, Valençay ★ $
dry, medium-bodied, medium acidity, no oak **drink now–3 years**
Twenty percent Chardonnay (a rarity in the Loire) provides lushness; Sauvignon Blanc takes care of the refreshing elements.

red wines

Cabernet Franc is the dominant red grape in the Loire. Red Sancerres are made from the Burgundian grape, Pinot Noir. They tend to be light-bodied wines with good acidity, but they rarely outpace simple Burgundies in quality.

at the table

Often overlooked, Loire Valley reds are some of the most food-friendly in all of France. They complement rather than overwhelm and are as good with poultry as with red meat. The Loire is abundant with game, and the region's Cabernet Franc is the perfect companion to duck, pheasant, or venison. The wine's acidity can also cut through the fattiness of the region's famous charcuterie, especially pork rillettes, and it is excellent with rich variety meats like sweetbreads or calf's liver. Red Sancerre is simpler but does well with shellfish dishes, like Cajun-style shrimp or seafood risotto.

the bottom line The world's ignorance is your gain. The best Loire reds rarely sell for more than $30, and most stay in the $16 to $22 range.

CABERNET FRANC

Except for Bordeaux's famous Château Cheval Blanc, the greatest Cabernet Francs are made in the Loire Valley. Though basically similar, there are some differences in the Cabernet Francs from the various appellations: Chinon suggests raspberries; Bourgueil, strawberries; Saumur, smoke and red currants; Anjou, cherries.

what to buy CABERNET FRANC

1996	1997	1998	1999	2000
★★★★	★★★	★★★	★★	★★

recommended wines

2000 Charles Joguet Clos du Chêne Vert, Chinon ★★★★ $$$
dry, medium-bodied, medium tannin, medium acidity drink now–8 years
Truly one of the world's great Cabernet Francs. It's shy at first, but once it gets some air, pepper and cherry flavors emerge.

1998 Domaine Cognard-Taluau Malgagnes, St-Nicolas-de-Bourgueil ★★★ $$
dry, medium-bodied, medium tannin, medium acidity drink now–6 years
Bourgueil's St. Nick doesn't slide down chimneys, but he does have a knack for making wine as spicy and plummy as a Christmas pudding.

1999 Domaine Pierre Breton Les Galichets, Bourgueil ★★★ $$
dry, medium-bodied, medium tannin, medium acidity drink now–6 years
The deep fruit and earth flavors here really scream for a lamb stew, but the wine is nice for casual sipping, too.

1999 Château de Fesles Vieilles Vignes, Anjou ★★ $
dry, medium-bodied, medium tannin, high acidity drink now–6 years
These old vines must have taken up smoking in their middle age. Filled with smoky and mouthwatering cassis flavors.

2000 Clos Roche Blanche, Touraine ★★ $
dry, medium-bodied, medium tannin, medium acidity drink now–2 years
Unusual for a Cabernet Franc: smooth sailing from start to finish.

1998 Langlois-Château, Saumur ★★ $
dry, light-bodied, medium tannin, high acidity drink now–4 years
A wine designed for food. Fruit and mineral flavors that won't overwhelm what's on the plate.

other red wines & rosés

It's not surprising that Sancerre grows Pinot Noir, since it is closer to Burgundy than to the rest of the Loire Valley. Pinot Noir from Sancerre is a comparative bargain, as is the small amount of Gamay that comes from the region. A few noteworthy rosés are also made in the Loire Valley, particularly in Sancerre, Anjou, and the Touraine.

recommended wines

1999 Philippe Raimbault Les Godons Sancerre, Sury-en-Vaux 🍷 ★★★ $$
dry, medium-bodied, medium tannin, high acidity drink now–3 years
Here's a Pinot Noir with the usual cherry flavor tarted up with a bit of spice and smoke.

2000 Philippe Raimbault Sancerre Rosé, Sury-en-Vaux 🍷 ★★★ $$
dry, medium-bodied, high acidity drink now
The strawberry flavor is so strong, you'd think they threw a few bushels of berries in with the grapes. Delicious.

1999 Alain Demon La Perrière Réserve, Côte Roannaise 🍷 ★★★ $
dry, medium-bodied, medium tannin, medium acidity drink now–2 years
Beaujolais's Gamay turns up in the Loire with strawberry and pepper flavors.

2000 James Paget Touraine Rosé, Azay-le-Rideau ★ $
dry, medium-bodied, high acidity **drink now**
Full of fruit and lots of acidity, this Grolleau-based wine is perfect as an aperitif and great with dinner as well.

the midi

French wine was born in the Midi—the regions bordering the Mediterannean—back in Roman times. And from the nineteenth century until the present, enormous quantities of wine have been produced in the area. Frankly, most of it has been bad. In the 1970s, better vinification techniques and the planting of higher-quality grapes brought improvements.

languedoc-roussillon

A land that has long produced cheap, traditional wines, Languedoc (lahn-guh-doc) today is the most anarchic wine region in France. The wines of the many vintners who aren't following traditional rules are classified as lowly Vins de Pays (see page 80), but no one seems to mind. The excitement these winemakers have stirred up has caught the attention of traditional vintners—whose wines have also improved—and of producers outside Languedoc. Bordeaux's Rothschilds have built a winery down there; so have the Mondavis of California.

grapes & styles

The large majority of Languedoc wine is red, and the Carignan (cah-ree-n'yahn) grape makes up the bulk of the harvest. Carignan is sometimes maligned, but when it's treated right, it can produce spicy, berry-flavored wines with good body. The wines of Corbières are among the best that use a large proportion of Carignan. Usually, other grapes—like dark Mourvèdre, smoky Syrah, spicy Grenache, and aromatic Cinsault (san-so)—

figure prominently in the blend. Grenache, though not yet big on its own, is used to make Rhône-style wines in Costières de Nîmes and is being made into the deliciously hearty, Spanish-style wines of Collioure, near the Spanish border.

White wines are definitely secondary in the region, but international varietals like Sauvignon Blanc and Chardonnay are exported and are easy to find, along with some Viognier and a few local varietals, like Maccabéo, Muscat, Grenache Blanc, and Picpoul.

on the label

The most common designation is the broadest, Vin de Pays d'Oc, which means the wine can come from anywhere within the region. Many labels also indicate the names of varietals, particularly when the wine is made with a popular international grape, like Cabernet Sauvignon or Merlot. These wines tend to be inexpensive and quite well made, though a bit commercial. Most of the more interesting wines are blends rather than varietals.

Vin de Pays wines that include the name of a place, like Vin de Pays de l'Hérault, are a step up. The most famous of these is Vin de Pays from the producer Mas de Daumas Gassac in Hérault. Wines from the large appellation Coteaux du Languedoc, as well as the twelve sub-appellations that fall within it, including St-Chinian, Pic St-Loup, and Faugères, just get better and better. Other appellations—like Corbières, Minervois, Collioure, or Costières de Nîmes (by the Rhône Valley)—offer terrific wines that reflect the styles of their neighbors yet have their own identities.

at the table

The heartier reds (like those from the broad designation Vin de Pays d'Oc, those from the smaller Collioure and Costières de Nîmes, and some from Minervois and Coteaux du Languedoc) should be paired with hearty food. Try these wines with grilled rosemary-and-garlic-marinated meats, lamb stews, or robust cassoulet. Gentler reds, like many from Corbières and Minervois, are perfect for grilled pork, veal chops, or charcuterie. They're also nice with a grilled vegetable platter. Drink the white wines from the region with lean fish, like sea bass, haddock, or red snapper. They complement oysters on the half shell, steamed clams, crab cakes, or seared sea scallops, too.

the bottom line Languedoc-Roussillon used to be the land of bargain wines that were on the rustic side. Today most bottles from this region are still a steal, with wonderful, sophisticated wines to be found for as little as $9. Among the more esteemed appellations, Collioure has wines that are currently getting serious attention from wine drinkers around the world, so you'll have to plan on spending around $24. Though Vin de Pays wines are theoretically of a lower classification than Appellation Contrôlée wines, they're not always less expensive. The Rothschilds' Languedoc wine, Baron'arques, is a Vin de Pays and sells for $50.

what to buy LANGUEDOC-ROUSSILLON

1997	1998	1999	2000
★★	★★★★	★★★★	★★★

recommended red wines

1998 Baron'arques,
Vin de Pays de la Haute Vallée de l'Aude ★★★ $$$
dry, full-bodied, medium tannin, medium acidity **drink in 2–10 years**
Bordeaux's Rothschilds offer a wine that combines the intense flavors of southern France with the finesse of Bordeaux.

1998 Domaine du Mas Blanc Docteur Parcé
Clos du Moulin, Collioure ★★★ $$$
dry, full-bodied, medium tannin, medium acidity **drink now–8 years**
In this wine, intriguing aromas of cedar and tobacco are followed by a lovely baked-cherry flavor.

1999 Mas de Daumas Gassac,
Vin de Pays de l'Hérault ★★★ $$$
dry, full-bodied, medium tannin, medium acidity **drink in 3–10 years**
The Grand Cru of Languedoc? With a great balance of fruit, mineral, and smoke flavors, we think it's pretty close.

1999 Domaine Deshenrys Abbaye Sylva-Planta La Closerie,
Faugères ★★★ $$
dry, full-bodied, medium tannin, high acidity **drink in 2–10 years**
One of Languedoc's finest producers tames rugged, mountain-grown grapes into a wine of great finesse. Delicious.

1998 Domaine du Mas Blanc Docteur Parcé Cosprons Levants, Collioure ★★★ $$
dry, full-bodied, medium tannin, medium acidity **drink now–8 years**
A lovely wine. Perfect for steak.

1999 Domaine Lacroix-Vanel Clos Mélanie, Coteaux du Languedoc ★★★ $$
dry, full-bodied, full tannin, medium acidity **drink in 2–10 years**
Full everything—body, flavor, tannin—all in admirable balance.

1999 Domaine Sarda-Malet Réserve, Côtes du Roussillon ★★★ $$
dry, full-bodied, full tannin, medium acidity **drink now–8 years**
A beautiful wine. Makes us want some spit-roasted lamb to go with it.

MONDAVI IN LANGUEDOC

Several years ago, Robert Mondavi built Vichon winery in Languedoc to produce inexpensive wines for the U.S. market. It is a success, but now Mondavi wants to start a winery whose products will rival any in the world. To that end, the company found land in a public forest near Aniane. The Mondavi proposal, which would have led to vineyard cultivation within 123 acres of pristine woodlands, was initially approved. But then local opposition mounted, inspired both by a desire to protect the environment and by fears of McDonaldization (where there are Americans. . .). The mayor who supported the proposal was defeated for reelection by a candidate who ran on an anti-Mondavi platform. Shortly thereafter, the city council voted down the plan. Mondavi is considering other options.

1998 La Cuvée Mythique, Vin de Pays d'Oc ★★★ $$
dry, full-bodied, medium tannin, medium acidity **drink now–6 years**
Loads of fruit, herb, and mineral flavors, with a nice smokiness.

1998 Mas Blanchard, Coteaux du Languedoc ★★★ $$
dry, full-bodied, full tannin, medium acidity **drink now–10 years**
This massive wine simply overwhelms us with the fullness of both its body and its flavor.

1998 Mas de Chimères, Coteaux du Languedoc ★★★ $$
dry, full-bodied, full tannin, medium acidity **drink now–8 years**
Mostly Syrah, the savory, smoky scents are sensational.

1999 Château d'Oupia, Minervois ★★★ $
dry, full-bodied, medium tannin, medium acidity **drink now–4 years**
Great bang for the buck in this delicious fusillade of fruit, spice, and smoke.

1999 Château Mourgues du Gres Les Galets Rouges, Costières de Nîmes ★★★ $
dry, medium-bodied, medium tannin, medium acidity **drink now–5 years**
From the area where the Languedoc borders the Rhône, this Syrah equals all but the best from the neighboring region. A wonderful wine.

1999 Château St-Martin de la Garrigue Cuvée Tradition, Coteaux du Languedoc ★★★ $
dry, medium-bodied, medium tannin, medium acidity **drink now–6 years**
Here's truth in labeling: This wine is infused with aromas of the scrubby wild herbs *(garrigue)* that pervade the countryside in southern France.

1999 Château Viranel, St-Chinian ★★★ $
dry, full-bodied, full tannin, medium acidity **drink now–8 years**
Mostly Syrah, this compelling wine delivers terrific northern-Rhône style for a fraction of the price.

1999 Domaine du Grand Arc Cuvée des Quarante, Corbières ★★ $$
dry, medium-bodied, medium tannin, medium acidity **drink now–6 years**
The kind of wine we'd want when grilling game over olive-wood charcoal and dried rosemary branches in the south of France.

1999 J.M. Boillot Les Roques, Vin de Pays d'Oc ★★ $$
dry, full-bodied, medium tannin, low acidity **drink now–4 years**
One of Burgundy's grand masters relaxes in Languedoc, making this delicious, fruity wine.

1999 Château de Paraza, Minervois ★★ $
dry, medium-bodied, light tannin, medium acidity **drink now–2 years**
Fantastic flavor in an easy-to-love wine that costs just six bucks.

1999 Château La Roque Pic St-Loup, Coteaux du Languedoc ★★ $
dry, full-bodied, medium tannin, medium acidity **drink now–4 years**
This pepper- and berry-flavored wine is just right for pepper-crusted anything.

1999 Domaine des Blagueurs Syrah/Sirrah, Vin de Pays d'Oc ★★ $
dry, full-bodied, medium tannin, medium acidity **drink now–3 years**
An enjoyable wine from iconoclastic Californian winemaker Randall Grahm.

1997 Mas Amiel, Côtes Catalanes ★★ $
dry, medium-bodied, medium tannin, medium acidity **drink now–8 years**
Lovely raspberry and herbal flavors. A special wine.

1998 Moulin de Gassac Terrasses de Guilhem, Vin de Pays de l'Hérault ★★ $
dry, medium-bodied, medium tannin, medium acidity **drink now–2 years**
Good berry, herb, and spice flavors. Really good.

1999 Domaine du Grand Arc La Fleurine, Corbières ★ $
dry, medium-bodied, medium tannin, medium acidity **drink now–2 years**
A mélange of cherry, rose, and smoked-earth flavors, all for a bargain price.

recommended white wines

1999 Gérard Bertrand Cigalus, Vin de Pays d'Oc ★★★ $$$
dry, full-bodied, medium acidity, medium oak **drink now–10 years**
Full of lush fruit flavors. Mouthwatering.

2000 Mas de Daumas Gassac, Vin de Pays de l'Hérault ★★★ $$$
dry, full-bodied, medium acidity, medium oak **drink now–8 years**
Terrifically complex. We wish more of this were available.

1999 Mas Mortiès, Coteaux du Languedoc ★★★ $$
dry, medium-bodied, medium acidity, light oak **drink now–5 years**
Lovely citrus flavors evolve into the essence of ripe pears. Truly stunning.

2000 Domaine Miquel Viognier, Vin de Pays d'Oc ★★ $$
dry, medium-bodied, medium acidity, no oak **drink now–3 years**
Charming pear and apple notes, plus a touch of spice.

2000 Bérail-Lagarde Roque Sestière, Corbières ★★ $
dry, medium-bodied, medium acidity, no oak **drink now**
Pear and orange flavors make this a great wine for summer.

1999 Domaine Deshenrys Alliance, Vin de Pays des Côtes de Thongue ★★ $
dry, light-bodied, medium acidity, no oak **drink now–2 years**
Five grape varieties yield a fruit salad's worth of flavors.

1999 Domaine de la Baume Chardonnay, Vin de Pays d'Oc ★ $
dry, medium-bodied, medium acidity, light oak **drink now–2 years**
We liked this more than many Chards at five times the price.

provence

Once a land of rough reds drunk by locals and frivolous rosés enjoyed by Riviera jet-setters, Provence is now the home of powerful yet elegant reds and intelligent rosés, both of which are enjoyed by connoisseurs everywhere. Like the wild-herb covered hills of the region, Provence wines are often wonderfully aromatic.

grapes & styles

Bandol, perhaps the best-known grape-growing area of Provence, is the only appellation in France where the Mourvèdre grape dominates. The wines here are full-bodied and bold. They're also high in tannin and can benefit from ten years or more of bottle-aging. Grenache, Cinsault, Carignan, Syrah, and, increasingly, Cabernet Sauvignon are also planted in Provence, finding their way into wines that are often as full in body but usually less tannic than those of Bandol. The most familiar of these come from Les Baux and Coteaux d'Aix-en-Provence.

Rosés are made primarily from Cinsault, Grenache, and Mourvèdre. With rare exceptions, they should be drunk within a year of release. White wines are usually blends. The region's most famous white is Cassis, which, despite the name, has nothing to do with black currants. It is light-bodied and sometimes has a little sparkle.

on the label

As in most of France, Provençal wine labels favor appellation names over grape varieties. Bandol reds must be made from at least 50 percent Mourvèdre. Whites may contain as much as 40 percent Sauvignon Blanc. Other appellations in the region, such as Coteaux d'Aix-en-Provence and Les Baux, require minimum and maximum percentages of certain varieties of local grapes.

at the table

If you see *Provençal* at the end of any dish on a menu, you'll do well to order a wine from Provence. The flavors of Provence—such as rosemary, garlic, tomato, and olive—marry beautifully with the region's aromatic wines. Leg of lamb or roasted pork is as good a match as you can get for the reds. Rosés are perfect for *Brandade de morue*. For whites: bouillabaisse or grilled fish.

the bottom line Bandol reds run $18 to $45. Those at the top end of the price range are some of the best wines in France. Wines from Les Baux de Provence are lower: $11 to $30, though the best one, Domaine de Trévallon red, sells for $45. Most rosés are $10 to $20; the best cost $35. A few whites can be found, usually for around $10, the best for $35.

what to buy PROVENCE RED WINES

1996	1997	1998	1999	2000
★★★	★★★	★★★★	★★★	★★★

recommended red wines

1998 Domaine de Trévallon, Vin de Pays des Bouches du Rhône ★★★★ $$$
dry, full-bodied, medium tannin, medium acidity **drink now–8 years**
Bureaucratic difficulties led to this wine being classified as Vin de Pays. Ignore the classification. This is one of France's best.

1998 Domaine de la Bastide Blanche Fontagnieu, Bandol ★★★ $$$
dry, full-bodied, full tannin, medium acidity **drink in 3–10 years**
A big, bold wine, with barnyard aromas and lovely blackberry and bitter-chocolate flavors.

1998 Domaine du Gros' Noré, Bandol ★★★ $$$
dry, full-bodied, full tannin, medium acidity **drink in 3–10 years**
This is already compelling, but just wait 'til you try the wine after it's matured a bit.

1994 Domaine Le Galantin Longue Garde, Bandol ★★★ $$
dry, full-bodied, full tannin, medium acidity **drink in 3–10 years**
Odd to describe—lanolin and coal—but easy to love. Have it with spit-roasted meat to understand why.

1998 Domaine de la Tour de Bon, Bandol ★★ $$
dry, full-bodied, medium tannin, medium acidity **drink now–8 years**
This wine is very smooth, and it has loads of blackberry flavors and a delicious smokiness.

1997 Triennes Cabernet Sauvignon, Vin de Pays du Var ★★ $
dry, medium-bodied, medium tannin, medium acidity **drink now–5 years**
Bordeaux's great grape in the hands of fine Burgundy winemakers. Good.

recommended white & rosé wines

1999 Domaines Ott Château Romassan Cuvée Marine Rosé, Bandol ★★★★ $$$
dry, medium-bodied, medium acidity **drink now–5 years**
About as far from White Zin as one can go with a rosé. We're completely taken by the dry mineral earthiness of this wine.

1999 Domaines Ott Clos Mireille Blanc de Blancs, Côtes de Provence ★★★ $$$
dry, full-bodied, high acidity, light oak **drink now–5 years**
Not a simple picnic wine. This is sophisticated stuff full of the flavors of orange peel, nuts, and honey.

1999 Triennes Viognier, Vin de Pays du Var ★★★ $$
dry, light-bodied, medium acidity, light oak **drink now–5 years**
What happens when two great Burgundy winemakers collaborate in the south of France? This lovely, refreshing wine.

2000 Château Routas Rouvière Rosé, Vin de Pays du Var ★★★ $
dry, medium-bodied, high acidity **drink now**
Great strawberry flavors excellently balanced by acidity make this the perfect summer house wine.

1999 Les Vignerons de Grimaud Rosé Cuvée du Golfe de St-Tropez, Côtes de Provence ★★★ $
dry, light-bodied, medium acidity **drink now**
One sip transports us to the Riviera. The taste of fresh strawberries tempered with oyster-shell minerality.

2000 Domaine Eric Texier Marsanne, Cassis ★★ $$
dry, medium-bodied, high acidity, no oak **drink now–2 years**
Most Cassis is not worth giving much thought, but Texier's demands attention.

2000 Château du Rouët Cuvée Réservée Rosé, Côtes de Provence ★★ $
dry, medium-bodied, high acidity **drink now**
Charming fruit and spice flavors paired with a strong tannic grip.

2000 Château de Roquefort Rosé Corail, Côtes de Provence ★ $
dry, light-bodied, medium acidity **drink now**
Light, with a slight fruity kick. A perfect casual summer wine.

rhône valley

The northern and southern Rhône have entirely dissimilar topography and climate and, therefore, support different grapes. In fact, if vineyards didn't border the Rhône River pretty much continuously along its north–south path through France, the Rhône Valley probably would not be considered a single region. Rhône wines, whether northern or southern, are part of the Côtes-du-Rhône appellation.

northern rhône

grapes & styles

Syrah dominates in the northern Rhône, with different styles in the various subregions outlined below. Three white grapes are cultivated in the region: Marsanne, Roussanne, and, the most famous, Viognier (vee-oh-n'yay).

Hermitage and Cornas The steep, difficult terrain of Hermitage (air-mee-tahj) and Cornas (cor-nahss) both challenges vines to survive and allows for long exposure to the sun, yielding especially flavorful grapes that produce intense, tannic red wines that often require a decade or more of aging. Hermitage at one time commanded the highest prices in France. Fashions may have changed, but the quality of the wines has only gotten better (and there's still plenty of demand). Hermitage's whites, made from Marsanne and Roussanne, are also full-bodied and require age. In Cornas, in addition to traditional reds, wines that are ready to drink earlier are being made by innovative winemakers like Jean-Luc Colombo, who removes the stems to reduce tannin.

Côte-Rôtie From the terraced hills of the Côte-Rôtie come wines that are as fine as those of Hermitage and Cornas, though certainly less bold.

Crozes-Hermitage and St-Joseph The more gently sloped parts of the region, Crozes-Hermitage and St-Joseph, produce simpler, less tannic wine, meant to be enjoyed young. St-Joseph is lighter-bodied as well.

Condrieu A small appellation at the top of the region, Condrieu is dedicated to the production of wines from Viognier grapes. Château-Grillet is a vineyard within Condrieu so special that it has been given its own appellation.

at the table

The tannic reds of the northern Rhône demand hearty foods. Drink Hermitage and Cornas with gamey meats like venison or wild boar, or, better yet, a hunter's stew that combines game with wild mushrooms. Not in a gamey mood? Try the wines with a well-aged roast prime rib of beef. Being a bit softer, Côte-Rôtie combines well with lamb or strong-flavored birds, like duck. Crozes-Hermitage and St-Joseph are great with kebabs, whether meat or vegetable, or pasta with a tomato-based sauce. The white wines of the region are truly special. Try one with a holiday bird like roast goose or turkey, or with a whole baked fish with herbs.

the bottom line Strong demand and relatively small supply bring high prices for the best northern Rhône wines. However, these high prices seem reasonable considering the quality they buy. Hermitage and Cornas start at around $35 and go up to $65 (more for the rarest bottles). Côte-Rôtie starts higher, at about $40. St-Joseph and Crozes-Hermitage can be picked up for $18, going to $30. Whites, even rarer than reds, start at $35, going to $65 for Château-Grillet—if you can find it, that is.

what to buy NORTHERN RHONE REDS

1996	1997	1998	1999	2000
★★★	★★★	★★★	★★★	★★★

recommended red wines

1998 Vincent Paris, Cornas ★★★★ $$$
dry, full-bodied, full tannin, medium acidity **drink now–10 years**
Vincent Paris's skill shows clearly in this full, elegant wine with its flavors of fruit and smoke.

1997 E. Guigal, Hermitage ★★★ $$$$
dry, full-bodied, full tannin, medium acidity **drink in 2–10 years**
We expect power from Hermitage, and this delivers with a burst of smoke, licorice, berry, and spice flavors.

1998 Domaine de Bonserine Côte Brune, Côte-Rôtie ★★★ $$$
dry, full-bodied, full tannin, medium acidity **drink in 3–10 years**
Typical of this producer—full and concentrated.

1998 E. Guigal, Côte-Rôtie ★★★ $$$
dry, full-bodied, full tannin, medium acidity **drink in 3–10 years**
A spicy, fruity Syrah from one of the region's most prominent producers. It has a good mineral quality as well.

1999 J.L. Chave Offerus, St-Joseph ★★★ $$
dry, full-bodied, full tannin, medium acidity **drink in 2–8 years**
Goes well beyond the typical St-Joseph. Fruity and earthy.

1998 M. Chapoutier Les Meysonniers, Crozes-Hermitage ★★★ $$
dry, medium-bodied, medium tannin, medium acidity **drink now–10 years**
Unusually good for a Crozes-Hermitage, this delivers complex flavors.

1998 Pierre Gonon, St-Joseph ★★★ $$
dry, full-bodied, medium tannin, medium acidity **drink now–5 years**
Gonon's hillside vineyards in mostly flat St-Joseph are the source of this fine wine with smoke and deep cherry flavors.

1999 Jean-Luc Colombo Le Prieuré, St-Joseph ★★ $$
dry, medium-bodied, medium tannin, medium acidity **drink now–6 years**
Colombo again shows why he's considered one of the region's most innovative producers. Sumptuous fruit and cedar flavors.

1999 Paul Jaboulet Aîné "Les Jalets," Crozes-Hermitage ★★ $$
dry, medium-bodied, medium tannin, medium acidity **drink now–3 years**
Luscious cherry flavor highlighted by a dusting of spice.

recommended white wines

1998 Château-Grillet, Condrieu ★★★★ $$$$
dry, full-bodied, medium acidity, medium oak **drink in 5–20 years**
There are few wines we'd recommend buying regardless of price, but here's one. It's singularly complex.

2000 E. Guigal, Condrieu ★★★ $$$
dry, full-bodied, medium acidity, light oak **drink now–10 years**
Buy at least two bottles, one to enjoy now and the other in several years.

1997 E. Guigal, Hermitage ★★★ $$$
dry, full-bodied, high acidity, medium oak **drink now–10 years**
Dried fruit, nut, and spice flavors as well as good minerality.

1999 Paul Jaboulet Aîné, St-Péray ★★ $$
dry, medium-bodied, medium acidity, light oak **drink now–2 years**
St-Péray wines are rare in the U.S., and this is a fine one.

southern rhône

Whereas the climate is temperate in the north, it becomes distinctly more Mediterranean in the southern Rhône, and vines produce abundantly. Ninety-five percent of Rhône wines are made here, and the region is second only to Bordeaux in volume of wines designated Appellation Contrôlée.

grapes & styles

Though Grenache is the primary grape, several others are grown in the south. Châteauneuf-du-Pape, the region's most famous appellation, allows up to thirteen different red and white grapes in its wines, and appellations such as Gigondas (jee-goh'n-dahss), Vacqueyras (vah-kay-rahss), and Lirac follow similar rules.

on the label

The classification system in the southern Rhône includes:

Côtes-du-Rhône The most basic wines of the Rhône Valley use this broad designation.

Côtes-du-Rhône Villages The wines from seventy-seven villages throughout the Rhône Valley can use this designation as long as they satisfy certain requirements concerning crop yields (low) and alcohol levels (high). Of the seventy-seven, sixteen are permitted to add their name to the label, for example, Côtes-du-Rhône Villages Rasteau.

Crus The best appellations can use their name without the designation Côtes-du-Rhône. The most well-known is Châteauneuf-du-Pape. Gigondas, Vacqueyras, Lirac, and Tavel are also given this privilege.

Satellite Appellations There are several areas on the periphery of the southern Rhône that produce wines in a similar style. The appellation name appears on the label, for example: Côtes du Ventoux.

at the table

The Grenache-based reds, with their fruity, herbaceous, and sometimes spicy notes, are admirably flexible. They're able to stand up to a simple charred steak and also to match the spiciness of a Moroccan tagine. Full-bodied Châteauneuf-du-Pape, Gigondas, Vacqueyras, and Lirac seem to have been made for garlic-studded leg of lamb. They're also great for moussaka or the Greek specialty *pastitsio,* a casserole made with pasta, ground lamb, cheese, and tomatoes. The region's white wines are dry, but because of their fruitiness, they can give the impression of sweetness. The whites will complement a variety of seafood dishes, including bouillabaisse and grilled calamari. They're also good with herb- or ash-covered chèvre.

the bottom line Prices of southern Rhône reds are still relatively low. Basic Côtes-du-Rhône starts at $9 but isn't especially interesting. Spend a couple of dollars more for a Village wine, especially one with a named village. Rasteau and Beaumes-de-Venise offer terrific value for about $13. Châteauneuf-du-Pape starts at about $12, but the high $20s is where real quality can be found; some exceptional examples hit $75 a bottle. Gigondas used to be a less expensive alternative to Châteauneuf-du-Pape, but word got out, and it is now similarly priced. Look to Vacqueyras or Lirac for solid wines from $15 to $20. The wines from the Satellite Appellations are even less known, and often as well made. These can be bargains. Look for reds from Côtes du Ventoux.

what to buy SOUTHERN RHONE REDS

1997	1998	1999	2000
★★★	★★★★	★★★	★★★★

recommended red wines

1998 Château La Nerthe, Châteauneuf-du-Pape ★★★★ $$$
dry, medium-bodied, medium tannin, medium acidity **drink now–5 years**
One of the few producers who still use all of Châteauneuf's thirteen permitted grape varieties. This is a great, traditional wine.

1998 E. Guigal, Châteauneuf-du-Pape ★★★★ $$$
dry, full-bodied, full tannin, medium acidity **drink now–10 years**
Warm weather ripened the grapes to almost Port-like lushness in 1998 and resulted in intense wines like this one.

1999 Lucien Barrot et Fils, Châteauneuf-du-Pape ★★★★ $$$
dry, full-bodied, full tannin, medium acidity **drink in 2–10 years**
Don't know if they have cookouts in the southern Rhône, but if so, this smoky, berry-flavored wonder would be the perfect wine.

1998 Jean-Luc Colombo Les Bartavelles, Châteauneuf-du-Pape ★★★ $$$
dry, full-bodied, medium tannin, medium acidity **drink now–8 years**
It's earthy, as is common in Châteauneuf, but this also offers strong blackberry flavor that's out of the ordinary.

1998 M. Chapoutier La Bernardine, Châteauneuf-du-Pape ★★★ $$$
dry, medium-bodied, full tannin, medium acidity **drink now–8 years**
Smoky aroma and good wild huckleberry flavor.

1999 Domaine Bressy-Masson Cuvée Paul Emile, Côtes-du-Rhône Villages Rasteau ★★★ $$
dry, full-bodied, full tannin, medium acidity **drink now–5 years**
A blend of old-vine Grenache and Syrah yields a great wine with berry, apple, and spice flavors.

1999 Domaine de l'Oratoire Saint Martin Cuvée Prestige, Côtes-du-Rhône Villages Cairanne ★★★ $$
dry, full-bodied, full tannin, medium acidity **drink now–10 years**
A wine so thick with fruit and mineral flavors that it almost feels as though you could chew it.

1999 Domaine des Coteaux de Travers Cuvée Prestige, Côtes-du-Rhône Villages Rasteau ★★★ $$
dry, full-bodied, medium tannin, medium acidity **drink now–6 years**
Mulberry, pomegranate, and spice flavors make this a wine we'd be happy to sip any time.

1998 Domaine des Grands Devers,
Côtes-du-Rhône Villages Valréas ★★★ $$
dry, full-bodied, medium tannin, medium acidity **drink now–6 years**
Power and elegance. Concentrated berry flavors that come off smooth despite their strength.

1998 Domaine du Roucas de St-Pierre
Le Coteau de Mon Rêve, Gigondas ★★★ $$
dry, full-bodied, full tannin, medium acidity **drink now–10 years**
A wonderful wine. Cherry flavor complemented by a robust earthiness. Excellent price for the quality, too.

1998 E. Guigal, Gigondas ★★★ $$
dry, full-bodied, medium tannin, medium acidity **drink in 2–15 years**
As Gigondas prices continue to rise, we especially appreciate the value in this classic, loaded with berry flavors.

1997 Le Mas des Collines, Vacqueyras ★★★ $$
dry, full-bodied, full tannin, medium acidity **drink now–8 years**
One sip takes us to the south of France, with unbridled fruit, earthiness, and flavors of wild herbs.

1999 Petrus de Roy, Côtes du Ventoux ★★★ $$
dry, full-bodied, full tannin, medium acidity **drink now–8 years**
Worried about not getting enough minerals? Reach for this: intense minerality with full berry flavor.

1999 Domaine de la Ferme Saint Martin Cuvée Princesse,
Côtes-du-Rhône Villages Beaumes-de-Venise ★★★ $
dry, medium-bodied, medium tannin, high acidity **drink now–4 years**
We'd pay much more for this, with its deep berry, earth, and smoke flavors.

1999 Domaine Pélaquié, Côtes-du-Rhône ★★★ $
dry, full-bodied, medium tannin, medium acidity **drink now–4 years**
Why can't all Côtes-du-Rhône be this good? A beauty.

1999 Barton & Guestier Tradition,
Châteauneuf-du-Pape ★★ $$
dry, medium-bodied, medium tannin, medium acidity **drink in 3–10 years**
Perhaps not the best Châteauneuf-du-Pape, but it offers delicious drinking for a relatively modest price.

1999 Domaine Alary Daniel et Denis,
Côtes-du-Rhône Villages Cairanne ★★ $$
dry, medium-bodied, medium tannin, medium acidity **drink now–5 years**
Look no further for something to drink with meaty braised oxtails or short ribs.

1999 Domaine Pélaquié, Lirac ★★ $$
dry, full-bodied, medium tannin, medium acidity **drink now–5 years**
A lyrical Lirac that starts like a lullaby with lovely berry aromas and then explodes into a symphony of mineral-rich *terroir.*

1999 Domaine Favards, Côtes-du-Rhône ★★ $
dry, medium-bodied, light tannin, medium acidity **drink now–3 years**
A delicious, fruit-filled but spicy and stony wine that gives a lot more than its low price suggests.

1998 E. Guigal, Côtes-du-Rhône ★★ $
dry, medium-bodied, medium tannin, medium acidity **drink now–5 years**
A standard for a reason: The cherry and spice flavor and mouth-filling body work every time.

1999 Paul Jaboulet Aîné Parallèle 45, Côtes-du-Rhône ★★ $
dry, medium-bodied, medium tannin, medium acidity **drink now–2 years**
One of the most widely available Rhône wines. It's not complex, but it offers pleasant fruit and light spice flavors.

1999 Perrin Réserve, Côtes-du-Rhône ★★ $
dry, full-bodied, medium tannin, medium acidity **drink now–4 years**
Lip-smacking berry flavor from start to finish.

1998 Domaine des Grands Devers Enclave des Papes, Côtes-du-Rhône ★ $
dry, medium-bodied, medium tannin, medium acidity **drink now–4 years**
Here's a perfect wine for casual occasions, with simple fruit flavors and leather and smoke notes.

1999 La Vieille Ferme, Rhône Valley ★ $
dry, medium-bodied, medium tannin, medium acidity **drink now–3 years**
It's simple, but this blend of four Rhône grapes covers all the bases.

1999 Marc Chevillot, Côtes-du-Rhône ★ $
dry, medium-bodied, light tannin, medium acidity **drink now**
Not spectacular, but for six bucks, it sure tastes good.

recommended white wines

1999 Domaine de l'Oratoire Saint-Martin Haut-Coustias, Côtes-du-Rhône Villages Cairanne ★★★ $$$
dry, medium-bodied, medium acidity, light oak **drink now–4 years**
Grenache Blanc and Clairette grapes partner in this flavorful wine.

2000 Chante Cigale, Châteauneuf-du-Pape Blanc ★★★ $$
dry, medium-bodied, medium acidity, medium oak drink now–8 years
This wine is a floral-scented wonder, full of lovely fruit, mineral, and slightly bitter flavors.

2000 Domaine Pélaquié, Côtes-du-Rhône Villages Laudun ★★ $
dry, medium-bodied, medium acidity, light oak drink now–2 years
Five Rhône varieties go into this highly perfumed wine that tastes like baked pears and apples topped by a squeeze of lime.

1999 E. Guigal, Côtes-du-Rhône ★★ $
dry, medium-bodied, medium acidity, light oak drink now–2 years
Tastes a bit high in alcohol at first; a little time in the glass allows its appealing citrus and nut flavors to come out nicely.

the southwest

Le Sud-Ouest, land of Cyrano de Bergerac, produces wines that are about as swashbuckling as they get in France. The region stretches from the southernmost edge of Bordeaux to the Basque country. It is here that some of France's heartiest reds are found—black and tannic.

grapes & styles

For red wines, two regions stand out: Cahors (cah-or) and Madiran (mah-dee-rahn). The wines are typically intense. Recent innovations have toned down the power of some Cahors, but many traditional wines with stick-to-the-teeth tannin are still around. Madiran is even more tannic than Cahors due to its main grape, Tannat. Jurançon (joo-rahn-sohn) is known for its hearty, spicy whites; red wine of indifferent quality is also made in the area. Bergerac, immediately south of Bordeaux, makes reds and whites that closely resemble its neighbor's basic wines. In Gascogne, blends are made from local and international varieties. Grapes that are normally distilled into brandy (Colombard and Ugni Blanc) find their way into pleasant, medium-bodied whites. In other regions, such as Côtes de St-Mont, indigenous varieties are blended to produce refreshing whites.

at the table

Cahors and Madiran are perhaps best sampled with lamb stew, especially one that includes black olives. Madiran's powerful taste absolutely requires strong, meaty flavor—if not lamb, then beef cuts like hanger steak and braised short ribs. Or try it with the region's famous cassoulet. Use Bergerac as you would the simplest Bordeaux, for instance with plain grilled or sautéed steaks. Jurançon white and white blends will stand up to chunky country pâté and the mustard and cornichons that come with it.

the bottom line Southwest wines are a terrific bargain. Cahors and Madiran can be picked up for under $10, though it might be worth the money to spend more, especially if you can find an older vintage. Age helps these wines—a lot. Blends from Côtes de Gascogne and Côtes de St-Mont are also less than $10. Bergerac runs $8 to $14. Jurançon is usually right around $10, but a few of the best will cost substantially more.

recommended red wines

1997 Alain Brumont Château Montus, Madiran ★★★★ $$$
dry, medium-bodied, medium tannin, medium acidity **drink now–10 years**
A superb, powerful wine with fruit and smoke flavors.

1997 Château Lagrezette Cuvée Dame Honneur, Cahors ★★★★ $$$
dry, full-bodied, full tannin, medium acidity **drink in 2–10 years**
Want to find out what the best Cahors used to be like? Pull the cork on this and indulge.

1997 Alain Brumont Château Bouscassé, Madiran ★★★★ $$
dry, full-bodied, full tannin, medium acidity **drink now–10 years**
Heavy with cherry, mineral, and smoke flavors. Excellent.

1999 Château de La Colline Bergerac, Bergerac ★★ $$
dry, full-bodied, medium tannin, medium acidity **drink now–5 years**
You'll enjoy the berry and cocoa flavors in this. The low price doesn't hurt either.

1999 Château Barrejat Tradition, Madiran ★★ $
dry, full-bodied, full tannin, medium acidity **drink in 3–10 years**
An aptly named Madiran. It is indeed traditional, full of bold fruit flavors and tons of tannin.

1999 Domaine du Mage, Côtes de Gascogne ★★ $
dry, full-bodied, medium tannin, medium acidity **drink now–5 years**
A blend: plum flavor from Merlot; minerality from Tannat.

recommended white wines

1999 Clos Lapeyre Vieilles Vignes Sec, Jurançon ★★ $$
dry, medium-bodied, high acidity, light oak **drink now–3 years**
The Pyrenees aren't usually tropical fruit territory, but this wine has lovely hints of passion fruit and citrus.

2000 Domaine de Rieux, Côtes de Gascogne ★★ $
dry, medium-bodied, high acidity, no oak **drink now**
Cognac's grape Ugni Blanc is turned into this simple, refreshing summer wine bursting with apple and lemon flavors.

1999 Domaine du Mage, Côtes de Gascogne ★★ $
dry, medium-bodied, medium acidity, no oak **drink now**
Lowly grapes elsewhere, Ugni Blanc and Colombard come together in a snappy wine with tropical fruit flavors.

1999 Plaimont Colombelle, Côtes de Gascogne ★★ $
dry, medium-bodied, medium acidity, light oak **drink now**
This is made from the lowly Colombard grape, but handled well, as it is here, the wine can be nice.

1999 Plaimont Les Vignes Retrouvées, Côtes de St-Mont ★★ $
dry, medium-bodied, medium acidity, light oak **drink now**
Made from three heirloom grape varieties, this is a wonderfully unique wine, with grassy, yeasty, and lime flavors.

italy

With more than 2,000 grape varieties and millennia of experience, Italian vintners produce an unmatched diversity of wine. But a single attitude prevails: Wine is food, as essential to a meal as bread. And what food it is, getting better with every vintage.

grapes & styles

Sangiovese (san-joh-VAY-zeh), the main component of Chianti, is the most-planted grape in Italy. Nebbiolo, Barbera, Dolcetto, Primitivo, Negroamaro, Aglianico, and Cannonau all shine in various regions. Common white varieties are Malvasia, Pinot Grigio, Vermentino, and Greco di Tufo. Styles range from the light whites of the Alps to the tannic reds of Barolo and Barbaresco.

on the label

Wine labeling is diverse in Italy. Some bottles are identified by their place of origin—for example, Barolo and Barbaresco. Others are named for a region-specific style, such as Veneto's Amarone. Others are identified by grape variety and place—for instance, Barbera d'Asti, made in Asti from Barbera grapes. Some, especially those from the German-influenced parts of the north, stress grape variety.

northern italy

Bordering four countries—France, Switzerland, Austria, and Slovenia—the regions of northern Italy provide a microcosm of virtually all wine styles.

piedmont

red wines

The noble grape of Piedmont is Nebbiolo. It's made into the legendarily powerful Barolo and the gentler Barbaresco, which is no pushover itself. Meant for years of aging, Barolo and Barbaresco correspond in power and elegance to the finest Grand Crus of Burgundy. Barbera (bar-BEAR-ah) is the most common grape in Piedmont, and the wine made from it is considerably less tannic than that produced from Nebbiolo. Dolcetto (dohl-CHET-oh) makes simpler wine than Barbera.

Charming and light- to medium-bodied, Dolcetto is comparable to Beaujolais. Freisa (FRAY-zah) is even less complex and often has a touch of sweetness. Among international varieties are Merlot, Cabernet Sauvignon, and Pinot Noir.

at the table

There's no better match for well-aged Barolo or Barbaresco than a risotto *alla piemontese* with a generous shaving of white truffles on top. Actually, anything with aromatic truffles or, less expensively, truffle oil would marry well with these wines. You can also serve them with prime steak or beef or game braised in red wine. Barbera and Dolcetto labeled Superiore, indicating at least one year of barrel aging, can be matched with the standard array of red meats or with wild mushroom ravioli. Simpler versions are perfect for burgers, grilled chicken, or pork chops. Light-bodied Freisa is a flexible wine, good with pork or poultry and all but the most delicate fish.

the bottom line You can't get around the fact that Barolo and Barbaresco are expensive, starting at $35 and going to over $100 for some single-vineyard wines. Nebbiolo-based wines from other parts of Piedmont can be a bargain, though. Look for Nebbiolo delle Langhe for wonderful wines starting at around $15. Many top Barolo producers make these simpler wines for considerably less than their more prestigious kin. Some Barbera and Dolcetto can be found for $9. More interesting bottles from excellent producers run $15 to $30 and are worth it. Less common but worth seeking are Freisa wines, which run about $15.

BAROLO & BARBARESCO

Until a few years ago, Barolos were aged in large oak or chestnut barrels for a minimum of three years, which produced wines that were too tannic to drink for over ten. But fears that some of the wines' fruit flavors were being lost to the wood have dropped the required aging to two years. The story is similar for Barbaresco, which is to be expected, since so many winemakers work in both of these neighboring areas. Wines from both Barolo and Barbaresco are commonly labeled with vineyard designations.

what to buy BAROLO & BARBARESCO

1992	1993	1994	1995	1996
★★	★★★	★★	★★★★	★★★★

1997	1998	1999
★★★★	★★★	★★★

recommended wines

1997 Alfredo Prunotto Bussia, Barolo ★★★★ $$$$
dry, full-bodied, full tannin, high acidity **drink in 5–20 years**
A blockbuster wine, so full of fruit, spice, and licorice flavors that you might want to indulge now. Better to put it away for a decade.

1997 Conterno Fantino Parussi, Barolo ★★★★ $$$$
dry, full-bodied, full tannin, medium acidity **drink in 3–15 years**
Very dry, with intense fruit flavors precisely balanced between power and finesse.

1997 Gaja, Barbaresco ★★★★ $$$$
dry, full-bodied, full tannin, high acidity **drink in 3–30 years**
If money is no object, buy all of this you can find.

1996 Giacomo Conterno Cascina Francia, Barolo ★★★★ $$$$
dry, full-bodied, full tannin, high acidity **drink in 5–20 years**
Great, powerful wine. Absolutely world class.

1997 Pio Cesare Ornato, Barolo ★★★★ $$$$
dry, full-bodied, full tannin, medium acidity **drink in 10–25 years**
Ornato is made only in the best years. Full of concentrated fruit flavors.

1996 Anselma Vigna Rionda Serralunga d'Alba, Barolo ★★★★ $$$
dry, full-bodied, full tannin, high acidity **drink in 5–15 years**
It's a tango of berry and sage flavors with the fruit leading from the start and pleasingly bitter herbal notes kicking in on the finish.

1997 Poderi Luigi Einaudi, Barolo ★★★★ $$$
dry, full-bodied, full tannin, medium acidity **drink in 5–15 years**
A big wine with rose, licorice, and deep cherry flavors.

1996 Produttori del Barbaresco Asili Riserva, Barbaresco ★★★★ $$$
dry, medium-bodied, full tannin, high acidity **drink in 3–15 years**
Made by a co-op that shows how it should be done. Nice cherry flavor.

1996 Giuseppe Cortese Rabajà, Barbaresco ★★★★ $$
dry, full-bodied, full tannin, high acidity **drink in 5–25 years**
Here's a great Barbaresco, designed to last a generation like in the old days.

1998 Ca'Rome' Sori Rio Sordo, Barbaresco ★★★ $$$$
dry, full-bodied, full tannin, medium acidity **drink in 2–12 years**
Deep fruit flavors with mineral notes for complexity.

1997 Ca'Rome' Vigna Cerretta, Barolo ★★★ $$$$
dry, full-bodied, full tannin, medium acidity **drink now–12 years**
Seemingly blah when first poured, a bit of air brings luscious fruit flavors to the fore. Almost ready now, but age will make it a lot better.

1996 Bersano, Barolo ★★★ $$$
dry, full-bodied, full tannin, medium acidity **drink in 3–15 years**
A macédoine of fruit flavors: cranberry, cherry, even notes of pineapple and tamarind.

1997 La Spinona Bricco Faset, Barbaresco ★★ $$$
dry, full-bodied, full tannin, medium acidity **drink in 3–12 years**
Smoky, with tart fruit flavors from start to finish.

BARBERA & DOLCETTO

The best examples of Barbera can fill in for Barolo or Barbaresco and are drinkable much earlier—after three years versus five to ten or more. Barbera and Dolcetto often include their place of origin in their name—for example, Barbera d'Asti or Dolcetto d'Alba.

what to buy BARBERA & DOLCETTO

1992	1993	1994	1995	1996
★★	★★★	★★	★★★★	★★★★

1997	1998	1999
★★★★	★★★	★★★

recommended wines

1997 Villa Giada Bricco Dani Superiore, Barbera d'Asti ★★★★ $$$
dry, full-bodied, medium tannin, medium acidity **drink now–8 years**
Like a square dance of flavors as herbs and minerals do-si-do around cherry and spice.

1999 Anselma, Dolcetto d'Alba ★★★★ $$
dry, full-bodied, full tannin, medium acidity **drink in 3–10 years**
Warning: Not your simple, fruity Dolcetto. One sip of this smoky, spicy, musky wonder could alter your view of Dolcetto forever.

1999 Pecchenino Sirì d'Jermu, Dolcetto di Dogliani ★★★ $$$
dry, full-bodied, full tannin, high acidity **drink in 2–10 years**
Full of blackberry and bitter chocolate flavors. Simply delightful.

1999 Prunotto Costamiole, Barbera d'Asti ★★★ $$$
dry, medium-bodied, medium tannin, medium acidity **drink now–8 years**
When the piggy bank is low but your yen for Barolo high, allow this to fill in.

1998 Marchesi di Barolo Ruvei, Barbera d'Alba ★★ $$$
dry, full-bodied, medium tannin, medium acidity **drink now–8 years**
Toast and concentrated blackberry flavors. Delicious.

1999 Castello di Neive Messoirano, Dolcetto d'Alba ★★ $$
dry, medium-bodied, medium tannin, high acidity **drink now–5 years**
A wine that shows Dolcetto's range, with deep cherry and earth flavors, an almost *frizzante* lightness, and bitter tannin.

1999 La Spinona Vigneto Qualin, Dolcetto d'Alba ★★ $$
dry, medium-bodied, medium tannin, high acidity **drink now–5 years**
Red cherry, some rose, some spice. Lots of acidity.

1998 Vicara Superiore, Barbera del Monferrato ★★ $
dry, full-bodied, medium tannin, medium acidity **drink now–5 years**
This wine is almost southern Italian in its rose and spice flavors, but its sophisticated, silky texture places it back in Piedmont.

2000 Prunotto, Dolcetto d'Alba ★ $$
dry, medium-bodied, medium tannin, high acidity **drink now–2 years**
Simple cherry and walnut flavors make a very pleasant wine.

other red wines

Freisa is a nice simple quaffing wine, often (though not always) slightly sweet and sometimes a bit effervescent. Among the more serious red wines being produced in the area are the 100 percent Nebbiolos and the blends, some of which include international grape varieties.

recommended wines

1998 Gaja Sorì San Lorenzo, Langhe ★★★★ $$$$
dry, full-bodied, full tannin, high acidity **drink in 5–20 years**
Piedmont's most revered winemaker again does the unexpected, blending a bit of Barbera with noble Nebbiolo. Among the finest wines we've ever tasted.

1999 Conterno Fantino Monprà, Langhe ★★★ $$$
dry, full-bodied, full tannin, high acidity **drink in 3–10 years**
A "Super Piedmont" blend of powerful grapes—Nebbiolo, Barbera, and Cabernet Sauvignon—makes a big wine.

1998 Vicara Rubello, Monferrato ★★★ $$
dry, medium-bodied, medium tannin, high acidity **drink in 2–10 years**
Here's a surprisingly lively blend of three varieties: Barbera, Nebbiolo, and Cabernet Sauvignon.

1996 Nervi Vigneto Molsino, Gattinara ★★ $$$
dry, medium-bodied, medium tannin, medium acidity **drink now–10 years**
This 100 percent Nebbiolo revels in the old-fashioned, earthy flavors that make wines made from this grape variety so special.

1996 Coppo Mondaccione, Piedmont ★★ $$
dry, medium-bodied, medium tannin, medium acidity **drink now–3 years**
One of our favorite northern Italian varieties, Freisa, usually light-hearted and almost floral, is a bit more serious here, with cherry and smoke flavors.

white wines

Whites made from the Cortese (cor-TEH-zeh) grape around the town of Gavi are notable. Less common is the Arneis (ahr-NAY'Z) grape, which can make even more interesting wines. Try particularly those from around Roero (roh-AIR-oh). Inevitably, Chardonnay has burst onto the scene as well, the best known being from the area around Langhe.

at the table

People who drink Gavi in those seafood restaurants near Genoa know what they're doing. It's light and tart, perfect with grilled octopus, sea bass, or really almost any white fish. Gavi is also good with light chicken dishes, pasta in pesto sauce, roasted vegetables or other selections from the antipasti cart, and even with salads. Arneis has the same essential qualities and goes equally well with any of the suggestions for Gavi. Langhe Chardonnays, with their higher acidity levels, are more food-friendly than those from California. Try one with a light pasta dish, such as agnolotti filled with chicken and prosciutto or fusilli with fresh spinach and ricotta.

the bottom line If Piedmont whites suffer from one problem, it's cost. The fact that Piedmont is one of the most prosperous parts of Italy pushes prices up, though certainly not to an outrageous point. Gavis start at $13, Arneis at $15, and both go up to around $30. Chardonnays cost more, ranging from $25 to over $50.

recommended wines

1999 Gaja Gaia & Rey, Langhe ★★★ $$$$
dry, full-bodied, medium acidity, medium oak **drink 2–12 years**
The concentrated flavors of this Chardonnay will take your breath away (if the price tag hasn't already).

2000 Giacosa, Roero Arneis ★★★ $$$
dry, light-bodied, high acidity, no oak **drink now–2 years**
Arneis means "difficult" in the local dialect, but this wine is easy to love, with delicate pear and apple notes and lots of minerals.

1999 Paolo Scavino Sorriso, Piedmont ★★★ $$$
dry, light-bodied, high acidity, light oak **drink now**
When Chardonnay and Sauvignon Blanc get together, the former usually dominates, but it's Sauvignon's turn here. Refreshing apple and citrus flavors.

2000 Broglia La Meirana, Gavi di Gavi ★★★ $$
dry, full-bodied, high acidity, no oak **drink now–2 years**
The perfect first wine before one of Piedmont's giant reds, this is lush with peach and tropical fruit scents, just right for a seafood risotto.

1998 Coppo Monteriolo Chardonnay, Piedmont ★★★ $$
dry, full-bodied, medium acidity, medium oak **drink now–6 years**
We're skeptical of Italian Chardonnay, but a few more examples like this wine, with subtle tropical fruit flavor and moderate oak, might turn us into believers.

friuli-venezia giulia & trentino-alto adige

In terms of culture, Friuli-Venezia Giulia (free-OO-lee veh-NET-zee-ah JOO-lee-ah) and Trentino-Alto Adige (tren-TEE-no AHL-toe AH-dee-jay) are barely Italian. Friuli, bordering Austria and Slovenia, shows the effects of past rule by the Romans, Byzantines, Venetians, and Hapsburgs. People in Alpine Trentino-Alto Adige, which borders Switzerland and Austria, speak a dialect of German, live in houses worthy of Hansel and Gretel, and make wine from Germanic grape varieties. These two regions produce the most exciting white wines in Italy, as well as some of the most interesting reds.

white wines

In Friuli-Venezia Giulia, Pinot Grigio and Traminer (as Gewürztraminer is often called here) are excellent, but the full-bodied Tocai Friulano (toh-KYE free-oo-LAH-no) is most interesting. Sauvignon Blanc is also a winner in the region.

Pinot Grigio does exceptionally well in Trentino-Alto Adige, where it is made into wines with lots of fruit flavor, balanced with good acidity. Santa Margherita, the wildly popular brand of Pinot Grigio, comes from here. But perhaps more attention should be paid to the region's Traminer, and Müller-Thurgau, which possess a Lamborghini-like raciness of fresh flavors and exhilarating acidity.

at the table

Pinot Grigio and Sauvignon Blanc are tailor-made for seafood. Try them with *frutti di mare* pasta full of mussels and clams or with grilled fish. Traminer and Müller-Thurgau are also excellent with seafood, but their hint of sweetness makes them perfect matches for pasta with a fruity olive oil and garlic. Native Friulians enjoy the heavy-bodied Tocai Friulano with white meats, such as veal and pork.

the bottom line Simple Pinot Grigio and Sauvignon Blanc are about $10, serious ones in the mid-$20s. Most Tocai Friulano is just under $20; $25 for the best. Traminer and Müller-Thurgau are $10 to $20.

recommended wines

1997 Gravner Breg, Collio ★★★★ $$$$
dry, full-bodied, high acidity, medium oak **drink now–10 years**
A Pandora's box of flavors that threatens delicious havoc when opened.

1999 Bastianich Tocai Friulano, Colli Orientali del Friuli ★★★★ $$$
dry, light-bodied, medium acidity, medium oak **drink now–10 years**
New York restaurateurs Lidia and Joe Bastianich return to their Friulian roots to offer a complex wine with notes of orange peel, apricot, and papaya.

1998 Vie di Romans Piere Sauvignon, Isonzo del Friuli ★★★ $$$
dry, medium-bodied, high acidity, no oak **drink now–2 years**
This shows that Italy is one of the great Sauvignon producers of the world.

1999 Pojer E Sandri Vigna Palai, Trentino ★★★ $$
dry, medium-bodied, high acidity, no oak **drink now**
A great Müller-Thurgau, with an unusual mix of flavors: pungent grass and pear.

1999 Franz Haas Manna, Alto Adige ★★★ $
dry, full-bodied, medium acidity, no oak **drink now**
Unique, with smoky, spicy, and savory qualities and some floral notes.

1999 Peter Zemmer Gewürztraminer, Alto Adige ★★ $$
dry, medium-bodied, high acidity, no oak **drink now–3 years**
A straightforward, bone-dry Gewürz with lemon, floral, and mineral flavors.

2000 Pighin Pinot Grigio, Grave del Friuli ★★ $$
dry, light-bodied, high acidity, no oak **drink now**
A great house wine for summer, with lemony flavor and brisk acidity.

1999 Pojer E Sandri Traminer, Trentino ★★ $$
dry, medium-bodied, medium acidity, no oak **drink now–3 years**
Lots of roses, with an interlude of orange and spice flavors.

2000 Puiatti Pinot Grigio, Collio ★★ $$
dry, medium-bodied, high acidity, no oak **drink now**
Exceptional Pinot Grigio with nice, restrained citrus flavors and mineral notes.

2000 Santa Margherita Pinot Grigio, Alto Adige ★★ $$
dry, medium-bodied, high acidity, no oak **drink now**
Could the millions who buy this best-selling Italian wine be wrong? Maybe about other things, but not about this.

2000 Kris Pinot Grigio delle Venezie, Trentino-Alto Adige ★★ $
dry, medium-bodied, high acidity, no oak **drink now**
One of Alto Adige's finest producers offers an easy-to-drink Pinot Grigio that should put other makers on notice.

red wines

Though white wine country, Friuli-Venezia Giulia and Trentino-Alto Adige also make interesting reds. Merlot does well. Refosco and Schioppettino (skyo-peh-TEE-no) are Friuli's most aromatic local varieties.

at the table

Drink Refosco and Schioppettino with roasted meats; black-pepper-crusted pork loin would do nicely. Serve Merlot when you would Bordeaux or Burgundy: with beef tenderloin, roast rack of lamb, or sharp cheeses, like Vermont cheddar or aged Gorgonzola.

the bottom line Reds are a mixed bag as far as price is concerned. Because they're relatively unknown, they can be bargains. Merlots rivaling many from California can be found for $10. Refosco is a good buy; a few of them sell for $10, though better bottles are around $25. The finest Schioppettino costs $30.

recommended wines

1994 Ronchi di Cialla Schioppettino di Cialla, Colli Orientali del Friuli ★★★★ $$$
dry, full-bodied, medium tannin, medium acidity **drink now–5 years**
A local hero of a grape, Schioppettino is brawny, with flavors of toasted nuts, pomegranates, plums, and herbs.

1997 Livio Felluga Sossó Riserva Merlot, Colli Orientali del Friuli ★★★ $$$
dry, medium-bodied, medium tannin, medium acidity drink now–10 years
This reserve-quality Merlot offers all the full cassis and plum flavors we love in great examples of the varietal.

1994 Ronchi di Cialla Refosco di Cialla, Colli Orientali del Friuli ★★★ $$$
dry, medium-bodied, medium tannin, high acidity drink now–3 years
Age has somewhat diminished this Refosco, but smoky, cherry, and floral characteristics remain in full measure.

1997 Pojer E Sandri Rosso Faye, Trentino ★★★ $$
dry, full-bodied, full tannin, high acidity drink now–10 years
The classic duet of Cabernet and Merlot is joined by indigenous Lagrein. Blackberry, pepper, and vanilla, with a local riff of spice notes.

1998 Scarbolo Riserva Refosco, Grave del Friuli ★★★ $$
dry, full-bodied, full tannin, medium acidity drink now–8 years
This wine shows Friuli's lusty side—full of spice, dried fruit, smoke, and coffee-like flavors.

1998 Formentini Tajut Merlot, Collio ★★ $$$
dry, full-bodied, full tannin, high acidity drink now–6 years
Not the more typical velvety, plum-scented Merlot. Collio's soil gives puckery tannin and adds pepper to the plum.

1999 Formentini Cabernet Franc, Collio ★★ $$
dry, full-bodied, full tannin, high acidity drink now–6 years
Collio's soil adds pepper even to Merlot, so you can imagine what it does to typically peppery Cabernet Franc. A nice balance of flavors.

1998 Tiefenbrunner Merlot, Alto Adige ★★ $
dry, medium-bodied, medium tannin, medium acidity drink now–7 years
The fruit flavors and tannin are in good balance. This is an elegant, smoky version of Merlot.

1999 Villa del Borgo Refosco, Friuli ★★ $
dry, medium-bodied, light tannin, high acidity drink now
Here's a wine that's easy to drink, with smooth blackberry and smoky, almost meaty flavors.

1999 Lagaria Merlot delle Venezie, Trentino ★ $
dry, medium-bodied, medium tannin, high acidity drink now–2 years
With tart fruit flavors more like cherries than plums, this isn't typical for Merlot, but we like it fine. Good acidity makes it great with food.

the veneto

One of the most productive winemaking regions of Italy, the Veneto has been both blessed and cursed by its success. It sells a lot of wine, but much of it is over-produced in quantity and underwhelming in quality. Valpolicella and Soave in particular suffer from low reputations. Still, there are many excellent wines to be found.

white wines

The multi-terrained zone of Soave (s'WAH-veh) dominates white wine production. Made by large companies, most Soaves are thin and tart. However, smaller producers using grapes from the hillside Soave Classico regions are making some excellent, medium-bodied wines. Some good Pinot Grigios are made, too.

at the table

The best use for a simple Soave might be in a spritzer or wine punch. Soave Classico was made for scampi. Serve Pinot Grigio with lean fish, blends with shellfish.

the bottom line Spending more than $8 for a simple Soave is a waste. Plunk down a few dollars more for a Classico—it's worth it. A few single-vineyard versions will cost between $22 and $35 and will show you how good Soave can be. There are several Pinot Grigios available for around $10. Various blends sell for about $22.

recommended wines

1999 Leonildo Pieropan Calvarino,
Soave Classico Superiore ★★★ $$
dry, medium-bodied, high acidity, no oak **drink now–4 years**
A single-vineyard wine from Soave's greatest proponent of quality offers tangy lime and mineral flavors.

1999 Tamellini Anguane, Soave Classico Superiore ★★★ $$
dry, full-bodied, high acidity, no oak **drink now–2 years**
Forget about all those lemon-water Soaves, this is the real thing, with the lush aromas and flavors of peaches and pears.

1999 Tamellini Le Bine, Soave Classico Superiore ★★★ $$
dry, full-bodied, high acidity, no oak **drink now–4 years**
Le Bine's mineral-rich but otherwise poor soil results in a completely different wine from Anguane's (above), with apple and—what else?—mineral flavors.

2000 Bertani Duè Uvè, Veneto ★★★ $
dry, medium-bodied, medium acidity, no oak **drink now**
Pinot Grigio and Sauvignon Blanc dance a tango of peppery lemon flavors that dip seductively into the realm of peach and pineapple.

2000 Maculan Pino & Toi, Veneto ★★ $
dry, full-bodied, medium acidity, no oak **drink now–4 years**
'Pino' for Pinots Grigio and Bianco, 'Toi' for Tocai. Maculan's skill shown in his sweet wines is clearly up to the more modest task of making dry whites.

2000 Bolla, Soave ★ $
dry, light-bodied, medium acidity, no oak **drink now**
Though not spectacular, this wine is good for casual occasions. It has nice, lively fruit flavors.

2000 Folonari Pinot Grigio delle Venezie, Veneto ★ $
dry, light-bodied, high acidity, no oak **drink now**
This doesn't go beyond tart apple and lemon flavors, but it certainly does the trick for mild fish.

red wines

The primary red wine of the Veneto is Valpolicella (vahl-poh-lee-t'CHELL-ah). Most of the simple Valpolicellas are thin and astringent. Those made in Valpolicella Classico are usually better, and those labeled Superiore are the best of all. When it's good, Valpolicella is medium-bodied and aromatic. Amarone (ah-mah-ROE-neh), a subspecies of Valpolicella, is made from partially dried grapes. Compared to plain Valpolicella, Amarone generally offers more of everything: more flavor, fuller body, and a higher level of alcohol.

at the table

Valpolicella Classico is a good match for lasagna, spicy pork sausage, or polenta with Bolognese sauce, but when you get into Superiore and especially Amarone, go for more robustly flavored dishes. A Moroccan lamb tagine with prunes, for instance, or braised lamb shanks with sweet spices like clove and cinnamon, would be perfect. And Amarone complements Gorgonzola beautifully.

the bottom line Bypass basic Valpolicella that costs more than $10—unless it has a vineyard name on the label. Classicos are only a couple of dollars more and they're much better. Superiore is another notch up in both quality and cost. Most Amarones are priced between $30 and $50. However, as new styles are (relatively) less intense, you may want to pay extra for vintages before 1993. Amarones from a couple of top producers cost over $100. They are worth trying if you can afford them. Several producers have experimented with Cabernet Sauvignon and Merlot, but results and prices vary—from $11 to well over $50.

recommended wines

1998 Maculan Fratta, Veneto ★★★★ $$$$
dry, full-bodied, medium tannin, medium acidity drink in 5–15 years
In this great wine full of berry, spice, and licorice flavors, Cabernet Sauvignon and Merlot get some of the same treatment as the Corvina used for Amarone.

1997 Allegrini, Amarone della Valpolicella Classico ★★★★ $$$
dry, full-bodied, full tannin, medium acidity drink in 3–15 years
At the moment, this is as expressionless as a master poker player. It's in no hurry to show you what it's got, but in time it'll be a royal flush of a wine.

1996 Santi Proemio, Amarone della Valpolicella ★★★ $$$$
dry, full-bodied, medium tannin, medium acidity drink now–10 years
Lovely fruit as well as somewhat bitter spice and herb flavors. Not for everyone, but we love it.

1995 Acinum, Amarone della Valpolicella Classico ★★★ $$$
dry, full-bodied, medium tannin, medium acidity drink now–8 years
Relatively full, with berry flavors and hints of tobacco and spice.

1996 Bolla, Amarone della Valpolicella Classico ★★★ $$$
dry, full-bodied, full tannin, high acidity **drink now–8 years**
A classic Amarone, with spice, rose, and honey notes wafting through a base of deep cherry flavor.

1995 Cesari Il Bosco,
Amarone della Valpolicella Classico ★★★ $$$
dry, full-bodied, full tannin, medium acidity **drink now–10 years**
An espresso-thick Amarone of the old school. Deep flavors like smoke, cassis, chocolate, and leather, prettied up by hints of lavender.

1997 Masi Costasera,
Amarone della Valpolicella Classico ★★★ $$$
dry, full-bodied, medium tannin, medium acidity **drink in 3–10 years**
Fruit, spice, smoke, and leather flavors so well balanced that they become one.

1995 Sartori Corte Bra, Amarone della Valpolicella ★★★ $$$
dry, full-bodied, full tannin, medium acidity **drink now–10 years**
Really lovely spice and floral aromas. Spice, fruit, mineral, and smoke flavors.

1997 Villa Novare Ognisanti,
Valpolicella Classico Superiore ★★★ $$$
dry, medium-bodied, full tannin, medium acidity **drink now–5 years**
Quite dry, with lots of fruit, spice, vanilla, and rose notes.

1999 La Montecchia Godimondo Cabernet Franc,
Veneto ★★★ $$
dry, full-bodied, medium tannin, medium acidity **drink now–5 years**
A Cabernet Franc on steroids. The variety's typical peppercorn flavor is so magnetic it almost pulls you into the glass. Plenty of fruit flavor as well.

1997 Acinum Ripasso, Valpolicella Classico Superiore ★★ $$
dry, full-bodied, medium tannin, high acidity **drink now–6 years**
Frugality to good effect: The spent must (pulp) from making Amarone is combined with ordinary Valpolicella, adding an extra dimension.

1998 Cesari Mara Vino di Ripasso,
Valpolicella Classico Superiore ★★ $$
dry, full-bodied, medium tannin, high acidity **drink now–5 years**
Not as big as the Cesari Amarone above, but still relatively lush, with cherry, some spice, and light floral notes balanced by good acidity.

1998 Zenato, Valpolicella Classico Superiore ★★ $
dry, full-bodied, medium tannin, high acidity **drink now–4 years**
The kind of easy-drinking, lush-fruit-and-a-hint-of-spice type wine we wish every ordinary Valpolicella could be.

central italy

Northern Italy is lauded for its sophistication, and southern Italy for its soul, but the heart of Italy lies in its six central regions. It's difficult to imagine Italian cuisine without Parmigiano-Reggiano or prosciutto di Parma, both of which are from central Italy, not to mention the wines of the area, such as Lambrusco, Chianti, Orvieto, and Frascati.

tuscany

It isn't surprising that Frances Mayes's *Under the Tuscan Sun* sold so many copies. Americans are simply obsessed with Tuscany—its food, its wine, its lifestyle. Tuscan restaurants are everywhere in the U.S., and Chianti has graduated from light, astringent plonk in straw-covered bottles to a wine that must be taken seriously.

red wines

The Tuscan sun really shines on red wines. The Sangiovese (san-joh-VAY-zeh) grape dominates, usually blended with other red or white grapes. Sangiovese-based wines are typically medium- to full-bodied with good acidity.

CHIANTI

The heart of Tuscan wine country, Chianti is a large region, bigger than Bordeaux. It is divided into seven zones with varying reputations. The most famous is Chianti Classico, between Florence and Siena. Chianti Rufina and Chianti Colli Senesi, both near Florence, are also well regarded. Wines distinguished by the word *Riserva* on the label are those that have been aged the longest before bottling.

at the table

Basic Chianti is simple, light-bodied, pleasingly fruity, and astringent. Use it to wash down pizza, spaghetti and meatballs, or linguine with red clam sauce. Wines from designated subregions are fuller in body and flavor. Serve them with chicken cacciatore or roasted pork loin flavored with rosemary. Save Riservas for venison or a good steak, perhaps *bistecca alla Fiorentina.*

the bottom line The basic stuff will run you $9 to $12; those from Chianti Classico, $15 to $18, with Riservas starting at around $20 and going to $35. Wines from Chianti subregions like Rufina or Colli Senesi are often a good value.

what to buy CHIANTI

1992	1993	1994	1995	1996
★★	★★★	★★★	★★★★	★★★

1997	1998	1999
★★★★	★★★	★★★

recommended wines

1997 Melini Massovecchio Riserva, Classico ★★★★ $$$
dry, full-bodied, medium tannin, high acidity **drink now–10 years**
A concentration and depth of flavor that left us speechless. Sip while contemplating the meaning of life.

1997 Monsanto Il Poggio Riserva, Classico ★★★ $$$$
dry, full-bodied, full tannin, high acidity **drink now–10 years**
Aging in small oak barrels, in the modern style, brings vanilla and caramel to this big wine. Great now, but in a few years…wow.

1999 Badia a Coltibuono, Classico ★★★ $$
dry, medium-bodied, medium tannin, medium acidity **drink now–10 years**
There's a certain lively and refreshing quality to this wine that is rare in Chianti. Deep cherry and violet flavors, spiced up by a little cedar.

1997 Cecchi Messer Pietro di Teuzzo Riserva, Classico ★★ $$$
dry, full-bodied, full tannin, high acidity **drink now–10 years**
A lusty wine full of cherry, tar, and leather flavors accented by the vanilla that comes from aging in small oak barrels.

1997 Monsanto Riserva, Classico ★★ $$
dry, medium-bodied, medium tannin, medium acidity drink now–6 years
Though not as concentrated as its sister wine, Il Poggio (page 155), this has the sort of charm any Tuscan could appreciate.

1999 Piazzano Rio Camerata, Chianti ★★ $$
dry, medium-bodied, full tannin, high acidity drink now–5 years
Sometimes we just need something simple; not one-dimensional, but not terribly complicated. Here's a Chianti with an easy-to-like range of flavors.

1997 Puiatti Casavecchia Il Sogno, Classico ★★ $$
dry, medium-bodied, medium tannin, high acidity drink now–5 years
The motto on the bottle says it all: "Save a tree, drink Puiatt. No oak-aged wines." Score one point for humor and ten for beautiful, pure fruit flavors.

1999 Rocca delle Macie, Classico ★★ $$
dry, medium-bodied, light tannin, medium acidity drink now–5 years
Aromas reminiscent of a bowl of berries. Here is a pure expression of Sangiovese, uncomplicated by oak aging.

1998 Colognole, Rufina ★★ $
dry, medium-bodied, medium tannin, high acidity drink now–5 years
A great find for lovers of classic Chianti. Bracing acidity and pronounced but smooth tannin.

1997 Il Valore Riserva, Classico ★★ $
dry, medium-bodied, light tannin, medium acidity drink now–5 years
A real steal. This is a smoky, traditional Chianti at an old-fashioned price.

1998 Spalletti, Chianti ★★ $
dry, light-bodied, light tannin, medium acidity drink now–3 years
Intriguing, earthy aromas and flavors. A complete charmer.

1999 Villa Giulia Alaura, Classico ★★ $
dry, medium-bodied, light tannin, medium acidity drink now–6 years
With flavors of fruit and spice, this is a modern-style Chianti. Very nice.

1999 Fontaleoni, Colli Senesi ★ $
dry, medium-bodied, medium tannin, medium acidity drink now–2 years
It's hard to find a delicate Chianti these days. Here's one with berry flavors and spice, and the price is right, too.

1999 Straccali, Chianti ★ $
dry, light-bodied, light tannin, high acidity drink now–2 years
Charming cherry aromas and a color to match. This wine is particularly nice when slightly chilled.

MONTALCINO

Twenty years ago, the wines of Montalcino (mohn-tahl-t'CHEE-no), a town south of Siena, were largely overlooked. Today, Montalcino's Brunello (one of several clones of Sangiovese) is among the most sought-after wines from Italy. Brunellos are famously tannic and full-flavored. As with Chianti, those labeled Riserva are the top of the line. Rosso di Montalcino, sometimes referred to as Baby Brunello, needs less aging.

at the table

An ideal combination is Brunello with roasted game birds wrapped in prosciutto or bacon. Partridge and wild duck are classic partners, but Brunello with crusty prime rib or roast leg of lamb would also be excellent. Vegetarians can pair Brunello with hearty bean-based dishes. The full-bodied but less powerful Rosso can be enjoyed with lamb chops, braised turkey legs, grilled quail, or sharp cheeses.

the bottom line Brunello is expensive, period. Noteworthy bottles start at $45 and go over $100 for top Riservas. Rosso di Montalcino is less expensive and can be good. Look for wines ranging between $18 and the mid-$20s.

recommended wines

1995 Il Poggiolo Beato, Brunello di Montalcino ★★★★ $$$$
dry, full-bodied, full tannin, high acidity **drink now–10 years**
It's tempting to drink this top-notch Brunello now, but patience will be rewarded.

1996 Lisini, Brunello di Montalcino ★★★★ $$$
dry, full-bodied, full tannin, medium acidity **drink in 5–10 years**
Full of cherry and spice flavors, this is the Brunello by which we judge all others.

1996 Biondi-Santi, Brunello di Montalcino ★★★ $$$$
dry, full-bodied, medium tannin, medium acidity **drink now–15 years**
Biondi-Santi, the father of Brunello, has created another beautiful wine.

1996 Poggio Antico Altero, Brunello di Montalcino ★★★ $$$$
dry, full-bodied, medium tannin, medium acidity **drink now–10 years**
A thoroughly modern style of Brunello, with two years aging in cask and two in the bottle instead of three and one. Nice cherry and herb flavors.

1995 Castiglion del Bosco, Brunello di Montalcino ★★★ $$$
dry, full-bodied, full tannin, medium acidity **drink in 3–15 years**
Cherry and raspberry made more interesting by brown sugar, leather, and cedar flavors.

1996 Col d'Orcia, Brunello di Montalcino ★★★ $$$
dry, full-bodied, medium tannin, medium acidity **drink now–8 years**
After six years, the tannin has settled down and the cherry and spice flavors have come forward. Good.

1996 Castello Banfi, Brunello di Montalcino ★★ $$$$
dry, medium-bodied, full tannin, medium acidity **drink in 3–12 years**
A combination of sweet fruit and tart, spicy flavors like tamarind come together harmoniously in this powerful wine.

1999 Calbello, Rosso di Montalcino ★★ $$$
dry, medium-bodied, medium tannin, medium acidity **drink now–5 years**
In kindergarten, we made a cranberry-orange relish for Thanksgiving. We finally found the wine to go with it. Good with turkey, too.

1999 Il Poggione, Rosso di Montalcino ★★ $$$
dry, full-bodied, full tannin, medium acidity **drink now–5 years**
A great introduction to the magic that is Montalcino, with plum flavors that go on and on through the long finish.

1998 Castello Banfi, Rosso di Montalcino ★★ $$
dry, full-bodied, medium tannin, medium acidity **drink now–5 years**
True to the Banfi style, this tasty wine emphasizes fruitiness with a handful of spice notes.

1999 Col d'Orcia, Rosso di Montalcino ★★ $$
dry, medium-bodied, medium tannin, high acidity **drink now–6 years**
Fruit, flowers, and a whole chest full of cedar.

1999 Le Macioche, Rosso di Montalcino ★ $$
dry, medium-bodied, medium tannin, medium acidity **drink now–4 years**
Enjoyable cherry flavors. Interesting earthiness.

OTHER SANGIOVESE-BASED WINES

There's a great deal more to Tuscan Sangiovese than just Chianti and Brunello, wonderful as they are. Explore the wines of less-known areas, especially those that follow, for attractive quality-to-price ratios.

Vino Nobile di Montepulciano (veen-no NOH-bee-leh dee mon-teh-pool-t'CHA-no) Once one of Italy's most famous wines, Vino Nobile is based on a strain of Sangiovese grown around the town of Montepulciano. It is generally fuller-bodied than Chianti. Between the 1960s and the 1980s, the region's wines declined. Improvements in production have raised the quality considerably and the reputation moderately, to the advantage of consumers.

Carmignano (cahr-mee-n'YAH-no) Wines from this area are usually fuller-bodied and more tannic than Chiantis, but have less acidity. This is a place to watch.

Morellino di Scansano (mor-el-EEN-o dee skahn-SAN-o) "Little cherry" is the translation of Morellino, which is full-bodied and tastes like—what else?—cherries.

what to buy OTHER SANGIOVESE-BASED WINES

1994	1995	1996	1997	1998	1999
★★★	★★★★	★★★	★★★★	★★★	★★★

recommended wines

1997 Badia a Coltibuono Sangioveto, Tuscany ★★★★ $$$$
dry, medium-bodied, medium tannin, medium acidity drink in 2–20 years
There are other great Tuscan wines, but none better than this perfect example of what mature Sangiovese can be.

1995 Castellare I Sodi di San Niccolò, Tuscany ★★★★ $$$
dry, full-bodied, full tannin, medium acidity drink in 3–20 years
Whereas others rely on French varieties to make their Tuscans "super," Castellare calls on local Malavasia Nera to support Sangioveto. Superb.

1998 Aia della Macina Terranera Riserva, Morellino di Scansano ★★★ $$$
dry, full-bodied, medium tannin, medium acidity drink now–10 years
With a name like Morellino (little cherry), you'd expect cherry flavors, and indeed, you get loads of them, plus lots of spices.

1998 Fattoria Le Pupille Riserva, Morellino di Scansano ★★★ $$$
dry, medium-bodied, light tannin, high acidity drink now–7 years
From the most famous producer of Morellino. Sure to please.

1996 Carpineto Riserva, Vino Nobile di Montepulciano ★★★ $$
dry, full-bodied, medium tannin, high acidity **drink now–10 years**
A superb example of its type, the austerity of this wine is softened by nice berry flavors.

1998 Fattoria del Cerro Vigneto Antica Chiusina, Vino Nobile di Montepulciano ★★ $$$
dry, medium-bodied, full tannin, medium acidity **drink now–10 years**
Although many such wines are not very *nobile,* this one does an admirable job of living up to its name.

1999 Dei, Rosso di Montepulciano ★★ $$
dry, medium-bodied, medium tannin, medium acidity **drink now–5 years**
Before wine becomes Vino Nobile, it is Rosso. This one's lovely.

1997 Tenuta della Seta, Vino Nobile di Montepulciano ★★ $$
dry, medium-bodied, medium tannin, medium acidity **drink now–8 years**
A delicious wine with cassis flavor.

1998 Tenuta di Capezzana, Carmignano ★★ $$
dry, full-bodied, medium tannin, high acidity **drink now–7 years**
Allow a few minutes for the sulfur to dissipate before enjoying the cherry and chocolate flavors here.

1999 Conti Contini Sangiovese, Tuscany ★★ $
dry, full-bodied, medium tannin, light acidity **drink now–6 years**
Intense plum aromas and concentrated earthy flavors make for a winning international style.

1999 Fattoria Ambra Barco Reale, Carmignano ★★ $
dry, medium-bodied, medium tannin, medium acidity **drink now–5 years**
We turn to a Carmignano like this when we want the smoky flavors of Tuscany without Chianti's astringency.

1999 Rocca delle Macie Rubizzo Sangiovese, Tuscany ★ $
dry, medium-bodied, light tannin, medium acidity **drink now–3 years**
A pure expression of the Sangiovese grape, this is a great choice for pasta in an olive-oil-based sauce.

SUPER TUSCANS

It started in the late 1960s when a Bordeaux-loving Tuscan started tinkering around with locally grown Cabernet Sauvignon and small French-oak barrels. This resulted in Sassicaia (sah-see-CAH-yah), a wine the likes of which had never been made in Tuscany—lots of flavor, body, and tannin, yet with a silky texture and relatively little astringency. This wine didn't fit into any official categories and had to be classified as lowly Vino da Tavola, but its accolades started a revolution in Tuscany. Some winemakers turned to new grape varieties and vinification techniques. Others combined old and new. The new-style wines were dubbed Super Tuscans and became wildly popular with consumers willing to pay high prices for them. Today, nearly every major wine producer in Tuscany has introduced a similarly styled wine. As for Sassicaia, it's no longer a Vino da Tavola, having been given its own official designation a couple of years ago.

at the table

Full-bodied, tannic Super Tuscans go perfectly with a wide range of meats and meat dishes, including seared lamb chops with rosemary, grilled aged porterhouse steaks, braised lamb shanks, and roast rib of beef. Homemade gnocchi with hearty meat sauce would also be delicious. Non-meat-eaters should pair it with grilled seitan steaks or portobello mushroom burgers.

the bottom line One wouldn't expect wines regarded as *super* by American wine merchants and writers to sell for anything less than super-high prices. There are a couple of wines that slip in under $12, but the overwhelming majority cost $25 to $40, with more than a handful selling for $70 or more.

what to buy SUPER TUSCANS

1995	1996	1997	1998	1999
★★★	★★★	★★★★	★★★	★★★

recommended wines

1997 Castello Banfi Summus ★★★★ $$$$
dry, full-bodied, full tannin, medium acidity **drink in 5–20 years**
What do you get when you cross Cabernet Sauvignon, Syrah, and Sangiovese with the producer that brings us Riunite? Believe it or not, one of Italy's most sumptuous wines.

1997 Tenuta San Guido Sassicaia, Bolgheri ★★★★ $$$$
dry, full-bodied, full tannin, medium acidity **drink in 5–20 years**
From the father of all Super Tuscans comes the mother of all wines.

1997 Tenuta Caparzo Ca' del Pazzo ★★★★ $$$
dry, full-bodied, medium tannin, medium acidity drink now–7 years
This combination of Tuscany's Sangiovese and Bordeaux's Cabernet Sauvignon is everything a Super Tuscan should be.

1998 Antinori Tenuta Guado al Tasso Superiore, Bolgheri ★★★ $$$$
dry, full-bodied, full tannin, medium acidity drink in 3–15 years
A fruity stunner made from Cabernet Sauvignon, Merlot, and Syrah.

1997 I Balzini ★★★ $$$$
dry, full-bodied, full tannin, high acidity drink now–15 years
A super Super Tuscan with so many layers of super flavors that we only regret we can't afford to have this every day.

1997 Badia di Morrona "N'Antia" ★★★ $$$
dry, full-bodied, medium tannin, medium acidity drink now–10 years
Silky and elegant, this is a wine to savor over a romantic dinner.

1998 Biondi-Santi Sassoalloro ★★★ $$$
dry, full-bodied, medium tannin, medium acidity drink now–10 years
You don't expect cassis and chocolate flavors from Sangiovese, but in this wine from just outside Montalcino, that's what you get.

1998 Fattoria le Sorgenti Scirus ★★★ $$$
dry, full-bodied, full tannin, high acidity drink in 3–15 years
A concentrated blend of Cabernet and Merlot. Needs years to develop.

1996 Melini Coltri Two ★★★ $$$
dry, full-bodied, medium tannin, high acidity drink now–5 years
A very fine Cabernet Sauvignon and Sangioveto blend.

1998 Tenuta Oliveto Il Leccio, Rosso di Toscana ★★★ $$
dry, full-bodied, medium tannin, medium acidity drink now–10 years
With its cherry aroma and smooth tannin, this 100 percent Sangiovese-based wine is sure to seduce.

1997 Badiolo, Sangiovese di Toscana ★★ $$
dry, full-bodied, medium tannin, medium acidity drink now–5 years
Here's an archetype of the modern style, with concentrated flavors and silky smooth tannin.

1998 Banfi Centine ★ $
dry, medium-bodied, medium tannin, medium acidity drink now–3 years
Want to join the Super Tuscan club but don't want to pay the super-high dues? Try this bargain blend of Cabernet Sauvignon, Merlot, and Sangiovese.

THE COUNTER-REFORMATION

Easy-to-sell international grape varieties like Cabernet Sauvignon, Merlot, and Chardonnay are being planted around the world. Even Italy, with its proud ancient history of making wine from indigenous varieties, has succumbed to this phenomenon, most famously in the form of the Super Tuscans. But fearing that a vital heritage might be lost forever, a couple of organizations, Matura and Orchestra, have been formed to encourage producers to use local grape varieties. These groups provide enological, financial, and marketing advice and export services. Though the organizations are relatively young, response has been strong, and many indigenous-grape wines are now available in the U.S.

white wines

In Tuscany, white wine plays second fiddle to red. Trebbiano, the dominant white grape, is abundantly productive but makes wine that is generally insipid. In terms of the quality of the wines it produces, Vernaccia di San Gimignano (vair-NAH-t'chah dee san-d'jee-mee-n'YAH-no) is the most successful variety. Old styles are powerful wines. New styles are fruitier. Chardonnay has found its way into the region, with few obvious successes, although it has fattened the pocketbooks of several producers. A range of other varietals are produced as well. The best, often blends of indigenous and/or French varietals, can be excitingly aromatic and have unexpected flavors.

at the table

Drink old-fashioned Vernaccia di San Gimignano with a roasted capon or with a traditional Tuscan bean soup. New styles can be enjoyed with lighter dishes, perhaps stuffed zucchini blossoms or linguine with garlic and oil. An aromatic blend made from Sauvignon Blanc and Traminer makes an excellent match for red-pepper-flecked seafood pasta or a simple sautéed pork or veal chop.

the bottom line Indigenous varietals, such as Vernaccia di San Gimignano, can be a steal, with most under $12. Look for wines labeled Riserva. Those at around $20 are excellent. Other varietals and blends can be found for between $10 and $20. The few Tuscan Chardonnays worth buying cost about $25.

recommended wines

2000 Fattoria Le Pupille Poggio Argentato, Tuscany ★★★★ $$
dry, full-bodied, medium acidity, no oak **drink now–3 years**
Unusual anywhere, almost unheard of in Tuscany, this aromatic Sauvignon Blanc and Traminer blend is almost as intense as dessert wine, but is dry.

1999 Tenuta Le Calcinaie Vigna ai Sassi, Vernaccia di San Gimignano ★★★ $$
dry, medium bodied, medium acidity, no oak **drink now–3 years**
Here's the indigenous Vernaccia grape variety. It makes a wine with wonderful apple and mineral flavors.

1998 Tenuta del Terriccio Saluccio, Tuscany ★★ $$$$
dry, full-bodied, medium acidity, heavy oak **drink now–7 years**
If you like big, bold California Chardonnay, you'll love this richly flavored wine.

1999 Biondi-Santi Rivolo, Tuscany ★★ $$
dry, full-bodied, medium acidity, light oak **drink now–5 years**
Barrel aging does funny things to Sauvignon Blanc. Here it morphs into lemon poppy-seed cake in a glass.

1999 Fontaleoni, Vernaccia di San Gimignano ★★ $
dry, medium-bodied, medium acidity, no oak **drink now–2 years**
The pleasingly fruity qualities of this wine waft from nose to palate, but in the end, we just can't help thinking of lemon Pez. Fun!

1999 Nozzole Le Bruniche, Tuscany ★ $$
dry, full-bodied, high acidity, medium oak **drink now–3 years**
There's no real reason for a Tuscan Chardonnay, but if you're looking for a good, inexpensive Chard, this does fine.

2000 Banfi Le Rime, Tuscany ★ $
dry, light-bodied, high acidity, no oak **drink now**
You'll get the most pleasure from this simple wine with citrus and melon flavors if you let it get really cold before serving.

2000 Coltibuono Trappoline Bianco di Toscana ★ $
dry, full-bodied, high acidity, no oak **drink now**
From one of Chianti's finest estates, Badia a Coltibuono, this wine has gentle lime and pear-like flavors braced by vigorous acidity.

1999 I Campetti L'Accesa Malvasia di Toscana Bianco ★ $
dry, light-bodied, high acidity, no oak **drink now**
This is an easy-drinking wine, lightly but appealingly floral. Great with trout or other delicate fish.

other regions of central italy

Surrounding Tuscany are five other wine regions, each with its own traditions of winemaking.

Emilia-Romagna It has been said that the natives of this land of classic Italian cooking like their wine so much that little of the good stuff is exported. The fact is that most of the region's wine is less than inspiring. Lambrusco comes from here, not exactly an advertisement for quality. Still, some exports, such as Cabernet Sauvignon, are excellent, but they're difficult to find.

Umbria Best known for its white Orvieto, Umbria produces a lot that is thin and dull. But when done right, Orvieto can be excellent. In the last few years, Tuscan winemakers seeking new frontiers (and cheaper land) have set up shop in Umbria and are producing some really good Sangiovese.

The Marches Long known primarily for its distinctive white Verdicchio, the Marches region is undergoing a transformation due to new investments and ideas. Sangiovese is being produced here that can match many a Chianti. Wines from Rosso Piceno or Rosso Conero, which blend Sangiovese with Montepulciano (a grape not used in the town of the same name), can be full in both flavor and body.

Abruzzi The Montepulciano grape finds its greatest expression in the hands of a few winemakers from this region. Rich in aroma and tannin, Montepulciano d'Abruzzo is often a bargain. Quality whites made of Trebbiano d'Abruzzo (a different grape from Tuscan Trebbiano) can be outstanding.

Latium The best-known wine of Lazio (its Italian name) is the light, white, slightly fizzy Frascati, just the thing to help you enjoy *la dolce vita*.

the bottom line Wines from these regions are often overlooked in favor of those from Tuscany and therefore can be especially good values. Many reds fall in the $10 to $15 range. Lots of whites are under $10.

recommended red wines

1999 Lamborghini Campoleone, Umbria ★★★ $$$
dry, full-bodied, full tannin, medium acidity **drink now–7 years**
Fans of big California Cabernet Sauvignon can comfortably go Italian with this revved-up powerhouse of bold cherry flavor and lots of oak.

1997 Galli & Broccatelli Sagrantino di Montefalco, Umbria ★★★ $$
dry, full-bodied, full tannin, high acidity **drink now–10 years**
With earthy flavor and an endless berry finish, this wine makes it easy to understand why Sagrantinos have developed a cult-like following.

1998 Monteschiavo Conti Cortesi Rosso Conero, The Marches ★★★ $$
dry, full-bodied, medium tannin, medium acidity **drink now–3 years**
A compelling wine, with lusty cherry and sweet spice flavors and a dry finish.

1999 Tre Monti Tùrico Colli d'Imola Cabernet Sauvignon, Emilia-Romagna ★★★ $$
dry, full-bodied, medium tannin, medium acidity **drink now–5 years**
At last, a local wine that befits the gastronomic glories of Emilia-Romagna. Not a tannic monster, just smooth berry flavors and a hint of spice.

1999 Valori Riserva Montepulciano d'Abruzzo ★★★ $$
dry, full-bodied, medium tannin, medium acidity **drink now–10 years**
One of the finest Montepulcianos we've ever tasted. The fruit and oak flavors balance beautifully.

1998 Tenuta Cocci Grifoni Vigna Messieri Rosso Piceno Superiore, The Marches ★★ $$
dry, full-bodied, medium tannin, high acidity **drink now–5 years**
Give this some air before drinking so its submerged berry and herb flavors can surface.

1997 Galli & Broccatelli Rosso di Torgiano, Umbria ★★ $
dry, medium-bodied, medium tannin, medium acidity **drink now–5 years**
With seductive aromas of cherry pie and exotic spices, this one will make you want to dive right into your wine glass.

2000 La Monica Montepulciano d'Abruzzo ★★ $
dry, medium-bodied, light tannin, medium acidity **drink now–2 years**
A great choice for your next party. The forthright flavor will please the crowd without breaking the bank.

1999 Fazi Battaglia Sangiovese delle Marche ★ $
dry, medium-bodied, medium tannin, medium acidity **drink now–3 years**
A wine so smoky it's as if the grapes were crushed in a smokehouse. Sangiovese's typical cherry taste makes up the balance of the flavor.

1999 Testa Montepulciano d'Abruzzo ★ $
dry, medium-bodied, medium tannin, medium acidity **drink now**
Simple fruit and oak flavors make this a good wine for burgers. Five bucks a bottle makes it great.

recommended white wines

1999 Bucci Verdicchio dei Castelli di Jesi Classico, The Marches ★★★ $$
dry, full-bodied, medium acidity, light oak **drink now–5 years**
Full in body and in fruity, nutty flavor.

2000 Lungarotti Pinot Grigio, Umbria ★★ $$
dry, medium-bodied, medium acidity, no oak **drink now**
This Pinot Grigio, with its lime and apple aromas, is quite appealing.

1999 Cataldi Madonna Trebbiano d'Abruzzo ★★ $
dry, light-bodied, high acidity, no oak **drink now–2 years**
A more serious Trebbiano than most but still light enough to be a great companion to seafood and vegetarian dishes.

1999 Palazzone Terre Vineate Orvieto Classico, Umbria ★★ $
dry, light-bodied, high acidity, no oak **drink now**
After tasting so many dull Orvietos, all we can say about this is "finally!" Lovely fruit flavors in a light-bodied wine.

2000 La Monica Trebbiano d'Abruzzo ★ $
dry, light-bodied, high acidity, no oak **drink now**
This delicate wine shows why Trebbiano is Italy's most popular white grape.

southern italy

For Italy's southern wine regions, the sun has always been both friend and foe. Hot summers mean grapes ripen easily, with plenty of sugar, but not enough acidity. And the sun stews the fresh-fruit charm out of grapes fermented in traditional outdoor tanks. Now, though, such technology as temperature-controlled fermentation helps make extremely interesting wines.

apulia

More wine comes from Apulia than from any other region of Italy; thankfully, most of it will never grace these shores. But what does arrive stateside is good, sometimes excellent. Wines made from the Negroamaro grape can have the power of Côtes-du-Rhônes with even more aroma; Salice Salentino and Copertino are good examples. Primitivo, parent to our Zinfandel, makes wines that are similar to but less intense than the U.S. versions.

basilicata

Aglianico del Vulture (ah-lee-AH-nee-co del VOOL-too-reh) is Basilicata's one important wine. It's a spice- and rose-scented red, tannic when young but lovely after a few years of aging.

campania

Bold Aglianico reds and the aromatic whites Fiano di Avellino and Greco di Tufo give Campania a strong claim to being the best wine region in southern Italy. Falanghina, a favorite white grape in Roman times, today makes a dull wine of small consequence. Renewed interest is bringing some exciting exceptions.

sicily & sardinia

Long known for its sweet wines, Marsala and Moscato, Sicily is now showing its potential for dry bottlings. Hearty red blends are made from unseen-elsewhere and international grape varieties, while white wines mix indigenous varieties and Chardonnay. Sardinia has been a sleeper on the international wine stage, but excellent, full-flavored whites and reds are beginning to appear with more frequency. Tart Vermentino is notable among Sardinian white wines. Some of Sardinia's finest red wines, including the top-of-the-line Terre Brune (teh-ray BROO-nay), are made from the Carignano (Carignan) grape, introduced from Spain long ago.

white wines

at the table

Campania's white wines have a lot of presence and can go with an array of foods. Drink fuller-bodied Greco di Tufo with grilled mackerel or with veal Milanese. Lighter Fiano di Avellino can work with delicate fish or turkey cutlets piccata. Sicilian white blends are perfect for grilled fresh sardines or Sicily's famous fish dish *triglie di scoglio* (red mullet in onion sauce). One of Sardinia's best Vermentinos has a bright red prawn on the label, suggesting the ideal accompaniment: fresh shellfish, right out of the shell. Vermentino also complements dishes such as shrimp oreganata or shellfish Fra Diavolo and holds its own alongside strong-flavored fish, like fresh anchovies or sardines, mackerel or bluefish.

the bottom line The word is out on Campania white wines, and so they're no longer in the less-than-$10 category. However, they're still fine bargains at $12 to $15. Buy them now, before more people get the word. You'll find Sicilian blends for around $8, but the best bottles cost about $15 and are worth every penny. You can enjoy Vermentino's little-known charms for less than $10.

recommended wines

1999 Benito Ferrara San Paolo Greco di Tufo, Campania ★★★ $$
dry, full-bodied, high acidity, light oak **drink now–3 years**
A spicy, fruity wine with loads of presence. This will match as easily with a pork roast as it will with sea bass.

1999 Clelia Romano Fiano di Avellino, Campania ★★★ $$
dry, full-bodied, high acidity, light oak **drink now–3 years**
A wonderful fruity, herbal wine. This is one we'd serve with plank-roasted salmon, free-range turkey, or roast pork.

1999 Rapitalà Casalj, Sicily ★★★ $
dry, full-bodied, medium acidity, heavy oak **drink now–6 years**
Ancient Catarratto and modern Chardonnay made into a fine spicy oaky wine.

2000 Feudi di San Gregorio "Sannio" Falanghina, Campania ★★ $$
dry, full-bodied, medium acidity, no oak **drink now–6 years**
As with Condrieu from the Rhône, there's an interesting range of fruit, floral, and stone characteristics in this wine. Unlike Condrieu, this is a bargain.

2000 Argiolas Costamolino Vermentino di Sardegna, Sardinia ★★ $
dry, medium-bodied, medium acidity, no oak **drink now**
Only one grape variety, Vermentino, goes into this, but it has a tropical fruit cocktail's worth of flavors. Take a sip, and imagine you're relaxing in Tahiti.

2000 Corvo, Sicily ★ $
dry, light-bodied, high acidity, no oak **drink now**
Don't think too much about this one. Just get it really cold, pour, and let the refreshing lemon and pine flavors take over.

red wines

at the table

Southern wines are universally full-flavored and robust, so plan meals accordingly. Aglianico del Vulture makes a perfect match for lamb braised with apricots or prunes. Serve Primitivo when you would Zinfandel, such as with spit-roasted pork butt, garlic-rubbed lamb chops, or Italian meatballs. *Braciolone,* a typically Sicilian dish of beef rolled around bitter greens and cheese, is the perfect pairing for the island's reds.

the bottom line Terrific reds can be found hovering in the $10 range. A few extra dollars should buy you a bottle that's been aged a few years. Encouraged perhaps by higher Zinfandel prices in California, the cost of Primitivo wines is climbing, but you'll find good values between $15 and $18. Sardinia's best wine, Terre Brune, sells for around $35.

recommended wines

1998 Apollonio Primitivo, Apulia ★★★★ $
dry, full-bodied, medium tannin, medium acidity drink now–8 years
A stunning wine made from Zinfandel's kin, Primitivo. Luxuriate in the layers of flavor that would do California proud.

1999 Cantine del Notaio La Firma Aglianico del Vulture, Basilicata ★★★ $$$
dry, full-bodied, medium tannin, medium acidity drink now–10 years
Nothing at all like the rustic reds associated with Italy's south, this is a wonder of a wine with full fruit flavors set off by a little spice.

1996 Mastroberardino Radici Taurasi, Campania ★★★ $$$
dry, full-bodied, full tannin, medium acidity drink now–8 years
A powerful wine with intense flavors. This is for beef eaters.

1996 Terre Brune Carignano del Sulcis, Sardinia ★★★ $$$
dry, full-bodied, full tannin, medium acidity drink in 3–10 years
A wine we buy whenever we find it. We can't get enough of the bold roasted-fruit, spice, and tobacco flavors.

2000 Planeta La Segreta Rosso, Sicily ★★★ $$
dry, full-bodied, full tannin, medium acidity drink now–3 years
With intense cherry-brandy flavor, this inky, brawny wine is of the love-it-or-hate-it type. We love it.

1998 Azienda Agricola COS Cerasuolo di Vittoria, Sicily ★★ $$
dry, medium-bodied, medium tannin, low acidity drink now–3 years
Mixed-berry aromas, velvety tannin, and a bright ruby color make a wine reminiscent of good-quality Burgundy.

1997 Paternoster Aglianico del Vulture, Basilicata ★★ $$
dry, medium-bodied, full tannin, high acidity drink now–8 years
The Aglianico grape gives us a wine that is low in fruitiness and high in tannin but still well balanced.

1999 Salvatore Molettieri Irpinia Aglianico, Campania ★★ $$
dry, full-bodied, medium tannin, medium acidity drink now–5 years
Southern Italian to the core, this wine has an intriguing spiced-cherry taste strengthened by smoky tar flavors from the area's volcanic soil.

1999 Val Cerasa Etna Rosso, Sicily ★★ $$
dry, full-bodied, light tannin, high acidity drink now–5 years
It might take a while, but if more people taste the fruity pleasures of this wine, the ubiquitous Merlot may have to make room for Masclase and Cappuccio.

1998 Apollonio Copertino, Apulia ★★ $
dry, medium-bodied, light tannin, high acidity drink now–6 years
Not for the faint of heart. Courageous oenophiles will be rewarded by an unbelievable concentration of fruit and burnt sugar flavors.

1997 Candido Salice Salentino Riserva, Apulia ★★ $
dry, medium-bodied, light tannin, medium acidity drink now–2 years
A spaghetti-western wine, its fruitiness lassoed by smoke and leather aromas.

1998 Promessa Primitivo, Apulia ★★ $
dry, full-bodied, medium tannin, medium acidity drink now–4 years
They say Primitivo is the same as Zinfandel, but this big wine with spice and sandalwood flavors seems to be from another world.

1998 Rapitalà Nuhar, Sicily ★★ $
dry, medium-bodied, medium tannin, medium acidity drink now–3 years
A hit with everyone who tries it. And the low price tag makes this characterful Nero d'Avola wine perfect for parties.

1999 Cottanera Fatagione, Sicily ★ $$
dry, medium-bodied, light tannin, high acidity drink now–2 years
Made from native Sicilian grapes in a vibrant, modern style, this is Italy's answer to Beaujolais.

1997 Cantele Salice Salentino Riserva, Apulia ★ $
dry, full-bodied, medium tannin, high acidity drink now–5 years
The subtle charm of this wine lies in its lively acidity as well as Salice's trademark flavors of sour cherries and leather.

1999 Santa Lucia Castel del Monte, Apulia ★ $
dry, medium-bodied, medium tannin, high acidity drink now–2 years
A great pizza and pasta wine, full of acidity and honest fruit flavors.

1999 Terrale Primitivo, Apulia ★ $
dry, medium-bodied, medium tannin, medium acidity drink now–3 years
The fruit flavors are nicely complemented by the earthiness of black tea.

THE TEN MOST OVERLOOKED WINES

1. **Any white wine from Alsace** Rieslings and Gewurztraminers are our favorites, but all varieties from this region are great.

2. **Savennières** The Chenin Blanc from a subregion of Anjou in the Loire Valley, this is delicious when first released and becomes sublime with age.

3. **Cru Beaujolais** Nothing at all like the simple Nouveau quaffers, a Cru Beaujolais can have the depth of all but the best Burgundies at a fraction of the price.

4. **Rosé from the south of France** There's no reason to turn up your nose at this rosé. It's dry and enticingly aromatic.

5. **Dolcetto and Barbera from the best Piedmont producers** Delicious and beautifully made, these offer a taste of Piedmont without the cost of Barolo or Barbaresco.

6. **German Riesling** Beautifully balanced wines that are amazingly flexible with food, from vegetables to fish to game, and often the best answer for fusion cuisine and Asian dishes.

7. **Finger Lakes wine** Riesling and Gewürztraminer may be the best, but the Pinot Noir and Cabernet Franc are pretty terrific.

8. **Sparkling wine** Popping a cork is too much fun to save for celebrations, and many sparklers are inexpensive.

9. **Madeira** One of the most complex wines around. Great with rich soups as well as with desserts.

10. **Fino Sherry** Yes, Sherry. It's the perfect accompaniment to many savory dishes, from tapas to soups to garlicky roast chicken.

spain

In a world where international styles of wine are more dominant each year, Spain maintains its own identity. Until about fifteen years ago, American consumers largely overlooked the distinctive Spanish wines (with the exception of Sherry and Rioja). That has changed. The already high quality is always improving, and relatively low prices have led Americans to say *olé* to Spanish wines.

on the label

Wines marked Joven, Spanish for "young," have seen little if any time in oak barrels. Jovens can be eminently enjoyable wines, and nearly all are inexpensive. The aged wines, each requiring more time before release than the one before, are Crianza, Reserva, and Gran Reserva. The last is made with only the best grapes from good years.

BY ANY OTHER NAME

The two most important Spanish red grapes and the single most significant white remain virtually the same wherever they're grown, though the names of all three change:

Garnacha	Grenache (France), Cannonau (Sardinia)
Tempranillo	Tinto Fino (Ribero del Duero), Tinto del Pais (Ribero del Duero), Tinto de la Rioja (Rioja), Tinto de Toro (Toro), Cencibel (La Mancha and Valdepeñas), Tinta Roriz (Portugal)
Macabeo	Viura (Rioja), Maccabéo (France), Maccabeu (France)

rioja

red wines

Red Rioja (ree-oh-ha) is the pride of the region and can compete with the best wines in the world. It's full-bodied, velvety smooth, and flavorful, with excellent acidity. Tempranillo dominates the blend, and Garnacha is frequently used to contribute body and spiciness.

at the table

Almost anytime a full-bodied red is in order, Rioja will do beautifully. Roast leg of lamb and slow-roasted pork shoulder rubbed with garlic and spices are ideal matches. Try it also with flavorful vegetable stews, like ratatouille, or with the Spanish blue-veined cheese Cabrales.

the bottom line Rioja is one of the few places in the world that offer fully-aged, ten-year-old wines for under $25 a bottle. Look to Crianzas for values under $15, Reservas for three dollars more, and Gran Reservas for $23 to $30.

what to buy RED RIOJA

1993	1994	1995	1996
★★	★★★★	★★★★	★★★

1997	1998	1999
★★★	★★★	★★

recommended wines

1996 Cune Imperial Reserva ★★★★ $$$
dry, full-bodied, full tannin, medium acidity **drink now–15 years**
Solid Rioja. Fruitiness enhanced by vanilla and cocoa flavors. Very good drinking.

1996 Roda I Reserva ★★★★ $$$
dry, full-bodied, full tannin, medium acidity **drink now–20 years**
As if the deep fruit flavors weren't enough to make us love it, we're really taken by the earthiness of this excellent wine.

1995 Solabal Reserva ★★★★ $$
dry, full-bodied, full tannin, medium acidity **drink now–8 years**
A terrific Rioja with concentrated fruit flavors accented by musky notes.

1998 B. Sierra Cantabria Colección Privada ★★★ $$$
dry, full-bodied, medium tannin, medium acidity **drink now–10 years**
A unique, international-style Rioja. This is Rioja for the California Cabernet lover.

1996 El Coto de Rioja Coto de Imaz Selección Pedra Guasch Reserva ★★★ $$$
dry, full-bodied, medium tannin, medium acidity **drink now–15 years**
Fruit flavors come out loud and clear in this lightly spicy wine with currents of cocoa and espresso flavors.

1997 Bodegas Bretón Loriñon Reserva ★★★ $$
dry, full-bodied, full tannin, medium acidity **drink in 2–10 years**
Most Riojas are ready to drink as soon as they're released, but wait a couple of years for this wine to develop its full berry and spice flavors.

1994 López de Heredia Bosconia Reserva ★★★ $$
dry, full-bodied, full tannin, medium acidity **drink now–5 years**
A wine that deserves contemplation. Lots of fruit and flowers.

1994 Marqués de Cáceres Reserva ★★★ $$
dry, full-bodied, medium tannin, high acidity **drink now–5 years**
Great baked fruit flavors, hints of molasses, and excellent acidity.

1996 Bodegas Montecillo Reserva ★★ $$
dry, medium-bodied, full tannin, high acidity **drink now–10 years**
Saturated with toasted coconut and cherry flavors.

1996 Bodegas Riojanas Viña Albina Reserva ★★ $$
dry, medium-bodied, medium tannin, medium acidity **drink now–10 years**
A lovely wine that starts with a simple tune of fruity notes and ends with a crescendo of lively cherry and walnut flavors.

1997 Marqués de Arienzo Crianza ★★ $$
dry, medium-bodied, medium tannin, medium acidity **drink now–5 years**
A classic Rioja, with the taste of baked cherries and the coconut flavor that comes from aging in American oak barrels.

1991 Marqués de Arienzo Gran Reserva ★★ $$
dry, full-bodied, medium tannin, high acidity **drink now–8 years**
Is it the grandest Gran Reserva? No, but it shows what good fruit can become with years of oak aging; lots of mineral and cherry flavors.

1996 Marqués de Murrieta Ygay Reserva ★★ $$
dry, medium-bodied, full tannin, medium acidity **drink now–5 years**
Despite heavy tannin, rose and pomegranate flavors make this wine seem surprisingly light.

1997 Marqués de Cáceres ★ $$
dry, medium-bodied, full tannin, medium acidity **drink now–5 years**
A standard, with nice fruit flavors and a touch of oak. Good with roasted meat.

rosé wines

Rosés (*rosados* in Spanish) from Rioja can be some of the most fascinating pink wines in the world. It isn't uncommon to find Rioja rosés that are ten years old—refreshing but full-flavored and powerful.

at the table

With their full body and flavor and their good acidity, Spanish rosés complement a variety of dishes. They're excellent matches for pâtés, charcuterie, smoked trout, and antipasti. Try them also with tomato, mozzarella, and basil salad or fresh crab salad. They're great, too, with corned beef or BLT sandwiches.

the bottom line Spanish rosés are a bargain. You can get good quality for $8 or $9. Older rosés sometimes appear on the market for about $15. They can be terrific.

recommended wines

1991 López de Heredia Rosado ★★★★ $$
dry, full-bodied, high acidity **drink now–4 years**
One of the greatest wine-drinking experiences we've ever had. Really. Citrus, strawberries, spices, and a sherry-like nuttiness.

1999 Marqués de Cáceres Rosé ★★ $
dry, full-bodied, medium acidity **drink now**
Here's a wine that's exactly what you expect from a rosé. Refreshing, fruity, and charming. Chill, sip, and enjoy.

1999 Faustino V Rosado ★ $
dry, full-bodied, high acidity **drink now**
The antithesis of López de Heredia, with clear strawberry flavor that makes the wine seem almost sweet at first, though it's actually dry.

white wines

White Riojas are not widely known in the U.S. Both the young, light-bodied, and refreshing wines as well as the complex, aged wines offer terrific quality and value. Because they're right in line with contemporary tastes, the young wines are more common. Aged white Riojas, however, deliver delicious nutty, fruity, spice-laden flavors. If you come across a white Reserva or Gran Reserva, grab it.

at the table

Young white Riojas are high in acidity. Serve them very cold with mussels and clams steamed in white wine. Sip older wines with tapas; they have the power to stand up to sharp cheeses like manchego or Mahón, cured sardines, marinated olives, and even chorizo.

the bottom line White Riojas are a steal: Young ones come in under $10; older gems are only a few dollars more.

recommended wines

1987 R. López de Heredia Viña Tondonia Reserva Blanco ★★★★ $$$
dry, full-bodied, high acidity, light oak **drink now–5 years**
This spectacular wine should banish any notion that whites don't age well. Multilayered, balanced flavors that only time can bring.

1999 Bodegas Riojanas Monte Real ★★★ $
dry, full-bodied, medium acidity, medium oak **drink now–15 years**
Loads of baked fruit, with apple-pie spices and honeyed vanilla notes.

1998 Martinez Bujanda Conde de Valdemar Rioja Finca Alto de Cantabria ★★ $$
dry, medium-bodied, medium acidity, medium oak **drink now–2 years**
There's some spicy oak here as well as nice fruit flavors.

1999 El Coto ★ $
dry, full-bodied, medium acidity, no oak **drink now–2 years**
It's simple, but chill this really well and enjoy the citrusy refreshment.

ribera del duero

For more than a century, Ribera del Duero (ree-BAIR-ah del doo-EH-ro), the region around the Duero River, has been home to Vega Sicilia, Spain's most famous winery. But it wasn't until

1982, when critic Robert Parker lavished praise on another winery, Pesquera, that people really started paying attention to the Duero. Since then, there has been an explosion of activity in the area, with new wineries and an influx of investment capital. Reds dominate the region's production. Like Riojas, Ribera wines are based on a local variety of Tempranillo, but they are often blended with as much as 25 percent Cabernet Sauvignon. As a result, Riberas are a bit more tannic than Riojas, which is not necessarily a bad thing.

at the table

Ribera wines are particularly tasty with meaty cuts that have generous marbling to help mellow the tannin. Try prime steaks, beef short ribs, or crown roast of lamb.

the bottom line Wines from Vega Sicilia and Pesquera will run you $50 to $150, but you can find excellent wines from other producers for $15 to $30.

what to buy RIBERA DEL DUERO

1995	1996	1997	1998	1999
★★★★	★★★★	★★★	★★★	★★★

recommended wines

1996 Vega Sicilia Valbuena ★★★★ $$$$
dry, full-bodied, full tannin, medium acidity **drink in 5–20 years**
From the titan of Ribera del Duero comes a red wine painted black with black cherry, blackberry, smoke, and burnt sugar flavors.

1997 Viña Pedrosa Crianza ★★★ $$$
dry, full-bodied, full tannin, medium acidity **drink in 3–15 years**
Full and smoky with cherry and herb flavors. Very fine.

1998 Condado de Haza ★★★ $$
dry, full-bodied, medium tannin, medium acidity **drink in 3–15 years**
Lots of berries and also a taste like smoked meat that gives depth.

1998 Pesquera Crianza ★★★ $$
dry, full-bodied, full tannin, medium acidity **drink in 3–15 years**
Mellow fruit and vanilla, plus a bit of bitter coffee for sophistication.

1997 Ibernoble Crianza ★★ $$
dry, full-bodied, full tannin, medium acidity **drink in 5–15 years**
So dry it's almost powdery. Here's a heady brew of blackberry, herb, and burnt sugar flavors. This needs meat.

1999 Valdubón ★★ $$
dry, full-bodied, full tannin, medium acidity **drink in 3–10 years**
A wine so nice that we'd like to have it now, but it really needs a few years to meld its fruit, oak, and spice flavors.

navarre, penedès, priorato

Situated next to Rioja, Navarre enjoys little of its neighbor's glory despite its long history of wine production. The region has always focused on reds, though the rosés are better known. Penedès (peh-neh-DESS) and Priorato (pree-oh-RAH-toe) are Catalonia's most prominent wine regions and produce the most "international" wines in Spain. Penedès makes a good amount of red and white wines from local varietals, but its reputation comes primarily from its sparkling Cavas (see page 266). Priorato makes full-bodied, high-alcohol reds that inspire great demand.

at the table

Penedès whites are just the thing for Barcelona's famed paellas or langostinos. Try light-bodied, complex reds from Penedès with veal chops or Swedish meatballs. Powerful, peppery Priorato reds require similar food, like steak au poivre. Navarre reds would go beautifully with a variety of tapas, especially meatballs or a Spanish stew like *cocido madrileño,* made with beef or veal shank.

the bottom line It's hard to believe there's a place offering better value than Rioja, but Navarre might make that claim. The reds are similar in style to Riojas (if not quite as fine), but they are usually ignored nevertheless. Ten dollars buys you a very good bottle of wine. Penedès wines are also well priced, staying under $12. But with high demand and little supply, Priorato's wines are expensive. It's possible to find something good for $15, but you're more likely to see price tags in the $30 to $50 range.

recommended red wines

1998 Cims de Porerra Solanes, Priorato ★★★ $$$
dry, full-bodied, full tannin, high acidity **drink in 3–10 years**
Terrific Priorato doesn't come cheap, but at least this beautiful wine will leave you enough to pay for the steak it deserves.

1998 Morlanda Criança, Priorato ★★★ $$$
dry, full-bodied, full tannin, medium acidity **drink in 3–10 years**
Lush chocolate-cherry flavor. Just needs time for its tarry qualities to mellow.

1999 Guelbenzu Evo, Navarre ★★★ $$
dry, full-bodied, full tannin, high acidity **drink in 3–10 years**
A blend of 70 percent Cabernet Sauvignon with Tempranillo and Merlot. The result? A fine, fruity wine with wonderful toffee and mocha aromas.

1998 Vall Llach Embruix, Priorato ★★★ $$
dry, full-bodied, full tannin, medium acidity **drink now–8 years**
A pastry shop's worth of flavors from berry to coconut, vanilla to chocolate. Have with a braised meat dish.

1998 Beltran Crianza, Navarre ★★ $$
dry, full-bodied, full tannin, medium acidity **drink now–8 years**
Fruit flavors that almost seem sweet are nicely balanced by touches of spice and cedar.

1994 Bodegas Julián Chivite Colección 125 Gran Reserva, Navarre ★★ $$
dry, full-bodied, medium tannin, medium acidity **drink now–6 years**
A wine that has terrific appeal: a little smoky, a bit rough, but still elegant in its own way.

1999 Buil e Gine Gine-Gine, Priorato ★★ $$
dry, medium-bodied, medium tannin, medium acidity **drink now–10 years**
A veritable bargain, especially from Priorato, with clear cherry flavor from the first taste through the finish.

1995 Juvenals Cabernet Sauvignon Reserva, Penedès ★ $$
dry, full-bodied, medium tannin, medium acidity **drink now–5 years**
A peppery Penedès, relatively gentle for Cabernet. Just right for hearty paella.

1997 Torres Gran Coronas Cabernet Sauvignon, Penedès ★ $$
dry, full-bodied, full tannin, medium acidity **drink now–4 years**
Baked fruit and a generous handful of peppercorns to wake up your tastebuds.

recommended white wines

2000 Les Brugueres, Priorato ★★★ $$
dry, full-bodied, medium acidity, no oak **drink now**
A unique, remarkable wine that is as close to a Bellini as one can get without actually pouring Prosecco into a glass of white peach juice.

1999 Torres Gran Viña Sol Chardonnay, Penedès ★★★ $$
dry, full-bodied, medium acidity, light oak **drink now–5 years**
In this wine, 15 percent Parellada, an indigenous grape, adds a floral element to the passion fruit and peach flavors of this Chardonnay.

2000 Can Feixes Blanc Selecciò, Penedès ★★★ $
off-dry, full-bodied, medium acidity, no oak **drink now**
This exuberant wine has terrific floral and citrus flavors and just enough minerality on the finish.

1998 Juvenals Chardonnay, Penedès ★★ $$
dry, full-bodied, medium acidity, light oak **drink now–6 years**
Like a pear tart right from the oven. The spicy baked pear flavors permeate this wine, nicely balanced by oak and acidity.

other regions

Spain has other, less famous regions that deserve attention. Galicia on the Atlantic coast is noted for its whites, which range in style from simple, anonymous wines to the sought-after, full-bodied Albariños (ahl-bah-REE-n'yoh); those from Rías Baixas (ree-ahs bah-EEX-sahs) are especially in demand. Somontano, in the foothills of the Pyrenees, is known for its berry-flavored reds. Utiel-Requena, Alicante, Jumilla, and Ribera del Guadiana in the southern half of the country, has long produced rustic red wines in quantity. New vinification techniques have improved quality tremendously.

at the table

Simple whites from Galicia should be enjoyed with raw oysters and clams, whereas heavier Albariños are just right for lobster or crab, or anything you might eat with California Chardonnay. The reds of the South are for hearty foods: lamb stew with chickpeas, ratatouille, sharp sheep's milk cheeses.

the bottom line High demand and low production make Albariño relatively expensive. Count on paying between $24 and $35 a bottle. Somontano and southern reds are still unknown and, therefore, underpriced. They can be found for between $9 and $18.

recommended white wines

2000 Lusco Albariño, Rías Baixas ★★★ $$
dry, full-bodied, high acidity, no oak **drink now–2 years**
Almost as luscious as Key Lime pie, with creamy, limey flavors, plus hints of banana and nuts. Very good wine.

2000 Morgadío Albariño, Rías Baixas ★★ $$
dry, full-bodied, medium acidity, no oak **drink now–2 years**
A gentle wine with the scent of violets and a light, soothing pear flavor.

1999 Martínsancho Verdejo, Rueda ★★ $
dry, medium-bodied, medium acidity, light oak **drink now–4 years**
A wine that does all that most California Chardonnays dream of accomplishing, with pineapple flavor joined by hints of herbs and none of the usual flatness.

1999 Bodegas Inviosa Lar de Barros Macabeo, Ribera del Guadiana ★ $
dry, medium-bodied, medium acidity, no oak **drink now**
Served ice cold, this wine has the snap of an apple on a cool autumn day.

recommended red wines

1997 Ceremonia Tempranillo & Cabernet Sauvignon, Utiel-Requena ★★ $$
dry, medium-bodied, medium tannin, medium acidity drink now–7 years
A blast of toasted coconut flavor from American oak aging. But it's well-balanced by cherry flavor. Really enjoyable.

1994 Torre Oria Reserva Dominio del Derramador, Utiel-Requena ★★ $$
dry, medium-bodied, medium tannin, medium acidity drink now–4 years
Plums, red currants, cedar, and a touch of cayenne waft through this marvelous wine.

1996 Viña Vermeta Tinto Reserva Monastrell, Alicante ★★ $
dry, medium-bodied, medium tannin, medium acidity drink now–3 years
Mourvèdre is a different creature in Spain from what it is in France. It's called Monastrell and is often lighter and has berry flavors.

1998 Bodegas Inviosa Lar de Barros Tempranillo Crianza, Ribera del Guadiana ★ $
dry, medium-bodied, heavy tannin, high acidity drink now–2 years
A quaffer, with the flavors of strawberry jam bubbling in an oak vat. Good with burgers or grilled chorizo.

1999 Bodega Pirineos Montesierra, Somontano ★ $
dry, full-bodied, medium tannin, high acidity drink now–2 years
Not a complex wine, but it has enough bite to complement simple dishes well.

2000 Carchelo, Jumilla ★ $
dry, medium-bodied, medium tannin, medium acidity drink now–2 years
Fruity enough to be a Beaujolais, but Monastrell (Mourvèdre), Tempranillo, and Merlot add a bit more body. Drink and be happy.

1999 Viña Rey Tempranillo Vinos de Madrid, Madrid ★ $
dry, medium-bodied, full tannin, high acidity drink now–2 years
A good BBQ wine, with enough fruitiness to smooth out any spiciness, plus good acidity to balance sweet sauces.

portugal

In the 1990s, Portuguese winemakers launched a renaissance, upgrading facilities and adopting modern techniques. Thankfully, they did not replace their local grape varieties, which are diverse and make unique wines.

grapes & styles

For most people familiar with Portuguese wines, green means white. Vinho Verde (green wine)—light-bodied, tart, and slightly sparkly—is Portugal's best-known white. It's named *verde* because the grapes are picked before they are fully ripe and because the wines are drunk young. Meant to be consumed within a year after release, most Vinho Verde (VEEN-yoh VAIR-day) is made from undistinguished (and unidentified) varietals. But from the northwest corner of the country come Vinhos Verdes made from Alvarinho (Spain's Albariño). Alvarinho (ahl-vah-REE-n'yoh) Vinhos Verdes are different in style and quality. Fuller in body and flavor, these wines can be aged for several years. Whites from other regions of Portugal, such as Dão, Douro, Bucelas, and Alentejo, are often excellent as well.

Not so long ago, Portuguese reds were hearty and spicy, but often rather rough. Simple, rustic wines still exist, but several innovative producers, mostly in the Douro, Bairrada, and Dão regions, are turning out international-caliber wines maintaining a distinct Portuguese identity.

at the table

Simple, light-hearted Vinho Verde is an ideal summer wine. It's just the thing for steamer clams, fried calamari, fish and chips, or dinner salads. Fuller-bodied Alvarinho is an ideal match for more complicated shellfish dishes. Varietal whites from other regions will complement pork chops or lemon-flavored chicken. Look to the Douro, Bairrada, or Dão for hearty, aromatic reds to go with difficult-to-match spicy dishes like lamb shanks braised with

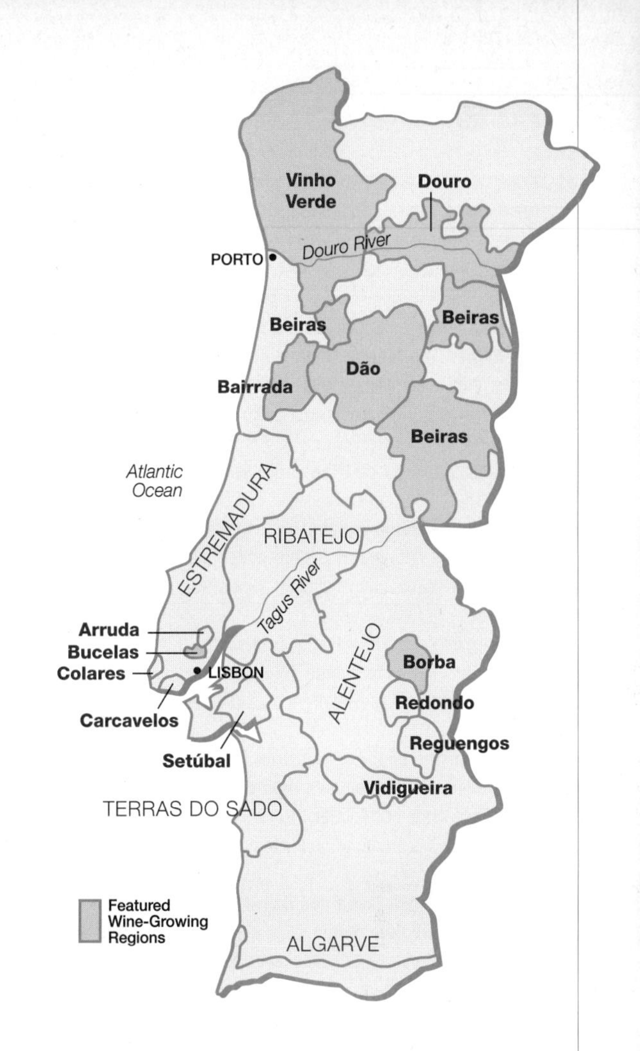

Moroccan spices, pork fajitas, or bean and meat stews such as Brazil's *feijoada.* More sophisticated red wines—those marked Reserva or Garrafeira—can be paired with game or prime rib.

the bottom line Most Vinho Verde is under $10. Alvarinho costs more, up to $20, but it's worth it. Look for whites from other areas in the $10 to $15 range. Once sleepers, the reds of Portugal are becoming known to more and more wine buyers. There are still good wines to be found between $8 and $12, but count on paying $15 to $18 for the better bottles, and up to $80 for the best made by innovative producers.

recommended wines

1998 Quinta do Crasto Vinha da Ponte, Douro ★★★★ $$$$
dry, full-bodied, full tannin, medium acidity **drink now–10 years**
Dense, dark, and delicious. We simply can't get enough of the tart black cherry, blackberry, and black pepper flavors.

1996 Quinta do Fojo "Fojo," Douro ★★★★ $$$$
dry, full-bodied, full tannin, medium acidity **drink in 5–20 years**
A wine designed to compete with the best in the world (and priced accordingly), full of lovely fruit and spice flavors. Cedar aromas.

1999 Luis Pato Quinta do Ribeirinho Baga, Bairrada ★★★★ $$
dry, full-bodied, medium tannin, medium acidity **drink now–15 years**
Lush berry flavors and velvety texture make this international in style; the smoke and spice flavors bring it straight back to Portugal. Excellent.

1999 Calheiros Cruz Tinta Roriz, Douro ★★★ $$$
dry, full-bodied, full tannin, high acidity **drink in 3–15 years**
Full of exotic flavors reminiscent of coconut, tamarind, mulberries, and spices.

1999 Vinha Antiga Escolha Alvarinho, Vinho Verde ★★★ $$
dry, full-bodied, medium acidity, light oak **drink now**
Proof that Vinho Verde need not be frivolous. With fruit and spice flavors and a bit of nuttiness, this is a wine worth contemplating.

1995 Caves Sao Joao Porta dos Cavaleiros, Dão ★★★ $
dry, full-bodied, medium tannin, high acidity **drink now–5 years**
Cavaleiros means horsemen, and the leather, roasted-meat, campfire-pit, and tobacco aromas are all there. The wine tastes, however, like cherries.

2000 J. P. Ramos Marquês de Borba, Alentejo ★★★ $
dry, full-bodied, medium acidity, no oak **drink now**
Doesn't taste particularly Portuguese, but a very good wine.

1999 Porca de Murça Reserva, Douro ★★★ $
dry, full-bodied, medium acidity, light oak **drink now–3 years**
Lush fruit flavors from Sémillon. Spicy and floral notes from native Gouveio and Cerceal grapes. A fine combination.

1999 Quinta de Pancas Special Selection Merlot, Estremadura ★★ $$$
dry, full-bodied, medium tannin, medium acidity **drink now–5 years**
A Merlot from Portugal? Yes, it's just so good we can't help recommending it.

1998 Quinta de Pancas Special Selection Touriga Nacional, Estremadura ★★ $$$
dry, medium-bodied, medium tannin, high acidity **drink now–8 years**
Loads of spice and cherry flavors, plus slight hints of coconut.

1997 Quinta da Murqueira Reserva, Dão ★★ $$
dry, medium-bodied, full tannin, high acidity **drink in 3–12 years**
Despite lively fruit flavors, the tannin makes this a wine to keep for a few years.

1999 Casa de Santar, Dão ★★ $
dry, medium-bodied, medium acidity, no oak **drink now**
A really interesting, bone-dry wine that would be perfect with smoked oysters.

1999 Catarina, Terras do Sado ★★ $
dry, full-bodied, high acidity, light oak **drink now–3 years**
A quarter Chardonnay contributes buttery flavor to the Portuguese varietals.

2000 Evel, Douro ★★ $
dry, full-bodied, medium acidity, no oak **drink now**
Four Portuguese varietals go into this lovely wine with very full fruit flavors.

1999 Quinta Seara d'Ordens, Douro ★★ $
dry, medium-bodied, medium tannin, high acidity **drink now–3 years**
Relatively simple, but for $8 the fruit flavors and the spice and vanilla from aging in oak are quite satisfying.

1999 Casa de Santar Castas de Santar, Dão ★ $
dry, medium-bodied, light tannin, medium acidity **drink now–3 years**
This wine has simple, appealing cherry flavor accented by a bit of spice.

1999 Caves Primavera Beira Litoral Baga, Beiras ★ $
dry, full-bodied, full tannin, high acidity **drink now–5 years**
Full cherry flavor and a meaty texture make this tannic wine a classic.

NV Fâmega, Vinho Verde (bottled in 2001) ★ $
dry, light-bodied, medium acidity, no oak **drink now**
Simplicity itself. Just get it really cold and knock it back when you're thirsty.

2000 Quinta da Romeira Arinto, Bucelas ★ $
dry, light-bodied, high acidity, no oak **drink now**
What can you get for $8? In this case, tasty apple and lemon flavors.

1999 Varanda do Conde Alvarinho/Trajadura, Vinho Verde ★ $
dry, medium-bodied, medium acidity, light oak **drink now**
Easy drinking. Great for casual occasions.

germany

Until thirty years ago, German wine found its place at formal dinner tables in America as frequently as did Burgundy or Bordeaux. But then changes in taste—helped along by World War II, cheaper imports from other countries, and big marketing of bad wine like Black Tower and Blue Nun—beat German wines black and blue in the U.S. Nowadays Americans have renewed their interest in German wines, particularly Rieslings. Prized for their fruitiness and laser-sharp acidity, these wines are supremely flexible; they complement foods that can be tricky to match, from spicy Asian dishes to fusion cuisine.

grapes & styles

Eighty percent of German wine is white, and Riesling reigns among the dozen or so varieties grown. It not only makes the finest German wine but is considered by many to be the world's white grape *sans pareil.* However, Müller-Thurgau is Germany's most-planted grape. If a German label doesn't include a grape name, chances are the wine is primarily Müller-Thurgau. But most fine wines are clearly marked varietals. They're beautifully aromatic, and the overwhelming majority of them see no oak at all. In response to market demands, both in Germany and abroad, winemakers are producing more dry wines.

on the label

Don't let long names in Gothic script scare you away from German wine. The labels are actually very informative, listing not only the winery name, but also the region, village, and sometimes the vineyard from which the grapes came. Varietal names are

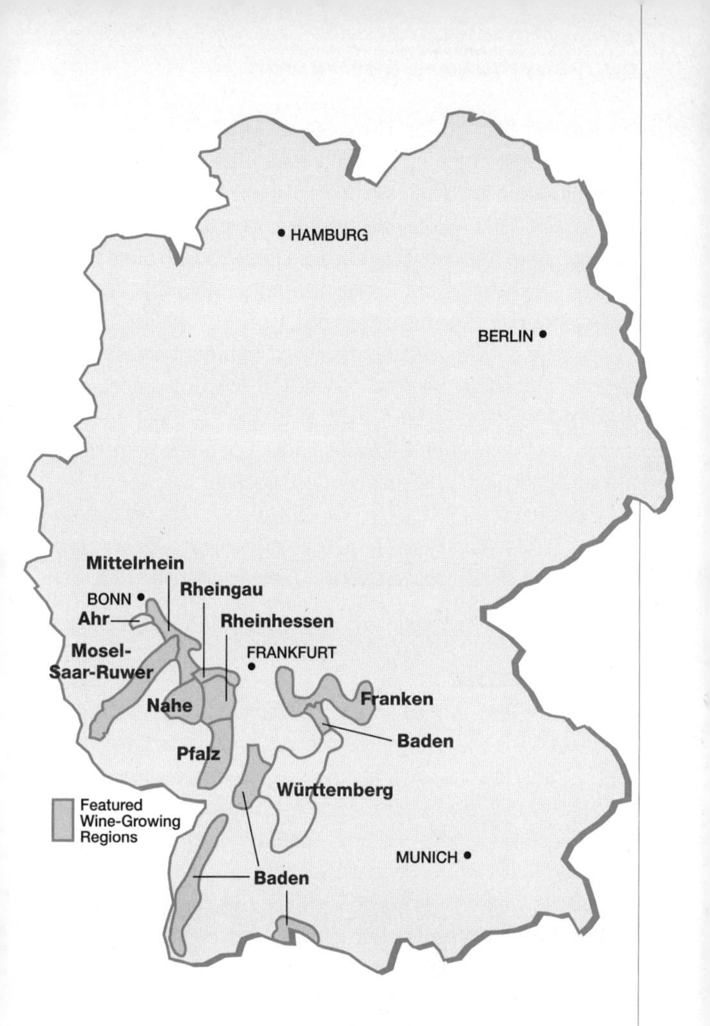

usually given, except in some well-known areas where the grape variety goes without saying. You may find the term *trocken,* meaning dry, or *halbtrocken,* half-dry, which is often just barely sweet. If there is no indication of dryness (check the back label, too), the wine is probably a touch sweet.

Wines are classified into categories denoting quality.

Qualitätswein bestimmter Anbaugebiete This designation, usually shortened to just Qualitätswein or QbA, is given to quality wine from a particular region.

Qualitätswein mit Prädikat (QmP) This is quality wine with distinction. Prädikat wines are further categorized according to the ripeness of grapes at harvest:

Kabinett (kah-bee-NET) wines are made from grapes with the least sugar of the categorized levels. They're consequently the lightest and frequently the driest of the Prädikat wines.

Spätlese (sh'PAY't-lay-zuh), or "late harvest," is the next category up from Kabinett. Spätleses are fuller-bodied, often with a touch of sweetness but sometimes completely dry. Spätlese wines labeled *trocken* are always dry.

Auslese (OUSE-lay-zuh), meaning "from the harvest," indicates that specially selected bunches of very ripe grapes were used. Ausleses are even fuller than Spätleses. Most are a bit sweet, approaching dessert-wine levels, but a few vintners ferment them dry and label them Auslese trocken.

Beerenauslese (BEAR-en-OUSE-lay-zuh), *Trockenbeerenauslese* (TRAW-ken-BEAR-en-OUSE-lay-zuh), and *Eiswein* (ice-vine) are all sweet dessert wines. (See Fortified and Dessert Wines, page 281.)

at the table

Luscious on their own as an aperitif, German whites are also an obvious choice to go with the standard array of fish and shellfish. But they are especially handy as excellent accompaniments for hard-to-pair sweet and spicy Asian dishes. Try one with Vietnamese spicy beef and green papaya salad, *pad thai,* or a ginger-and-chile-spiced fried whole snapper. Off-dry wines work particularly well with hot spices—their sweetness tames and beautifully complements chile peppers—as well as with Asian cuisine. Pair them too with your favorite Mexican food. You'll also be amazed how well they complement game, such as duck and even venison (though not if it has a red wine sauce), and they're among the few wines suitable for Indian food.

mosel-saar-ruwer

Famous for delicate Riesling (reece-ling) made from grapes growing on slopes so impossibly steep that laborers need harnesses to work in them, the Mosel produces wines that almost make you forget that Germany brews beer. Wines from the middle Mosel are often fuller-bodied and more flavorful than those from the upper and lower parts. Wines from the river's tributaries, the Saar and Ruwer, are generally less fruity and full than any of the Mosel wines, but they are still excellent.

the bottom line Good quality QbA Rieslings can be had for as low as $7 and go up to $12. Kabinett wines sell for $10 to $18, and most Spätleses for $12 to $25 (a few cost up to $40). Ausleses start at $16 and can go as high as $50.

what to buy MOSEL-SAAR-RUWER

1996	1997	1998	1999	2000
★★★★	★★★	★★★	★★★★	★★

recommended wines

2000 Joh. Jos. Christoffel Urziger Würzgarten Riesling Auslese ★★★★ $$$
off-dry, full-bodied, high acidity, no oak **drink now–10 years**
Big and beautiful, with a spice-cabinet's worth of flavors joining citrus notes.

1999 von Othegraven Kanzemer Altenberg Qualitätswein ★★★★ $$$
dry, medium-bodied, medium acidity, no oak **drink now–12 years**
Floral, apple, and citrus flavors thrive on a solid foundation of minerality.

1999 von Othegraven Kanzemer Altenberg Ungrafted Vine Riesling Auslese ★★★★ $$$
medium sweet, full-bodied, medium acidity, no oak **drink now–15 years**
A lovely floral wine sweet enough for dessert, but with grace and balance that also make it great for many fusion dishes.

2000 Fritz Haag Brauneberger Juffer-Sonnenuhr Riesling-Spätlese ★★★ $$$
dry, medium-bodied, high acidity, no oak **drink now–8 years**
We're taken by the lemon zest and floral flavors and the deep minerality.

2000 Selbach-Oster Zeltinger Sonnenuhr Riesling Auslese ★★★ $$$
off-dry, full-bodied, medium acidity, no oak **drink now–10 years**
Layers and layers of flavors, of which honeysuckle, apricot, and various earthy notes are just the start.

1999 Carl Schmitt-Wagner Longuicher Maximiner Herrenberg Riesling Auslese ★★★ $$
off-dry, full-bodied, high acidity, no oak **drink now–10 years**
A terrific, highly concentrated Auslese that is nearly fully dry. There's fruit, but it's the spice, floral, and mineral flavors that do the talking.

1999 Hoffman-Simon Estate Riesling Qualitätswein ★★★ $$
dry, medium-bodied, high acidity, no oak **drink now–5 years**
Higher ripeness levels than most Kabinett wines mean this non-classified Riesling is full of citrus flavors with anise highlights.

2000 Selbach-Oster Wehlener Sonnenuhr Riesling Kabinett ★★★ $$
dry, medium-bodied, medium acidity, no oak **drink now–8 years**
All of Selbach-Oster's wines are wonderful. This one is everything a Mosel Kabinett should be, with citrus and mineral flavors from start to finish.

1999 von Othegraven Maximus Riesling Qualitätswein ★★★ $$
dry, full-bodied, high acidity, no oak **drink in 3–15 years**
Give this a few years aging. The flavor will smooth out to a buttery nuttiness.

1999 Weingut Joh. Haart Piesporter Goldtröpfchen Riesling-Spätlese ★★★ $$
dry, full-bodied, medium acidity, no oak **drink now–10 years**
Intense, concentrated citrus flavors in good balance.

1999 Willi Haag Brauneberger Juffer Riesling Spätlese ★★★ $$
off-dry, full-bodied, medium acidity, no oak **drink now–10 years**
Citrus with added mineral complexity. We love it.

1999 Weingut Joh. Haart Piesporter Goldtröpfchen Riesling Qualitätswein ★★★ $
dry, medium-bodied, medium acidity, no oak **drink now–3 years**
Like a lemony grapefruit, with a bit of nuttiness thrown in.

2000 Dr. Loosen Erdener Treppchen Riesling Kabinett ★★ $$
off-dry, medium-bodied, high acidity, no oak **drink now–4 years**
As perfect for sipping by the pool as gracing a fine table. Fruit flavors brought out by excellent acidity make this a very flexible wine.

2000 Joh. Jos. Christoffel Urziger Würzgarten Riesling Spätlese ★★ $$
off-dry, full-bodied, high acidity, no oak **drink now–5 years**
This beautiful fruity and nutty wine comes from one of the Mosel's top-notch small producers.

1999 Schloss Saarstein Serriger Schloss Saarsteiner Riesling Spätlese ★★ $$
dry, full-bodied, high acidity, no oak **drink now–8 years**
Almost as pungent as Sauvignon Blanc at first; then the prominent herbal notes mellow into harmony with the tropical fruit flavors.

2000 Weingut Joh. Haart Piesporter Goldtröpfchen Riesling-Kabinett ★★ $$
off-dry, medium-bodied, high acidity, no oak **drink now–5 years**
Lime and tropical fruit aromas. Lush peach and faint pineapple flavors balanced by touches of typical Riesling petrol.

1998 Weingut Karl Erbes Urziger-Würzgarten Riesling Auslese ★★ $$
off-dry, full-bodied, high acidity, no oak **drink now–5 years**
A bargain Auslese, with full fruit flavors and acidity that engage your whole palate. Perfect with spicy Asian dishes.

1999 Weingut Karl Erbes Urziger-Würzgarten Riesling Spätlese ★★ $$
off-dry, full-bodied, high acidity, no oak **drink now–5 years**
Aromas and flavors of strawberries and peaches. The taste starts out sweet but finishes tart. Good.

1999 Wwe. Dr. Thanisch Riesling Qualitätswein ★★ $$
off-dry, medium-bodied, medium acidity, no oak **drink now–5 years**
Nice complexity of fruit, mineral, and nut flavors.

2000 Weingut Eilenz Ayler Kupp Riesling Kabinett ★★ $
dry, medium-bodied, medium acidity, no oak **drink now–5 years**
Lemon and orange on the nose, orange and peach on the palate.

1999 Willi Haag Riesling Qualitätswein ★★ $
off-dry, medium-bodied, medium acidity, no oak **drink now–5 years**
For lovers of intense, mineral-oil-flavored Rieslings, it's hard to get better than this, especially for the price.

2000 Weingut Eilenz Ayler Kupp Riesling Qualitätswein ★ $
dry, medium-bodied, medium acidity, no oak **drink now–2 years**
As tasty and refreshing as a fruit salad of citrus and pears. All in a liter bottle.

RECOMMENDED PRODUCERS

Fritz Haag, Egon Müller, C. von Schubert Maximin Grünhaus, Joh. Jos. Prüm, Dr. Loosen, Joh. Jos. Christoffel, Willi Schaefer, Dr. F. Weins-Prüm, Selbach-Oster, Karlsmühle, Heribert Kerpen, Merkelbach, Wegeler Erben, von Hövel, Schloss Saarstein

The warmest wine-producing region of Germany, the Pfalz supports grape varieties that don't do well in the rest of the country. Riesling still dominates, but here it is joined by Scheurebe (SHOY-reh-buh), Gewürztraminer (geh-VAIRTZ-tra-MEE-ner), and Weissburgunder (VICE-boor-gun-der), which, despite its German name, is scarce in the rest of the country. For years Pfalz winemakers seemed to take the easy way out, relying on the area's mild climate. Today there's a renaissance afoot leading to higher quality wines and making the region one of the most dynamic in Germany.

the bottom line As in most of Germany, Qualitätsweins sell for $7 to $12, Kabinetts for $10 to $18, most Spätleses for $12 to $25, and Ausleses for $16 to $50 (see Fortified and Dessert Wines, page 282).

what to buy PFALZ

1996	1997	1998	1999	2000
★★★★	★★★	★★★	★★★★	★★

recommended wines

2000 Müller-Catoir Gimmeldinger Mandelgarten Riesling Kabinett Trocken ★★★★ $$$
dry, medium-bodied, high acidity, no oak **drink now–15 years**
A great bone-dry wine with some fruit flavors and a punch of herbs and minerals.

2000 Müller-Catoir Neustadter Monchgarten Weissburgunder Kabinett Trocken ★★★★ $$$
dry, full-bodied, high acidity, no oak **drink now–15 years**
A beautiful bone-dry wine. In a country with so many fine winemakers, it's hard to say that anyone is the best, but if we were forced to choose…

1999 Weingut Dr. Bürklin-Wolf Ruppertsberg Gaisböhl Riesling Spätlese Trocken ★★★★ $$$
dry, full-bodied, medium acidity, no oak **drink now–15 years**
An upright model of German restraint, with lovely fruit and mineral notes.

1998 Weingut Dr. Bürklin-Wolf Wachenheimer Rechbächel Riesling Spätlese Trocken ★★★★ $$$
dry, full-bodied, medium acidity, no oak **drink now–15 years**
Amazing. Unmistakable passion fruit aromas leap from the bottle as soon as you pull the cork. Other tropical flavors soon join in.

1998 Weingut Jul. Ferd. Kimich Ruppertsberger Reiterpfad Gewürztraminer Spätlese ★★★★ $$
off-dry, full-bodied, medium acidity, no oak **drink now–12 years**
The Pfalz is one of the few regions in Germany that make excellent Gewürztraminer, and here's one we love.

1998 Josef Biffar Deidesheimer Hergottsacker Riesling Spätlese ★★★ $$$
off-dry, full-bodied, high acidity, no oak **drink now–10 years**
Here's a wine that is deeply and deliciously flavorful. It combines both fruity and floral aromas and flavors.

2000 Eugen Müller Forester Mariengarten Riesling Kabinett ★★★ $$
dry, medium-bodied, high acidity, no oak **drink now–8 years**
Spiced-apple and lemon complemented by lots of minerality.

2000 Weingut Kurt Darting Dürkheimer Hochbenn Riesling Kabinett ★★★ $$
off-dry, full-bodied, high acidity, no oak **drink now–5 years**
Lush for a Kabinett wine, full of honeyed-pear flavor balanced by great acidity.

2000 Weingut Kurt Darting Dürkheimer Spielburg Scheurebe Spätlese ★★★ $$
off-dry, full-bodied, high acidity, no oak **drink now–5 years**
Riesling is Germany's star, but if Scheurebe could always perform as well as it does here, we'd tell Riesling to watch its back.

1999 Lingenfelder Riesling Qualitätswein ★★ $$
dry, full-bodied, medium acidity, no oak **drink now**
A fruity wine that's great for casual occasions.

1999 Weingut Jul. Ferd. Kimich Deidesheimer Paradiesgarten Riesling Kabinett Halbtrocken ★★ $
dry, light-bodied, medium acidity, no oak **drink now–5 years**
Nutty aroma, but the flavor is lemon through and through.

RECOMMENDED PRODUCERS

Müller-Catoir, Koehler-Ruprecht, Dr. Bürklin-Wolf, Reichsrat von Buhl, Dr. von Bassermann-Jordan, Pfeffingen, Lingenfelder

rheingau

Germany's center of Riesling production, Rheingau is home to Schloss Johannisberg, a wine estate so famous that it lent its name (without being asked) to Rieslings grown in California, Johannisberg Riesling. It was several old estates—among them Schloss Johannisberg, Schloss Vollrads, and the oldest, Kloster Eberbach—that established (and in the 1970s and '80s nearly squandered) the reputation of Rheingau wines. More recently, winemakers like Robert Weil and Georg Breuer have taken the Rheingau to new heights.

the bottom line Rheingau wines once commanded some of the highest prices in Germany, but after a couple of decades of lax quality-control, their reputation and prices suffered. Things have gotten back on track in terms of quality, but luckily for us, prices on these wines remain low. Generally speaking, Qualitätsweins cost $7 to $12, Kabinetts go for $10 to $18, Spätleses can be had for $12 to $25, and Ausleses run $16 to $50.

what to buy RHEINGAU

1996	1997	1998	1999	2000
★★★	★★★	★★★	★★★★	★★

recommended wines

1999 Weingut Franz Künstler Hochheimer Hölle Riesling-Auslese-Trocken ★★★★ $$$$
dry, full-bodied, high acidity, no oak **drink in 5–15 years**
A great, great vintage offers a powerful wine with strawberry, tropical fruit, and deep mineral flavors.

1999 Georg Breuer Rüdesheim Berg Schlossberg Qualitätswein ★★★★ $$$
dry, full-bodied, medium acidity, no oak **drink now–20 years**
Power and balance; a macédoine of all manner of fruit flavors harmonizing with mineral notes.

1999 Weingut Franz Künstler Hochheimer Stielweg Riesling-Spätlese-Trocken ★★★★ $$$
dry, full-bodied, high acidity, no oak **drink in 3–10 years**
Rheingau wines used to be the most expensive and revered in the world. If more of them delivered the complexity of this one, they could be again.

1999 Georg Breuer Montosa Qualitätswein ★★★★ $$
dry, full-bodied, medium acidity, no oak **drink now–10 years**
Wonderful wine from an outstanding producer at a reasonable price. Buy whatever you can.

1999 Schumann Nägler Johannisberger Erntebringer Riesling Kabinett ★★★ $$
dry, full-bodied, high acidity, no oak **drink now–8 years**
Riesling that seems to have been crossed with a hazelnut tree. Toasted nut flavors start strong, give way to exotic fruit, and return on the finish.

1999 Weingut Robert Weil Riesling Kabinett Halbtrocken ★★★ $$
dry, full-bodied, high acidity, no oak **drink now–10 years**
With all the marzipan and orange notes, this would make the perfect German Christmas wine. It will make any day a holiday.

1999 Baron zu Knyphausen Kiedricher Sandgrub Riesling Spätlese ★★ $$
off-dry, medium-bodied, medium acidity, no oak **drink now–5 years**
Classic Rheingau Riesling, with citrus flavors joined by appealing (for many Riesling fans, including us) petrol notes.

RECOMMENDED PRODUCERS

Robert Weil, Georg Breuer, Weingut Johannishof, Franz Künstler, Josef Leitz, Schloss Johannisberg, Kloster Eberbach

CLASSIFIED RHEINGAU

France's classification system helps sort out the vineyards by labeling some of them Grand Cru or Premier Cru. Such categories have never been used in Germany, so consumers have had no way to know which vineyards were top quality, short of memorizing a long list of names. Beginning with the 1999 vintage, now in shops, twenty-nine exceptional vineyards in the Rheingau are allowed to use the new *Erstes Gewächs* (first growth) designation on their labels.

rheinhessen

Müller-Thurgau (MEW-lair TOOR-gau) grapes are prolific in the Rheinhessen, and the gentle topography of most of the region makes mechanized picking a cinch. This has led to factory-inspired Liebfraumilch: The Blue Nun has her home here in Rheinhessen, and it is here that the Black Tower looms. Some of Germany's best Rieslings are made from grapes grown on the steep slopes of the Rheinterrasse, a small subregion that runs along the Rhine. A few Silvaner (sil-VAH-ner) wines are also worth looking for.

the bottom line Only a handful of the Rheinhessen's best producers are able to escape the region's stigma and command prices as high as producers from other parts of the country, like Mosel-Saar-Ruwer and the Pfalz. So if you stay away from the mass-market Liebfraumilch, you'll find some really good deals. Qualitätsweins are priced around $8; Kabinett-level wines start at $8 and rarely command more than $13; Spätleses cost $11 to $20.

what to buy RHEINHESSEN

1996	1997	1998	1999	2000
★★★★	★★★★	★★★	★★★★	★★

recommended wines

2000 Bernhard Hackenheimer Kirchberg Scheurebe Kabinett ★★★ $$
off-dry, medium-bodied, high acidity, no oak **drink now–4 years**
When we need something unusual, Scheurebe always fills the bill. Here the grape offers strong herbal and grapefruit flavors and lots of minerals.

1999 Heyl zu Herrnsheim Niersteiner Pettental Riesling Spätlese Halbtrocken ★★ $$
dry, full-bodied, high acidity, no oak **drink now–8 years**
A good example to show why we love halbtrockens. Full fruit flavors so sumptuous that the wine seems sweet at first but is actually quite dry.

2000 J.u.H.A. Strub Niersteiner Paterberg Riesling Spätlese ★★ $$
off-dry, full-bodied, high acidity, no oak **drink now–5 years**
Luscious, slightly sweet fruit and spice flavors make this almost a dessert wine, but it's great with Thai food.

1999 Wittman Qualitätswein Halbtrocken ★★ $$
dry, medium-bodied, medium acidity, no oak **drink now–2 years**
A unique blend of Kerner and Müller-Thurgau, with lots of floral and herbal flavors and an appealing nuttiness.

2000 J.u.H.A. Strub Niersteiner Riesling Kabinett ★ $
dry, medium-bodied, high acidity, no oak **drink now**
Its liter bottle and zingy citrus flavors make this one of our longtime favorites. The fridge seems empty without it.

RECOMMENDED PRODUCERS
Gunderloch, Freiherr Heyl zu Herrnsheim, J.u.H.A. Strub, St. Antony

other regions

Areas that are less known outside Germany, such as Baden, Franken, the Nahe, and the Mittelrhein, also produce terrific wine. Baden makes wonderful Pinot Blanc and Pinot Gris. In Franken, a wide selection of grape varieties, from Müller-Thurgau to Gewürztraminer, is used with great success. The Upper Nahe produces some excellent Rieslings, but also Müller-Thurgaus and Silvaners. From the steep vineyards of the Mittelrhein come steely Rieslings.

the bottom line Good Baden wines cost from $12 to $20; spectacular ones go for $40 or more. Demand in Germany is high for Franken wines, so you won't find the bargains that you do from other regions; even the wines made with the unfairly maligned Müller-Thurgau start at $15 and go up to more than $30. Nahe and Mittelrhein prices are more typical: Qualitätsweins $7 to $12, Kabinetts $10 to $18, Spätleses $12 to $25, Ausleses $16 to $50.

recommended wines

1998 Dr. Heger Achkarrer Schlossberg
Pinot Blanc Spätlese Trocken Barrique, Baden ★★★★ $$$
dry, full-bodied, medium acidity, light oak **drink now–8 years**
A winery almost on the border with Alsace produces a wine that resembles an Alsace Grand Cru more than anything else in Germany.

1999 Hans Wirsching Iphofer Kalb
Traminer Spätlese, Franken ★★★ $$$
off-dry, full-bodied, high acidity, no oak **drink now–10 years**
An exciting wine with ripe, almost buttery tropical fruit flavors and loads of floral and mineral notes.

2000 Crusius Niederhäuser Felsensteyer
Riesling Spätlese, Nahe ★★★ $$
dry, medium-bodied, high acidity, no oak **drink now–3 years**
Fruit flavors made even more interesting by floral and mineral notes.

2000 Mathern Niederhäuser Felsensteyer
Riesling Kabinett, Nahe ★★★ $$
dry, medium-bodied, high acidity, no oak **drink now–8 years**
We don't detect hoplike flavors in many wines, but here's one filled with floral (including hops) and mineral flavors that's more refreshing than any Pilsner.

1998 Schneider Niederhäuser Klamm Riesling Auslese,
Nahe ★★★ $$
dry, full-bodied, high acidity, no oak **drink now–10 years**
The concentrated citrus, mineral, and earth flavors expected from an Auslese, without a high concentration of dollars required to taste them. Very good value.

1998 Winzergenossenschaft Thüngersheim
Müller-Thurgau Qualitätswein Halbtrocken, Franken ★★★ $$
dry, medium-bodied, medium acidity, no oak **drink now–5 years**
Lemon-lime flavors accented by a bouquet of herbs.

1999 Fürst Müller-Thurgau Kabinett Trocken, Franken ★★ $$
off-dry, medium-bodied, medium acidity, no oak **drink now–7 years**
Most quality Franken wines are close to bone-dry. This keeps a touch of sweetness, with mellow fruit flavors and refreshing pine notes.

2000 Weingart Bopparder Hamm Ohlenberg
Riesling Spätlese Halbtrocken, Mittelrhein ★★ $$
off-dry, medium-bodied, high acidity, no oak **drink now–5 years**
A great example of the glories of halbtrocken wines, full of concentrated fruit flavors but fermented nearly dry.

RECOMMENDED PRODUCERS

BADEN Dr. Heger, Andreas Laible

MITTELRHEIN Toni Jost, Ratzenberger, Weingart

NAHE Crusius, Diel, Dönnhoff, Kruger-Rumpf, Emrich-Schönleber

FRANKEN Burgerspital, Juliusspital, Wirsching, Fürst

GETTING FRANKEN'S GOAT

Most German wine, at least that which finds its way across the ocean, is in tall, flutelike bottles. A notable exception is the fine wine of Franken, which has enjoyed the exclusive right to use an unmistakable round and squat wine bottle known as the *bocksbeutel* ("goat's scrotum") since the early 1700s. The European Union, however, has ordered that producers in other parts of the continent may also use the bottle. The Franconians are up in arms. An appeal is now being made.

austria

Located smack in the middle of Europe, Austria is affected by several winemaking traditions. German influence is the most obvious, but Italian, Hungarian, Slovakian, and Slovenian sensibilities are also in evidence. Adhering to the strictest production standards in the world, Austrian vintners make wines of exceptional quality. The cross-pollination of traditions means the wines are diverse and at once reminiscent of and different from those made anywhere else.

grapes & styles

Austria is white wine territory, with the uniquely Austrian vine Grüner Veltliner (GROO-ner felt-LEE-ner) outnumbering other varieties. Most of it is made into simple wines enjoyed at local vintner-run wine taverns known as Heurigen. If Grüner Veltliner is the most common grape, Riesling (reece-ling) is the most noble. Rieslings here are full-bodied and aromatic. Less celebrated but still fine is Welschriesling, the second most common grape in the country. Weissburgunder (VICE-boor-gun-der; also known as Pinot Blanc), Sauvignon Blanc (sometimes called Muskat-Sylvaner), and Chardonnay (sometimes called Morillon) are other popular varieties. To meet international demand, plantings of the latter two have been increasing in recent years. Sometimes aged in oak (the word *barrique* is a giveaway), the best Weissburgunder and Chardonnay bear comparison to the wines of Burgundy. A few Austrian winemakers also grow Furmint (foor-mint), the grape of Hungary's famed Tokaji wine. Furmint wines can be reminiscent of Gewürztraminer.

on the label

Austrian wines are labeled by variety, region, and other designations that indicate the style of wine. Austria has a system similar to the German, using the Qualitätswein and Prädikatswein designations to indicate wines of good and excellent quality and the terms Kabinett (kah-bee-NET), Spätlese (sh'PAY't-lay-zuh), Auslese (OUSE-lay-zuh), Beerenauslese (BEAR-en-OUSE-lay-zuh), and Trockenbeerenauslese (TRAW-ken-BEAR-en-OUSE-lay-zuh) to indicate the ripeness level of the grapes when picked. However, given the Austrian preference for dry wines, an Austrian wine is likely to be drier than its German counterpart.

at the table

Grüner Veltliner can hold up to, and even enhance, ingredients like asparagus and artichokes, which are deadly matches for most wines. And it's a pleasure with shrimp, swordfish, or pork. Try Austrian Riesling with roast turkey, duck, rabbit, a Wiener schnitzel, or a wild mushroom goulash. Welschriesling, Weissburgunder, and Sauvignon Blanc pair well with freshwater fish or chicken. Chardonnay complements poached salmon.

the bottom line Austrian whites aren't cheap. Most Grüner Veltliners and Rieslings are priced above $25. Stick with the good producers and you'll be sure to get your money's worth. Welschrieslings and Weissburgunders go for $15 to $20. Sauvignon Blanc and Chardonnay sell for $20 to $25.

what to buy WHITE WINES

1996	1997	1998	1999	2000
★★★	★★★★	★★★	★★★★	★★★★

niederösterreich

Nearly 60 percent of Austrian wine is produced in the country's largest wine region, Niederösterreich, or Lower Austria. The area has six subregions: Weinviertel, Donauland, Traisental, Kamptal, Kremstal, and Wachau. From the latter three come some of Austria's most intense Grüner Veltliners and Rieslings.

recommended wines

2000 F.X. Pichler Smaragd Kellerberg Riesling, Wachau ★★★★ $$$$
dry, full-bodied, high acidity, no oak **drink now–15 years**
Is there a better Riesling in Austria? In the world? Hard to say.

2000 Hiedler Maximum Weissburgunder, Kamptal ★★★★ $$$
dry, full-bodied, high acidity, no oak **drink now–8 years**
The name says it all: maximum fruitiness, maximum minerality, maximum spiciness, all very well balanced.

2000 Nigl Ried Hochäcker Riesling, Kremstal ★★★★ $$$
dry, full-bodied, high acidity, no oak **drink now–10 years**
Brilliantly clear peach and lime flavors entwined in a labyrinth of mineral and herbal notes.

2000 Nigl Seftenberger Piri Privat Grüner Veltliner, Kremstal ★★★★ $$$

dry, full-bodied, high acidity, no oak **drink now–10 years**

Every once in a while we come across a wine that seems to make the world stop. With incredibly lush fruit and mineral flavors, this does just that.

2000 Weingut Bründlmayer Zöbinger Heiligenstein Riesling, Kamptal ★★★★ $$$

dry, medium-bodied, high acidity, no oak **drink now–10 years**

The lime, herb, and mineral flavors explode the second the wine hits the glass.

1999 Weingut Prager Smaragd Weissenkirchner Steinriegl Riesling, Wachau ★★★ $$$$

dry, full-bodied, high acidity, no oak **drink now–10 years**

If Austria ever organizes a hierarchy of Grand Cru wineries, Prager will certainly be in the top ranks. Here's an example that shows why.

2000 Jamek Federspiel Jochinger Pichl Riesling, Wachau ★★★ $$$

dry, medium-bodied, high acidity, no oak **drink now–3 years**

A wine of deception. A sniff promises peach and pear flavors. A sip delivers the taste of minerals and spices. Very good.

1999 Rudi Pichler Smaragd Kollmutz Grüner Veltliner, Wachau ★★★ $$$

dry, full-bodied, high acidity, no oak **drink now–10 years**

Vintners with 35 years' experience would be delighted to be able to make wines as intense as those made by this 35-year-old winemaker.

2000 Hiedler Loiser Berg Riesling, Kamptal ★★★ $$

dry, medium-bodied, high acidity, no oak **drink now–3 years**

Can a wine be described as happy? We'd say this one could, with its snappy acidity and lime and mango flavors as bright as a smile.

2000 Undhof Salomon Hochterrassen Grüner Veltliner, Kremstal ★★ $

dry, full-bodied, high acidity, no oak **drink now–5 years**

Marzipan and orange flavors that would make any Viennese pastry chef proud.

2000 Berger Grüner Veltliner, Kremstal ★ $

dry, light-bodied, high acidity, no oak **drink now**

Light, lovely lemon-lime flavors in a liter bottle at an equally light and lovely price.

RECOMMENDED PRODUCERS

Bründlmayer, F.X. Pichler, Franz Prager, Freie Weingartner, Loimer, Franz Hirtzberger, Nigl, E & M Berger, Hiedler, Rudi Pichler, Knoll

burgenland

Stretching along part of Austria's border with Hungary, Burgenland includes the subregions Neusiedlersee and Neusiedlersee-Hügelland, next to which is Carnuntum.

recommended wines

2000 Heidi Schröck Furmint, Neusiedlersee-Hügelland ★★★ $$
dry, medium-bodied, medium acidity, no oak **drink now–5 years**
Schröck is one the few Austrians to use Furmint, the grape of Hungary's Tokaji. It's used beautifully here, in a wine full of nutty, stony, and citrus-like flavors.

2000 Heidi Schröck Muscat, Neusiedlersee ★★★ $$
dry, medium-bodied, high acidity, no oak **drink now–5 years**
We love the flowery flavors of Muscat; when we find a dry one this good, we fall head over heels.

1999 Kracher Days of Wine & Roses Chardonnay/Welschriesling, Neusiedlersee ★★★ $$
dry, medium-bodied, high acidity, no oak **drink now**
Kracher is best known for its incredible range of intense sweet wines, but this lyrically named dry one sings right on key with invigorating herb and citrus flavors.

2000 Glatzer Classic Weissburgunder, Carnuntum ★★ $$
dry, medium-bodied, medium acidity, no oak **drink now**
Just a really nice wine with zingy flavors balanced by good acidity.

styria & vienna

Styria (Steiermark in German) produces a mere 5 percent of Austrian wines, but they are among the most distinctive in Austria. Ever-so-civilized Vienna makes more wine within its borders than any other capital city.

recommended wines

2000 Polz Steirische Klassik Sauvignon Blanc, Styria ★★★ $$$
dry, medium-bodied, high acidity, no oak **drink now–2 years**
A spirited display of grassy and lemon-lime flavors.

1999 Wieninger Nussberg Alte Reben, Vienna ★★★ $$
dry, medium-bodied, medium acidity, no oak **drink now–8 years**
From the land of Strauss, Freud, and Klimt comes a lush troika of Grüner Veltliner, Weissburgunder, and Welschriesling.

1999 E & M Tement Steirische Klassik Gelber Muskateller, Styria ★★ $$
dry, medium-bodied, high acidity, no oak **drink now–2 years**
Floral and spicy, with a bit of honey flavor. Lovely.

1999 Gross Steirische Klassik Sauvignon Blanc, Styria ★★ $$
dry, medium-bodied, medium acidity, no oak **drink now–3 years**
Here's a Sauvignon that combines all its best characteristics. There are fruit flavors, with herb, pepper, and other spice notes.

RECOMMENDED PRODUCERS

E & M Tement (Styria), Gross (Styria) Polz (Styria), Wieninger (Vienna), Schlumberger (Vienna)

switzerland

Until recently, the Swiss drank nearly all their wine. Now the country's winemakers are starting to look abroad for customers. The wines that have made it to the U.S. are impeccable.

grapes & styles

Of whites, Chasselas (shah'ss-lah) is most available. Others include Pinot Gris and Petite Arvine. Among reds, you'll see Merlot. Pinot Noir and Gamay are often blended into a wine called Dôle.

on the label

If a white wine isn't labeled by grape, assume it's Chasselas, called Fendant in Valais. Unlabeled reds are likely to be blends.

at the table

Chasselas from Neuchâtel is great with raw shellfish. Those from the Vaud are better with seafood in rich sauce. Valais Fendant will stand up to rich pâté or complement turkey. Pinot Gris can handle a fondue or turkey with all the fixings. Petite Arvine is good for pork or veal. Merlot is wonderful with roast beef or nutty cheeses; try it with cheese fondue. Drink Dôle with duck or lamb, or with the local raclette.

the bottom line The range is from $18 to $35.

recommended wines

1999 Jean et Pierre Testuz Grand Cru L'Arbalète, Dézaley ★★★★ $$$
dry, full-bodied, medium acidity, light oak **drink now–12 years**
A Chasselas-based wine, this Grand Cru is nicely fruity.

1999 Robert Gilliard "Pierre Ollaire" Petite Arvine, Valais ★★★★ $$$
dry, full-bodied, high acidity, no oak **drink now–8 years**
A complex wine with fruit, nut, and herb flavors and smoke and mineral notes.

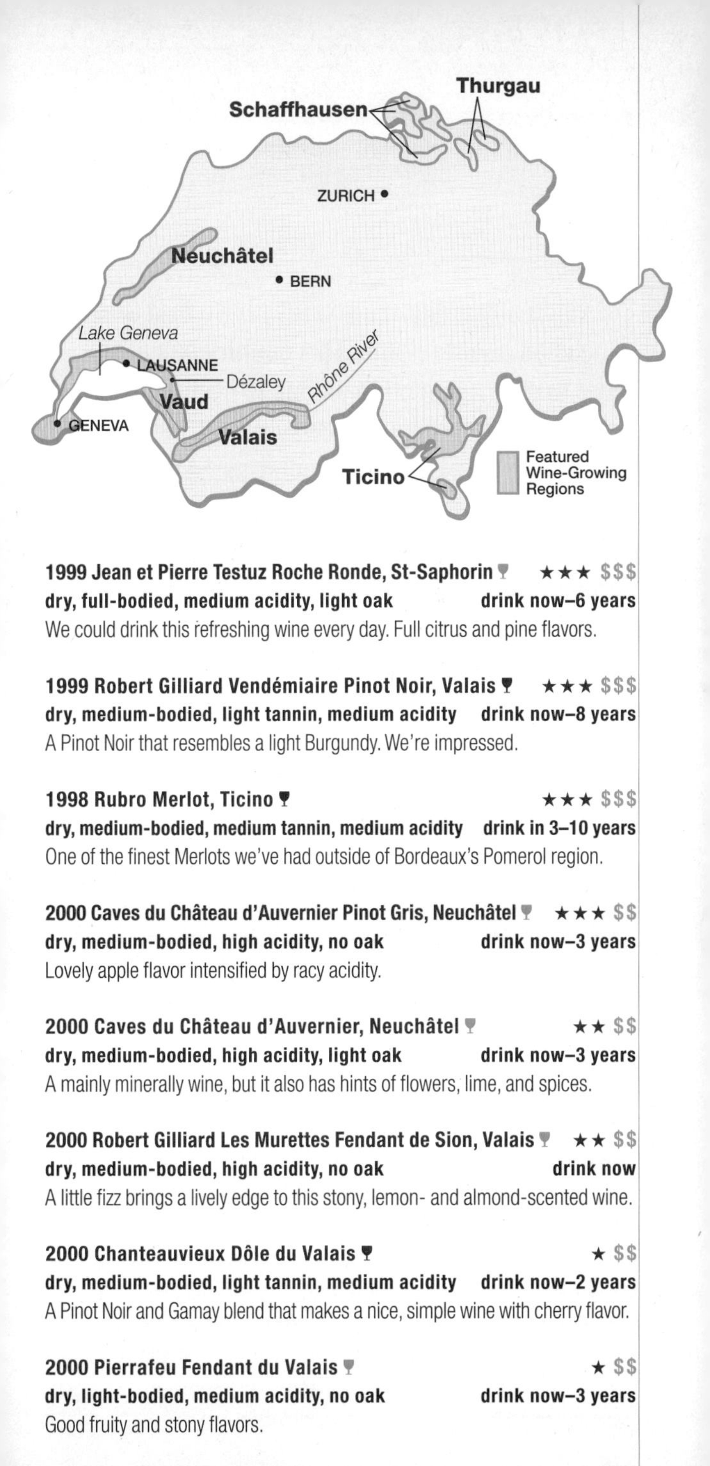

1999 Jean et Pierre Testuz Roche Ronde, St-Saphorin ★★★ $$$
dry, full-bodied, medium acidity, light oak **drink now–6 years**
We could drink this refreshing wine every day. Full citrus and pine flavors.

1999 Robert Gilliard Vendémiaire Pinot Noir, Valais ★★★ $$$
dry, medium-bodied, light tannin, medium acidity **drink now–8 years**
A Pinot Noir that resembles a light Burgundy. We're impressed.

1998 Rubro Merlot, Ticino ★★★ $$$
dry, medium-bodied, medium tannin, medium acidity **drink in 3–10 years**
One of the finest Merlots we've had outside of Bordeaux's Pomerol region.

2000 Caves du Château d'Auvernier Pinot Gris, Neuchâtel ★★★ $$
dry, medium-bodied, high acidity, no oak **drink now–3 years**
Lovely apple flavor intensified by racy acidity.

2000 Caves du Château d'Auvernier, Neuchâtel ★★ $$
dry, medium-bodied, high acidity, light oak **drink now–3 years**
A mainly minerally wine, but it also has hints of flowers, lime, and spices.

2000 Robert Gilliard Les Murettes Fendant de Sion, Valais ★★ $$
dry, medium-bodied, high acidity, no oak **drink now**
A little fizz brings a lively edge to this stony, lemon- and almond-scented wine.

2000 Chanteauvieux Dôle du Valais ★ $$
dry, medium-bodied, light tannin, medium acidity **drink now–2 years**
A Pinot Noir and Gamay blend that makes a nice, simple wine with cherry flavor.

2000 Pierrafeu Fendant du Valais ★ $$
dry, light-bodied, medium acidity, no oak **drink now–3 years**
Good fruity and stony flavors.

greece

Set aside any prejudice you may have that Greek wine is all about retsina. This country has a lot more to offer, from crisp whites to fruity reds, some ready to drink right away, others that need long aging. This is not surprising, since Greece's winemaking history goes back to the days when Pan played his flute for Zeus and Aphrodite. In addition, Greece has more indigenous grapes than nearly any other country in the world. If you want to experience a new take on the classics, Greek wines are for you.

grapes & styles

While Greece grows plenty of the international varieties—including Chardonnay, Sauvignon Blanc, Cabernet Sauvignon, and Merlot—most of the more interesting wines are those from indigenous varieties. The country's most common white is Savatiano, a grape once relegated to retsina. It is now being used to produce simple nonresinated whites. Another white grape, Assyrtiko (ah-SEAR-tee-koh), boasts electric acidity that highlights its fine mineral flavors. The most characteristic is grown on Santorini. Moscofilero grapes can produce wonderfully floral whites. Roditis varietals are typically light and floral and also have mineral characteristics.

Agiorgitiko (eye-your-YEE-tee-koh), grown all over Attica and the Peloponnese, produces ample amounts of cheap, plummy, quaffable red when grown in the flatlands; when grown on slopes, it can give an impressively tannic red that retains its beguiling plumminess. Xynomavro (ksee-NO-ma-vro), grown in the north in Naoussa, lives up to its name ("acid-black") when young, but with age—usually a decade or more—invites comparisons to Italian Nebbiolo in its earthiness.

white wines

at the table

Most Greek whites are made with Greek meze in mind, the innocuous flavor of the wine simply playing backup to the taste of the food. Think olives, salty cheeses, garlicky dips, and spicy dishes. An Assyrtiko, on the other hand, can grace a simple grilled snapper as easily as Greek meatballs served with *avgolemono.*

the bottom line Greek wines are some of the best values on the market. Everyday whites shouldn't set you back more than $12; fancier wines don't go much above $20.

recommended wines

NV Gai'a Estate Ritinitis Noble Retsina, Koutsi ★★★★ $
dry, medium-bodied, high acidity, medium oak **drink now**
A superb Retsina. This wine was based on research into what ancient Greeks drank. Don't mind the resin smell. Chill and serve with meze. It will be perfect.

1999 Boutari Barrel Fermented Kallisti, Santorini ★★★ $$
dry, full-bodied, medium acidity, medium oak **drink now–5 years**
You can practically taste Santorini's reputed hedonism in this thick and aromatic wine.

2000 Domaine Constantin Lazaridi Amethystos Fumé, Drama ★★★ $$
dry, medium-bodied, high acidity, medium oak **drink now–2 years**
A fine blend that would go perfectly with oregano-stuffed fish or with *horta,* Greece's wild-green dish. Intense lime, mineral, and herb flavors.

1998 Oenoforos Asprolithi, Pátras ★★★ $
dry, full-bodied, medium acidity, no oak **drink now–3 years**
Lest you think all Greek whites are simple sippers for picnics, here's a Roditis with hints of honey, nuts, and minerals. Worthy of taking to Olympus.

2000 Pape Johannou Vineyards Ai Lia Vineyard Assyrtiko, Corinth ★★ $$
dry, medium-bodied, medium acidity, no oak **drink now–2 years**
Assyrtiko is typified by floral, honeylike qualities; this is more like a grassy, pungent Sauvignon Blanc from New Zealand.

1999 Mercouri Estate Foloï Mercouri, Korakohori Ilias ★ $$
dry, light-bodied, medium acidity, no oak **drink now**
A fairly simple Roditis. Just the sort of thing to have with mild fish. Light lemon and mango flavors with a slightly bitter finish.

2000 Kourtakis Kourtaki Vin de Crete, Crete ★ $
dry, light-bodied, high acidity, no oak **drink now**
Here's a wine for casual occasions. Nice, gentle lemon flavor in this blend, plus a mineral-tinged edge.

2000 Tselepos Moschofilero, Mantinia ★ $
dry, light-bodied, high acidity, no oak **drink now**
With lemon, grass, and mineral flavors, plus a low price, this is just the wine for simple fish dishes.

red wines

at the table

The grapey goodness of southern reds is just the thing for a barbecue or for souvlaki. The more sophisticated pleasures of Xynomavro from the north suit rosemary-roasted leg of lamb or a Piedmontese wild mushroom pasta.

the bottom line As with the white wines, basic reds top out at around $10 and more elegant wines can be had for around $20.

recommended wines

1998 Palivou Vineyards, Neméa ★★★ $$
dry, full-bodied, full tannin, high acidity **drink now–10 years**
A wine with guts and lush black-cherry and rose flavors. This is a match for roast lamb.

1998 Chateau Pegasus, Náoussa ★★★ $
dry, medium-bodied, full tannin, high acidity **drink now–12 years**
Earthy yet elegant, this excellent wine is more reminiscent of a fine Nebbiolo from Piedmont (at a fraction of the price) than anything else from Greece.

1998 Boutari Agiorgitiko, Neméa ★★ $$
dry, full-bodied, medium tannin, medium acidity **drink now–3 years**
Loads of rustic, country charm in this smoky wine.

1999 Boutari Merlot/Xynomavro, Imathia ★★ $$
dry, medium-bodied, medium tannin, high acidity **drink now–8 years**
The high-acid Xynomavro grape is tempered by smooth berry flavors from Merlot in this nicely balanced, smoke-scented wine.

eastern europe

During the days of the Cold War, wines from the wide swath of territory known as Eastern Europe were largely unavailable in the U.S., due mainly to American politics (the wines have long been in Britain). The mission of the large, state-run wineries was to make decent, but not necessarily exciting, wines. Quality generally rose, but the reputations of the best wines declined from neglect. The fall of the Soviet empire in 1989 and the breakdown of state-controlled economies spurred interest in producing high-quality wines.

grapes & styles

Slovenia The Littoral (or Primorska) region bordering Italy makes splendid dry whites and lusty reds from local varieties. The Ljutomersko-Ormoske region bordering Austria makes dry whites from local varieties as well as international ones, like Sauvignon Blanc.

Hungary Known for its Tokaji Aszú (toh-KYE ah-SOO) dessert wines from the Furmint grape (see page 283), Hungary also makes terrific dry whites from the same variety and hearty reds from Bordeaux varieties.

Bulgaria The place for Cabernet Sauvignons that are as good as others costing three and four times the price, Bulgaria also produces good Merlot and some Chardonnay.

Croatia Apart from Slovenia, Croatia probably makes the finest wines in the former Yugoslavian countries. The best red, Plavac Mali (plah-votz mah-lee), is a relative of California's Zinfandel.

white wines

at the table

Serve white varietals when you would their kin from other countries. For something unusual with your holiday roast turkey and all the trimmings, try a dry Furmint (foor-mint).

the bottom line The combination of weak Eastern European economies and American unfamiliarity with the wines from these countries means a bonanza for knowledgeable bargain hunters. Dry whites rarely top $10 except for a few Slovenian wines, which sell for $11 or $12. The most exceptional sell for $20 to $30. Quality can still be inconsistent, but with low prices, one can afford an off bottle or two.

recommended wines

1999 Movia Sauvignon, Brda, Slovenia ★★★★ $$$
dry, medium-bodied, high acidity, light oak **drink now–5 years**
A magnificent Sauvignon with lush peach flavor and a floral aroma rather than the usual grassy scent.

1999 Movia Ribolla Gialla, Brda, Slovenia ★★★ $$
dry, full-bodied, medium acidity, medium oak **drink now–10 years**
Sharing a border with Italy's Friuli, Brda also shares many of the same grapes. Here's a lovely wine that would make any Friulian proud.

1999 Oremus Mandulas Furmint, Tokaji, Hungary ★★★ $
dry, medium-bodied, high acidity, no oak **drink now–2 years**
Tokaji, usually a luscious sweet wine, is dry here, but no less impressive. Wonderful fruity, herbal flavor, with crisp acidity.

1998 Grgic Posip Vinogorje Cara, Korcula, Croatia ★★ $$
dry, full-bodied, high acidity, medium oak **drink now–2 years**
Napa's Mike Grgich returns to his native Croatia to make this fine wine from the local Posip grape.

1999 Bataapati Chardonnay, Mocsenyi, Hungary ★★ $
dry, medium-bodied, high acidity, no oak **drink now–2 years**
Italian wine titans and a Hungarian distiller have formed a partnership aimed at reviving an old Hungarian winery. This citrusy wine is a nice result.

1999 Vini Chardonnay, Sliven, Bulgaria ★ $
dry, medium-bodied, high acidity, no oak **drink now**
Refreshing. Full of summer fruit and flowers.

red wines

at the table

Cabernet and Merlot are made in an international style, so think beef tenderloin, roasted leg of lamb studded with whole garlic cloves, or grilled wild mushrooms. Dry Plavac Mali is perfect with smoked ham or cured meats, such as prosciutto di Parma.

the bottom line Eastern European reds are just as cheap as whites, with prices hardly ever above the $10 mark. An exception to the rule, the Plavac Mali made by Croatian-born California winemaker Mike Grgich sells for $22, but you can do well for far less.

recommended wines

1995 Movia Cabernet Sauvignon, Brda, Slovenia ★★★ $$$
dry, full-bodied, full tannin, medium acidity **drink now–10 years**
This Cabernet is packed deliciously full with fruit, spice, oak, and mineral flavors. Really good.

1997 Grgic Plavac Mali, Dingac Peljesac, Croatia ★★ $$
dry, full-bodied, full tannin, medium acidity **drink now–3 years**
For a while, some people—including Napa's Mike Grgich—felt that Zinfandel was actually Croatia's Plavac Mali. He made this like a rich, old fashioned Zin.

1996 Vini Cabernet Sauvignon Reserve, Bulgaria ★★ $
dry, medium-bodied, medium tannin, medium acidity **drink now–3 years**
Cabernet is quite at home in Bulgaria, and it shows here. A nice balance of fruit flavors and hints of spice and cedar.

1998 Vini Merlot, Bulgaria ★★ $
dry, full-bodied, full tannin, medium acidity **drink now–4 years**
A good Merlot with plum flavor and notes of brown sugar and spice.

2000 Dunavar Cabernet Sauvignon Connoisseur Collection, Hungary ★ $
dry, medium-bodied, light tannin, medium acidity **drink now–2 years**
Spicy as a pot of goulash, fruity as cold cherry soup. This simple Cab offers easy drinking for casual pleasure. Try it slightly chilled.

1999 Dunavar Egri, Bikaver, Hungary ★ $
dry, full-bodied, medium tannin, medium acidity **drink now–3 years**
The literal translation is Bull's Blood. A blend of Bordeaux grape varieties with the Hungarian Kekfrankos, this wine has full berry flavor and a bit of spice.

1999 Rousse Merlot, Bulgaria ★ $
dry, full-bodied, medium tannin, medium acidity **drink now–2 years**
Nice balance of fruitiness and tannin.

middle east & northern africa

Wine has been a part of Middle Eastern culture since long before the biblical turning of water into wine. Lebanese wines enjoyed an enthusiastic following in Europe during the Middle Ages. From the late nineteenth century through the 1950s, France relied heavily on wines made in northern Africa to enhance its own characterless *vin ordinaire.* Indeed, wine from that region made up two-thirds of the international wine trade in the 1950s. Israel's best vineyards are planted in the Syrian Golan Heights. Though not always considered part of the Middle East, Turkey and Georgia are two other important wine producers in this general geographic area. The secular republic of Turkey has sponsored a wine industry since the 1920s, and wine has been part of Georgian culture for millennia.

grapes & styles

Morocco and Algeria Most northern African wines blend southern French varietals planted during the period of French rule from the late nineteenth century until 1962. The wines are full reds that resemble those from the Languedoc.

Israel The European varieties Sauvignon Blanc, Chardonnay, and Cabernet Sauvignon make the best Israeli wines. Sauvignon Blanc is probably the best of all.

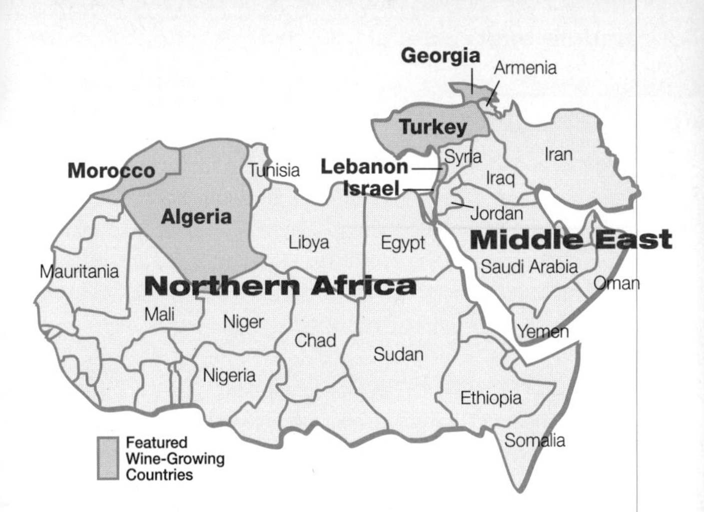

Lebanon The finest wines of the Mideast region come from Lebanon. European grape varieties such as Cabernet Sauvignon, Cinsault, and Syrah produce wines that would provoke jealousy from most Bordeaux vintners. Interesting dry whites, overwhelmingly blends, are produced from Sémillon (called Meroué here), Chardonnay, and a number of indigenous varietals.

Turkey Most Turkish wine available in the U.S. is red, dry, and medium-bodied, made from a combination of indigenous and southern French grape varieties.

Georgia Most Georgian wines—even reds—are semisweet, unusual for American palates, but interesting. Good dry wines are also made and are increasingly exported. Georgia grows dozens of indigenous grape varieties, but the country is perhaps best known for its Rkatsiteli (ruh-KAT-see-TEL-ee) a white variety that, though obscure in the U.S., is one of the four most widely planted white wine grapes in the world. Rkatsiteli wines are typically dry and medium-bodied.

at the table

You can use most northern African reds as you would a solid Côtes-du-Rhône. Drink them with spicy grilled sausages (*merguez* would be perfect), any type of couscous, chicken teriyaki, or hearty bean dishes. Lebanese reds are a more complex affair. The best ones can fill in for Bordeaux: think short ribs, meat lasagna, and roasted game birds. Pull out a Turkish red the next time you have shish kebabs, or Adana kebabs (made from ground lamb and chili peppers). Dry reds from Georgia match roast pork perfectly. The semisweet Georgian wines go well with cumin-rubbed Cornish hens or Moroccan-spiced chicken stew with prunes.

the bottom line Consumers are largely unaware of these wines, so bargains abound. Nearly all the northern African red wines are between $7 and $10. Most Lebanese reds sell for $10 to $18; whites cost $10 to $15. Turkish reds can be had for $8 to $12. Georgian dry wines sell for $5 to $10, semisweets for somewhat more, between $7 and $16. The higher price also gets you an impressive clay bottle.

recommended wines

1997 Chateau Kefraya Comte de M, Lebanon ★★★★ $$$
dry, full-bodied, full tannin, medium acidity **drink now–15 years**
Superb. Complex berry, spice, cedar, and smoke flavors.

1994 Chateau Musar, Bekaa Valley, Lebanon ★★★ $$$
dry, full-bodied, medium tannin, high acidity **drink now–6 years**
An unusual wine from the most famous winemaker in the Middle East. Very full, with spicy flavors and lots of acidity.

1998 Kavaklidere Kalecik Karasi, Ankara, Turkey ★★★ $$$
dry, medium-bodied, full tannin, high acidity **drink now–4 years**
The best Turkish wine we've tasted. Almost Burgundian.

1998 Chateau Ksara Cabernet Sauvignon, Bekaa Valley, Lebanon ★★★ $$
dry, full-bodied, full tannin, high acidity **drink in 3–10 years**
This will give you a big taste of the cedars of Lebanon. There's also cherry flavor for balance and anise and spice aromas.

1997 Golan Heights Winery Yarden Cabernet Sauvignon, Galilee, Israel ★★★ $$
dry, full-bodied, full tannin, medium acidity **drink now–12 years**
Could have come from Napa, full of fruity and chocolaty flavors. Very, very good.

ISRAEL'S GOLAN HEIGHTS WINE

Israel's most promising wine region, the Golan Heights, is not even officially Israeli. Captured from Syria in 1967 and annexed in 1981, the cool Golan Heights are considered occupied territory, and yet Israel has planted grapes and built a winery there. Today it produces the best wine in the country. But peace negotiations in 2000 came close to returning the Golan to Syria, raising the question of what will happen to the Israeli wine industry if Syria reassumes control of the area. A winery spokesman said that the company isn't worried and is even expanding. "If peace comes, we'll make the sacrifice. We can make wine in another part of the country. Hopefully, though, the Syrians would let us get the grapes from Golan."

NV "D" Khvanchkara, Georgia ★★★ $
off-dry, medium-bodied, medium tannin, medium acidity drink now–2 years
Good wine—very spicy with mixed fruit flavors.

1997 Chateau Kefraya, Lebanon ★★ $$
dry, full-bodied, full tannin, high acidity drink in 3–8 years
Lush berry flavor and a slight spiciness makes for superb drinking.

1998 Amazir Beni M'Tir, Morocco ★★ $
dry, full-bodied, medium tannin, medium acidity drink now–2 years
An exotic wine with spice, pomegranate, and tamarind flavors.

1998 Tbilvino Saperavi, Kakheti, Georgia ★ $$
dry, full-bodied, full tannin, medium acidity drink now–5 years
Appealing, refreshing fruit flavors.

1995 "D" Mukuzani, Kakheti, Georgia ★ $
dry, full-bodied, full tannin, medium acidity drink now–2 years
Smoky, meaty qualities with hints of cherry flavor. For the adventurous.

1998 Domaine El Bordj Coteaux de Mascara, Algeria ★ $
dry, full-bodied, medium tannin, medium acidity drink now–2 years
Fragrant as a rose and fruity as a berry patch.

1999 Kavaklidere Yakut Öküzgözü d'Elazig, Turkey ★ $
dry, medium-bodied, medium tannin, high acidity drink now–2 years
Looking for the perfect thing to go with grilled kebabs? Here it is.

1998 Les Celliers de Meknes Les Trois Domaines Guerrouane, Morocco ★ $
dry, medium-bodied, medium tannin, medium acidity **drink now**
Full fruit flavors balanced by good acidity. Just right for grilled *merguez.*

NV Sidi Mustapha Private Reserve, Marrakech, Morocco ★ $
dry, medium-bodied, medium tannin, medium acidity **drink now**
Charry, cherry, and cheap. Not bad for a few bucks.

white wines

at the table

Israeli Sauvignon Blanc goes wonderfully with vegetarian pasta dishes, seared sea scallops, or seafood risotto. Lebanese whites match well with grilled or baked ocean fish with plenty of herbs. Pair Rkatsiteli with any sautéed fish, like snapper or bass, or with a vegetable frittata.

the bottom line As with northern African reds, most whites cost between $7 and $10. Israeli Sauvignon Blanc can be found for $9 to $12. Rkatsiteli sells for $6, a price that should compel you to try it.

recommended wines

1996 Chateau Musar, Lebanon ★★★ $$
dry, full-bodied, medium acidity, medium oak **drink now–8 years**
Chateau Musar is famous for its reds, but its whites made from indigenous and international varieties are really more interesting.

1999 Tbilvino Gurjaani, Kakheti, Georgia ★★★ $
dry, full-bodied, high acidity, no oak **drink now–6 years**
Made from Rkatsiteli and Mtsvane grapes, this wine is so full of mineral, fruit, and nut flavors that it resembles an excellent Loire Valley Chenin Blanc.

1996 Tbilvino Tsinandali, Kakheti, Georgia ★★★ $
dry, full-bodied, high acidity, medium oak **drink now–3 years**
A thick, unusual white with fruit and lots of mineral flavors. Georgians would drink it with roast suckling pig.

1999 Golan Heights Winery Yarden Chardonnay, Galilee, Israel ★★ $$
dry, full-bodied, medium acidity, heavy oak **drink now–3 years**
A lot of oak here. Fortunately, there are enough tangy fruit flavors for balance.

1997 Kavaklidere Selection Beyaz Narince de Tokat, Turkey ★★ $$
dry, medium-bodied, medium acidity, no oak **drink now**
A lovely wine with scents and flavors of lemon and quince.

1999 Ksara Cuvée du Pape Chardonnay, Bekaa, Lebanon ★★ $$
dry, full-bodied, medium acidity, medium oak **drink now–5 years**
It's been said that tiny Lebanon, with its mountains, plains, and sea is a lot like California. Here's the proof.

2000 Carmel Valley Sauvignon Blanc, Dan, Israel ★★ $
dry, light-bodied, high acidity, no oak **drink now**
A grassy, lemony Sauvignon Blanc with bracing acidity.

1998 Old Tbilisi, Kakheti, Georgia ★★ $
dry, medium-bodied, medium acidity, no oak **drink now–2 years**
We love Rkatsiteli: It's aromatic and full of floral, fruit, mineral, and honey notes.

2000 Chateau Ksara Blanc de Blancs, Bekaa, Lebanon ★ $$
dry, light-bodied, medium acidity, no oak **drink now**
A Chardonnay, Sémillon, and Sauvignon Blanc blend. Refreshing.

1999 Kavaklidere Emir de Nevsehir, Çankaya, Turkey ★ $
dry, light-bodied, medium acidity, no oak **drink now**
A simple wine for casual times. Perfect when you grill fish in your backyard.

1998 Les Celliers de Meknes Les Trois Domaines Guerrouane, Morocco ★ $
dry, medium-bodied, medium acidity, no oak **drink now**
If you want a tart, mineral-laden wine that's great with fried fish, here it is.

ISLAM AND WINE

Orthodox Muslim practice forbids the consumption of wine, but more than a few hopeful imbibers have noted Qur'anic loopholes concerning this issue. In the four mentions of wine in the Qur'an, one presents wine in a positive light, two are cautionary, and the fourth is a prohibition. There are a variety of explanations for the different positions, but it is safe to say that some Muslims of a libertine nature focus on the positive one.

australia

About twenty-five years ago, richly flavored, full-bodied, well-priced Australian wines hit the American market. Most Australian wines exported to the U.S. were from large wineries and had a sameness about them. In the last five years, though, small producers dedicated to making wines that reflect Australia's varied microclimates have been sending to market exciting wines with evocative names, like Cockfighter's Ghost and Stumpy Gully.

on the label

Australian labels are a cinch. Grape varieties are almost always stated; even blends usually list the grapes. Wine regions are commonly included as well, but for many wines, especially inexpensive ones, regional designations such as South Eastern Australia are too broad to tell you much. More specific and meaningful designations to look for include Hunter Valley, Barossa Valley, Clare Valley, Yarra Valley, McLaren Vale, Coonawarra, Padthaway, and the Margaret River district.

white wines

CHARDONNAY

Australian winemakers, especially the bigger ones, churn out rivers of Chardonnay in the full-bodied, oaky style that so many love. However, just as California vintners, especially smaller ones, have backed away from the bigger-is-better approach to winemaking, so too have many Australians. It is now possible to find Chardonnays with finesse.

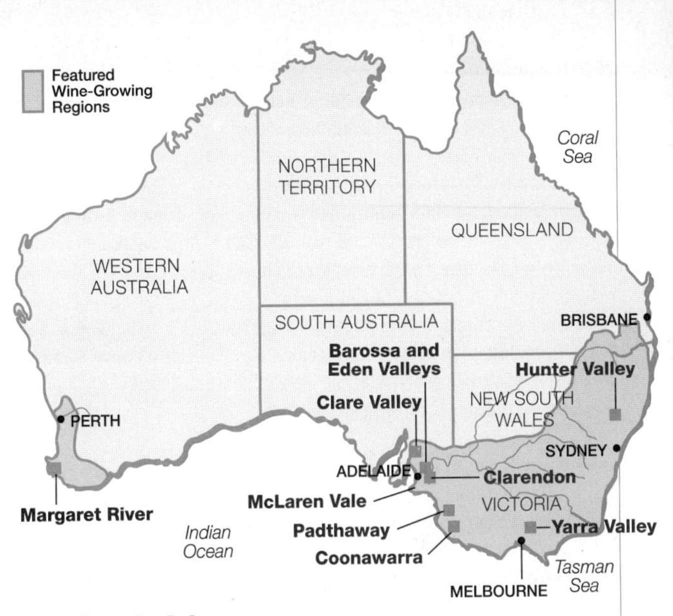

at the table

Though oaky Chardonnays often overwhelm whatever they're served with, they can be great with rich, creamy dishes like chowder, bisque, or pasta with cream sauce. Try a hearty lasagna with seafood and béchamel sauce. Serve subtler styles with a chef or Cobb salad, stir-fried shrimp or chicken, or sautéed or baked fish, like perch or bass. Either style can be served with chicken or turkey; you need to match the wine to the sauce. Both styles marry beautifully with Brie, Swiss, or Gouda.

the bottom line At under $10 a bottle, Australian Chardonnays are still hard to beat when it comes to good value in Chardonnays. Generally speaking, quality, even if high to start with, rises with each dollar you spend. Really interesting wines from small producers run $22 to $25.

recommended wines

1999 Clarendon Hills Hickinbotham Vineyard, Clarendon ★★★★ $$$
dry, full-bodied, medium acidity, medium oak **drink now–8 years**
Quite simply one of the best Chardonnays in the world, full of smoke, nut, orange, and mineral flavors.

2000 Rosemount Orange Vineyard, New South Wales ★★★★ $$
dry, medium-bodied, medium acidity, medium oak **drink now–8 years**
A multiplicity of delicious, full fruit and floral flavors. Just terrific.

1998 Penfolds Yattarna, South Australia ★★★ $$$$
dry, full-bodied, medium acidity, heavy oak **drink in 2–10 years**
This wine is so massively flavored that we liken it to a butterscotch and pineapple sundae. Give it a few years to calm down.

1999 Blue Pyrenees Estate Reserve, Victoria ★★★ $$
dry, full-bodied, high acidity, heavy oak **drink now–8 years**
We don't normally like a lot of oak, but here it's so well balanced with the flavors from the fruit that it's absolutely luscious.

1999 Shaw & Smith Unoaked, Adelaide Hills ★★★ $$
dry, medium-bodied, medium acidity, no oak **drink now–2 years**
With no oak, a chorus of bright fruit flavors take center stage.

1999 Tyrrell's Moon Mountain, Lower Hunter Valley ★★★ $$
dry, full-bodied, medium acidity, medium oak **drink now–8 years**
Bold flavors, yet in such perfect harmony and balance that none overwhelms the others.

2000 Tyrrell's Reserve, Hunter Valley ★★ $$$
dry, full-bodied, medium acidity, medium oak **drink now–5 years**
A classic New World Chardonnay with butter and pineapple flavors.

1999 Abbey Vale, Margaret River ★★ $$
dry, medium-bodied, high acidity, no oak **drink now–5 years**
This is more like an herb-laden Chablis than anything from Down Under.

2000 Lindemans Padthaway, Padthaway ★★ $
dry, full-bodied, medium acidity, medium oak **drink now**
Good all-purpose Chard, with nice, refreshing citrus flavors.

1999 Simon Gilbert Card Series, Hunter Valley ★★ $
dry, medium-bodied, medium acidity, light oak **drink now–2 years**
Loads of caramel and orange flavors and a snappy lime finish.

2000 Grant Burge Barossa Vines, Barossa ★ $
dry, full-bodied, medium acidity, no oak **drink now–1 year**
Well-balanced tropical fruit flavors—pineapple and passion fruit.

2000 Wolf Blass Barrel Fermented, South Australia ★ $
dry, medium-bodied, medium acidity, heavy oak **drink now–2 years**
Good for times when you want an oaky Chardonnay with everything in balance.

other white wines

Chardonnay may occupy the most shelf space, but many consider Semillon (pronounced SEM-uh-lahn in Australia) and Riesling (reece-ling) Australia's best whites. Both are lovely when young and are also suitable for aging up to ten years. Though frequently blended with Semillon, Sauvignon Blanc goes it alone as well. We're thrilled that Riesling, which Australians have kept to themselves for decades, is entering U.S. markets. Marsanne and Roussanne are also terrific, but they aren't easy to find.

at the table

Semillon has the body to stand up to rich seafood dishes and the acidity to balance them; try it with shellfish in a buttery saffron sauce. Sauvignon Blanc is a good match for a number of simpler seafood preparations, such as grilled shrimp, and has enough acidity to bring out the best in raw oysters and clams. Abundant in acidity, Riesling pairs wonderfully with everything from shellfish to mild fish like trout, heavier fish like tuna, and even hearty poultry, like duck and goose. Try it with a frisée and duck-confit salad or with Japanese spicy tuna rolls. In fact, Riesling complements dishes from many Asian cuisines, especially Vietnamese, Thai, and Korean.

the bottom line Usually ignored for higher-profile Chardonnay, many of these wines can be picked up for under $15. Those that cost more (and they're not a lot more) are generally superb.

recommended wines

2000 Grosset Polish Hill Riesling, Clare Valley ★★★★ $$$
dry, medium-bodied, high acidity, no oak **drink now–20 years**
Our verdict? Simple: This is one of the finest Rieslings in the world.

2000 Brokenwood Semillon, Lower Hunter Valley ★★★ $$
dry, full-bodied, medium acidity, no oak **drink now–8 years**
Clear, concentrated citrus-zest flavors swirl through this wine—one of the best Semillons in Australia.

1999 Frankland Estate Isolation Ridge Riesling, Western Australia ★★★ $$
dry, medium-bodied, high acidity, no oak **drink now–10 years**
From a remote part of western Australia comes a Riesling that can take on nearly any in the world. Sublime fruit, mineral, and honeysuckle aromas.

2000 Wirra Wirra Vineyards Scrubby Rise, McLaren Vale ★★★ $$
dry, full-bodied, high acidity, light oak **drink now–5 years**
A palate-cleansing combination of Semillon, Sauvignon Blanc, and Chardonnay with fruit, spice, and mineral flavors.

1998 Chateau Tahbilk Marsanne, Goulburn Valley ★★★ $
dry, full-bodied, medium acidity, no oak **drink now–10 years**
Intense fruit and nut flavors plus honey notes make this one of our favorite wines anywhere.

2000 Leasingham Bin 7 Riesling, Clare Valley ★★★ $
dry, medium-bodied, high acidity, no oak **drink now–10 years**
Let this breath for an hour. Spectacular floral, fruit, and spice flavors will emerge.

1999 Cape Mentelle Semillon Sauvignon Blanc, Margaret River ★★ $$
dry, medium-bodied, high acidity, light oak **drink now–2 years**
Fans of New Zealand Sauvignon Blanc will be delighted with this green demon, full of grass, lime, and jalapeño notes.

1999 Cockfighter's Ghost Verdelho, Hunter Valley ★★ $$
dry, medium-bodied, medium acidity, no oak **drink now**
A lovely wine with pungent herbal and tropical fruit flavors.

2001 Coldstream Hills Sauvignon Blanc, Yarra Valley ★★ $$
dry, medium-bodied, high acidity, no oak **drink now–2 years**
Tropical fruit flavors like passion fruit and kiwi stand out in this brisk wine.

2000 Penfolds Reserve Riesling, Eden Valley ★★ $$
dry, full-bodied, high acidity no oak **drink now–10 years**
An impressive, bone-dry Riesling, full of fruit flavors and mineral notes.

2000 Hill of Content Benjamin's Blend, Western Australia ★★ $
dry, medium-bodied, medium acidity, no oak **drink now**
An easy-drinking wine chock-full of fruit flavors.

2000 Penfolds Koonunga Hill Semillon Chardonnay, South Australia ★★ $
dry, medium-bodied, medium acidity, light oak **drink now–2 years**
A wine that seems inspired by a visionary dessert chef—raspberry and pineapple sorbet served with a green peppercorn sauce. It's good. Really.

red wines

SHIRAZ

If one thing has given the Australian wine industry an identity, it is Shiraz (the Rhône's Syrah), the most widely planted and most distinctive grape in the country. In Australia, Shiraz is usually made into mellow wine with full, fruity, spicy flavor. More complex versions have more than a little oak and tannin; these need years of age.

at the table

Simple Shiraz (shee-rahz) makes a great wine for barbecues; drink it with hamburgers, rotisserie chicken, or pork ribs. Tannic Shiraz is made for meat, like prime rib or a thick sirloin roast. Try more complex versions also with sharp and nutty cheeses, such as Parmigiano-Reggiano or Romano.

the bottom line There's a tremendous range of prices when it comes to Shiraz. Simpler ones sell for under $10; and you can find a number of solid wines at under $20. The most complex wines go for significantly more, with prices escalating to around $75. The most famous, Penfolds Grange, sells for $175 or more.

what to buy SHIRAZ

1996	1997	1998	1999	2000
★★★★	★★★	★★★	★★★	★★

recommended wines

1998 Mount Horrocks Watervale, Clare Valley ★★★★ $$$
dry, full-bodied, full tannin, medium acidity **drink in 3–15 years**
Big, complex, tannic, and worth the wait for it to be ready.

1998 Clarendon Hills Liandra, Clarendon ★★★ $$$
dry, full-bodied, full tannin, medium acidity **drink in 3–15 years**
Clarendon Hills' intense Shirazes are revered and rare. Here's one that meets all expectations for a relatively affordable price.

1999 Rosemount Estate Balmoral Syrah, McLaren Vale ★★★ $$$
dry, full-bodied, full tannin, high acidity **drink in 3–10 years**
A wine with identity issues: full berry flavor versus smoky tannin. Most Australian bottlings offer one or the other; this has both.

1999 Tyrrell's Reserve, McLaren Vale ★★★ $$$
dry, full-bodied, full tannin, medium acidity **drink in 3–10 years**
Big and brash, with bold blackberry taste and the bourbonlike flavor that comes from aging in American oak.

1999 Grant Burge Filsell, Barossa ★★★ $$
dry, full-bodied, full tannin, medium acidity **drink now–10 years**
Good blackberry, pepper, and cocoa flavors.

1998 Rufus Stone, McLaren Vale ★★ $$$
dry, full-bodied, full tannin, high acidity **drink in 2–8 years**
Very good Shiraz, lots of fruit flavor, for sure, but also exotic spices and mouth-puckering minerality.

1998 Blue Pyrenees Estate, Victoria ★★ $$
dry, full-bodied, medium tannin, medium acidity **drink now–8 years**
The interesting blackberry, menthol, and spice flavors all just seem to grow and grow.

1998 Penfolds Bin 128, Coonawarra ★★ $$
dry, full-bodied, full tannin, high acidity **drink in 3–10 years**
A strapping wine. Strong fruit, smoke, tobacco, and oak flavors.

1999 St. Hallet Faith, Barossa ★★ $$
dry, full-bodied, medium tannin, medium acidity **drink now–5 years**
Rich, full fruit flavors—delicious.

1999 Simon Hackett, McLaren Vale ★★ $$
dry, full-bodied, medium tannin, medium acidity **drink now–5 years**
A Shiraz that reminds you this grape is from the Northern Rhône. Not quite Hermitage or Cornas, but it would be at home nearby.

1999 Wynns Coonawarra Estate, Coonawarra ★★ $$
dry, full-bodied, full tannin, medium acidity **drink now–5 years**
Coonawara is known for deeply flavored Cabernets more than Shiraz, but here's one that deserves notice.

1999 Black Opal, South Eastern Australia ★★ $
dry, medium-bodied, medium tannin, medium acidity **drink now–2 years**
Good, all-purpose Shiraz. Fruity enough for casual drinking, but with enough tannin and acidity to accompany food. Cedar notes add interest.

2000 Banrock Station, South Eastern Australia ★ $
dry, full-bodied, medium tannin, medium acidity **drink now–2 years**
The kind of smooth, berry-packed wine that made Americans fall for Shiraz. Lovely drinking for a very nice price.

1998 Black Creek, South Eastern Australia ★ $
dry, medium-bodied, medium tannin, medium acidity **drink now–2 years**
Some fruitiness, some earthiness. A good deal for the price.

1999 Tyrrell's Wines Long Flat, South Australia ★ $
dry, medium-bodied, medium tannin, medium acidity **drink now**
Many inexpensive Shirazes are tasty but so fruity that they're difficult to pair with food. This one has nice acid balance that makes it great with meals.

CABERNET SAUVIGNON

Second to Shiraz in the number of acres planted, Cabernet Sauvignon in Australia makes wines that often have more blackberry flavor than you'd think would be possible to squeeze from a fruit that isn't actually a blackberry. Tannin is generally not as prominent as in Cabs from other countries, especially in the less-expensive wines. However, there are some distinctive (and tannic) bottles that go beyond simple fruit flavor.

at the table

A number of inexpensive Australian Cabernets are high in fruit and low in tannin, perfect for easy drinking. Sip them on their own or serve them with grilled sausages or meatloaf. Pair more complicated wines with lamb chops, beef tenderloin, venison or other game, or sharp cheeses, such as English cheddar. They also work well with meaty pasta dishes (think pasta Bolognese) and hearty legume or root-vegetable stews.

the bottom line Prices of Australian Cabernets are rising fast, but you'll still find some bottles from big producers at just under $13. The mid-range is creeping up from around $15 to near $20. Complex Cabernets can be found for around $30, definitely a bargain compared to many from California.

what to buy CABERNET SAUVIGNON

1996	1997	1998	1999	2000
★★★★	★★★	★★★	★★★	★★

recommended wines

1996 Montadam, Eden Valley ★★★★ $$$
dry, full-bodied, medium tannin, medium acidity **drink in 2–15 years**
The allure of long acclaimed Montadam generally escapes us, but this impresses with smooth Cabernet flavors that are rich yet restrained.

1999 Vasse Felix, Western Australia ★★★★ $$$
dry, medium-bodied, medium tannin, medium acidity **drink in 3–10 years**
It has all the full fruit flavor one expects from Down Under, but this serious wine also offers Graves-like minerality and Margaux-like finesse.

1996 Stonehaven Reserve, McLaren Vale ★★★ $$$
dry, full-bodied, full tannin, medium acidity **drink in 2–10 years**
Nothing missing here—fruit and strong floral flavors with herbal notes.

1998 Wynns Coonawarra Estate John Riddoch, Coonawarra ★★★ $$$
dry, full-bodied, full tannin, medium acidity **drink in 2–12 years**
Intense wine. Cassis and spice are complemented by cedar, earth, and mint.

1999 Black Opal, South Eastern Australia ★★ $
dry, full-bodied, medium tannin, medium acidity **drink now–2 years**
Easy to enjoy. Serve this smooth, fruit-filled wine at your next cookout.

1999 Wolf Blass Yellow Label, South Australia ★★ $
dry, full-bodied, medium tannin, medium acidity **drink now–2 years**
What a delicious wine! This is one to take when you're invited to a dinner party and want to give something good but not spend a lot.

2000 Lindemans Bin 45, South Eastern Australia ★ $
dry, medium-bodied, medium tannin, medium acidity **drink now–2 years**
Fruit flavors with a green pepper tinge in this always consistent wine.

other red wines

Some fine versions of Merlot are made in Australia, though it isn't as successful overall as it is elsewhere. Pinot Noir is becoming more common, with some great and some not-so-great results. Perhaps more interesting are the Rhône varieties, Grenache and Mourvèdre (often called Mataro), and blends.

the bottom line Merlot can be found for under $10, but unless you're desperate for cheap Merlot, skip it in favor of a better one or something else entirely. Good Pinot Noirs are a few dollars more. There are some good bottles of Grenache and Mourvèdre for around $20, though you can easily spend more. Blends start at $9, and the sky's the limit.

recommended wines

1999 Clarendon Hills Kangarilla Vineyard Old Vines Grenache, Clarendon ★★★★ $$$
dry, full-bodied, full tannin, medium acidity **drink in 2–10 years**
A portrait *en rouge*, composed of red cherry, raspberry, and currant flavors in a brick red wine.

1999 Rochford Macedon Ranges Pinot Noir, Victoria ★★★★ $$$
dry, medium-bodied, medium tannin, medium acidity **drink now–8 years**
The finest Australian Pinot Noir we've ever tasted. Beautifully balanced fruit, herb, and floral flavors dance together with great finesse.

1997 Grant Burge The Holy Trinity, Barossa ★★★ $$$
dry, full-bodied, full tannin, medium acidity **drink now–8 years**
A trinity of Grenache, Shiraz, and Mourvèdre in a Rhône-style wine.

1998 Penfolds Bin 389 Cabernet Sauvignon Shiraz, South Australia ★★★ $$
dry, full-bodied, full tannin, medium acidity **drink now–8 years**
Similarly inspired, and cut from the same cloth, here's the baby brother to Penfolds' legendary Grange. It's dense and delicious but needs lots of air.

1999 Primo Estate Il Briccone, Adelaide Plains ★★★ $$
dry, full-bodied, medium tannin, medium acidity **drink now–7 years**
Here's an Aus-Ital blend of lush Shiraz and fruity Sangiovese.

1999 Cape Mentelle Cabernet Sauvignon Merlot, Margaret River ★★ $$$
dry, full-bodied, full tannin, medium acidity **drink in 2–5 years**
There's some elegance here, but also the awkward (though oddly appealing) feeling of sucking on a chocolate, eucalyptus, and black cherry lozenge.

2000 Tyrrell's Wines Long Flat Red, Hunter Valley ★ $
dry, medium-bodied, medium tannin, medium acidity **drink now**
This is what we reach for when we're just tossing burgers on the barbie.

new zealand

The fine-wine industry in New Zealand is less than thirty years old. Despite this lack of experience, the country produces distinctive wines—from "what-in-the-world-is-in-this?" Sauvignon Blancs to classic Pinot Noirs that would please any red Burgundy lover.

on the label

Grape varieties are nearly always listed on New Zealand labels, along with the region and the vineyard. The great white wine areas are Hawke's Bay and Gisborne for Chardonnay, Marlborough for Sauvignon Blanc and Riesling. Martinborough and Central Otago are acclaimed for their Pinot Noir.

white wines

The complex fruit flavors in the generally light- to medium-bodied whites of New Zealand are preserved by fermenting and aging in stainless-steel tanks rather than oak barrels. A few producers are experimenting with wood, but to date their wines have not become as oaky as those from California and Australia.

SAUVIGNON BLANC

Not long ago, winemakers from other countries wishfully compared their often dull Sauvignon Blancs to those from France. Today, the benchmark for many vintners is New Zealand, where Sauvignon Blanc is the most lauded wine.

at the table

Its herbal, citrus, and peppery qualities make New Zealand Sauvignon Blanc one of the few wines that pairs easily with typically wine-killing asparagus, artichokes, and vinaigrette-dressed salads. But don't stop there. These wines work well with most non-meat dishes, especially herb-heavy ones, like pasta with pesto, gravlax, pizza Margherita with whole basil leaves, and herb-crusted fish. Sauvignon Blanc is also wonderful with fried chicken. Try spreading some goat cheese onto endive leaves and sprinkling them with coarse salt, cracked black pepper, and fresh herbs for an easy and delicious hors d'oeuvre that matches Sauvignon Blanc perfectly.

the bottom line You'll easily find simple wines for around $10. The price jumps to $18 for more complex ones. Some outstanding wines cost around $24.

recommended wines

1999 Caroline Bay, Marlborough ★★★ $$
dry, full-bodied, high acidity, no oak **drink now–5 years**
So what if the lush tropical fruit flavors—like those in a Riesling Auslese—aren't typical of New Zealand Sauvignon Blanc. We love this.

2000 Charles Wiffen, Marlborough ★★★ $$
dry, full-bodied, high acidity, no oak **drink now–3 years**
So aromatic, so floral, it's like knocking over a tray of cologne at the cosmetics counter. Full citrus and spice flavors and excellent acidity make for fine drinking.

2000 Cloudy Bay, Marlborough ★★★ $$
dry, medium-bodied, high acidity, no oak **drink now–2 years**
When you inhale the breathtakingly intense grapefruit aroma, you will understand what all other New Zealand Sauvignon Blancs aspire to.

2000 Mt. Difficulty, Central Otago ★★★ $$
dry, light-bodied, high acidity, no oak **drink now–2 years**
Tastes more of mellow fruit than the typical citrus and herbal flavors.

2000 Greenhough, Nelson ★★ $$
dry, medium-bodied, high acidity, no oak **drink now–1 year**
New Zealand, New Zealand, New Zealand. A wine that screams its origins. Herbal is the key word.

2000 Lynskeys Wairau Peaks, Marlborough ★★ $$
dry, medium-bodied, medium acidity, no oak **drink now–1 year**
So full of passion fruit flavors,Cupid could dip his arrows in this one.

2000 Mills Reef Reserve, Hawke's Bay ★★ $$
dry, medium-bodied, medium acidity, medium oak **drink now–5 years**
We feel that oak often overwhelms the flavor of New Zealand Sauvignon Blanc. But here's an oak-aged wine that holds its own.

2000 Whitehaven, Marlborough ★★ $$
dry, full-bodied, medium acidity, no oak **drink now–2 years**
Seems like someone crushed a few kiwifruits into this one. Interesting tropical fruit flavors and a little green pepper.

2000 Brancott Vineyards, Marlborough ★★ $
dry, medium-bodied, high acidity, no oak **drink now–2 years**
Take the same approach to this as you would to a ripe, pungent cheese: Ignore the strong aromas and indulge in the delicious flavors.

CHARDONNAY

Chardonnay almost never plays second fiddle to Sauvignon Blanc, but it definitely does in New Zealand. There is actually a lot more Chardonnay planted, and some excellent wines are made from it, but they lack the distinction of the country's Sauvignon Blancs.

at the table

With more fruity flavor, much higher acidity, and lighter body, New Zealand Chardonnays are a lot more versatile than those from Australia or California. Fish and shellfish are the obvious pairings. These Chardonnays are also very complementary to chicken dishes, no matter what the sauce. The high acidity makes them good with creamy sauces—that tartness cuts right through the cream to refresh the palate. And the fruitiness makes them nice sippers anytime.

the bottom line Many good New Zealand Chardonnays sell for a bit over $20, which is in line with those from California and Australia.

NECESSITY IS THE MOTHER OF DISTINCTION

One would rarely use the word *buttery* to describe any white varietal from New Zealand. Ironically, the country has its dairy farmers to thank for this welcome distinction from the style so prevalent in California and Australia, where oak barrels impart that butter flavor, among other characteristics. It would have been a financial hardship for New Zealand's nascent winemakers to import oak barrels from halfway around the world. But with a huge dairy industry, the country had a ready supply of inexpensive stainless-steel containers. Thus vintners are able to milk the grapes for all their luscious, grassy fruit flavors.

recommended wines

2000 Alpha Domus Unwooded, Hawke's Bay ★★★ $$
dry, medium-bodied, medium acidity, no oak **drink now–2 years**
A smooth and tasty, citrusy wine. Very good.

2000 Villa Maria Private Bin, East Coast ★★★ $$
dry, medium-bodied, medium acidity, medium oak **drink now–5 years**
Not too much of this or too much of that. Here's a wine that balances oak, fruit, mineral, herb, and acid elements almost perfectly.

2000 Charles Wiffen, Marlborough ★ $$
dry, full-bodied, medium acidity, light oak **drink now–2 years**
Comforting creamy, nutty, fruity flavors.

other white wines

New Zealand's bright sunshine and cool climate make for delightful Rieslings—light-bodied yet full of delicious fruit flavors balanced by zingy acidity. Gewürztraminer, Riesling's compatriot from Alsace, also does exceptionally well.

at the table

Riesling is an excellent match for moderately spicy Asian food: fish flavored with sesame oil, soy sauce, coriander, and mild chili paste; almost any sweet-and-sour or hot-and-sour dish; or lightly spiced Indian dishes like chicken *biryani* or tandoori shrimp. Alternatively, you can pair it with prosciutto and melon, shrimp cocktail, fresh crabmeat with a tangy sauce, or fried calamari. Gewürztraminer is also a natural with cuisines of the Near and Far East, but it's a shoo-in for rich poultry dishes like braised turkey legs, duck confit, and roast goose.

the bottom line Few New Zealand Rieslings and Gewürztraminers are imported into the U.S. because demand isn't high enough—yet. As a result, there aren't many bottles to choose from, but prices are nonetheless rather low. We don't expect things to remain this way for long; for now, though, you should be able to find a nice wine for between $10 and $15.

recommended wines

2000 Huia Gewürztraminer, Marlborough ★★★ $$
dry, medium-bodied, high acidity, no oak **drink now–4 years**
Exotica galore. Luscious aromas and flavors of rosewater, jasmine, pistachios, and spices.

2000 Huia Riesling, Marlborough ★★★ $$
dry, full-bodied, high acidity, no oak **drink now–6 years**
A lovely Riesling—honeysuckle aromas and full fruit flavors.

2000 Allan Scott Riesling, Marlborough ★★ $$
dry, medium-bodied, high acidity, no oak **drink now–5 years**
One of New Zealand's wine pioneers offers a beautiful, bone-dry bottling with refreshing fruit, floral, and spice flavors.

2000 Greenhough Riesling, Nelson ★★ $$
dry, medium-bodied, medium acidity, no oak **drink now–2 years**
A wine so smooth it's almost slippery—all the better to allow the tropical fruit flavors to slide down easily.

red wines

PINOT NOIR

Many people think New Zealand will soon be home to the finest Pinot Noir outside Burgundy. The most-planted red grape in the country, it does best in the cooler wine regions, like Martinborough and Central Otago.

at the table

Wherever it's made, Pinot Noir is one of the most versatile of wines. Seared medium-rare salmon (or salmon prepared any way, for that matter) is the perfect match, but try it also with a range of dishes: chicken and dumplings, pork burgers, or veal stew with spring vegetables.

the bottom line If there's a country that produces excellent-quality, inexpensive Pinot Noir, we don't know about it. Count on paying at least $20, up to the mid-$30s and higher.

recommended wines

1999 Martinborough Vineyard, Martinborough ★★★ $$$
dry, medium-bodied, medium tannin, medium acidity **drink now–10 years**
Where to place this Pinot? It has the smokiness of Burgundy, the fruitiness of California, and a bit of mysterious spiciness. Whatever, it's very, very good.

1999 Felton Road, Central Otago ★★ $$$
dry, medium-bodied, medium tannin, medium acidity **drink now–8 years**
Full strawberry and spice flavors remind us more of a Cru Beaujolais than a Burgundy, but that doesn't mean we're not impressed.

1999 Brancott Vineyards Reserve, Marlborough ★★ $$
dry, medium-bodied, medium tannin, medium acidity **drink now–8 years**
A luscious wine with loads of fruit flavor and a hint of cinnamon. Great with ham.

1999 Peregrine, Central Otago ★★ $$
dry, light-bodied, medium tannin, medium acidity **drink now–5 years**
Faint cherry aromas makes it seem like a simple sipping wine, but the balance of spicy fruit and acidity makes this a wine to plan a meal around.

other red wines

After Pinot Noir, Cabernet Sauvignon and Merlot are the most common reds from New Zealand. Many are uninspired, but there are some successes, particularly from Hawke's Bay and Wairarapa.

at the table

Merlot or Bordeaux-style blends from New Zealand are both good matches for any lamb preparation (a good thing, considering the country's sheep-to-human ratio is thirteen to one). Try either with spit-roasted leg of lamb from the barbecue. A platter of sharp or nutty cheeses like provolone, aged Gouda, and fontina is the perfect accompaniment. Serve Syrahs with rich meats.

the bottom line There are no bargains here. Count on paying at least $20 for a Merlot, up to the mid-$40s or higher for a good-quality blend.

recommended wines

1999 Goldwater Esslin Merlot, Waiheke Island ★★★ $$$$
dry, full-bodied, full tannin, medium acidity **drink in 2–8 years**
Not your average, easy-drinking, plummy Merlot; the focus here is on earthiness, with lots of mineral, smoke, and tar flavors and just a taste of cherry.

1998 Matariki Syrah, Hawke's Bay ★★★ $$
dry, full-bodied, full tannin, medium acidity **drink now–6 years**
A textbook (advanced, mind you) Syrah, full of fruit, smoke, tar, and vanilla flavors. Just right for braised lamb shanks.

1999 Alpha Domus "The Navigator," Hawke's Bay ★★ $$
dry, medium-bodied, medium tannin, medium acidity **drink now–5 years**
A Bordeaux-style blend from about as far from Bordeaux as you can get.

argentina & chile

South American wine didn't hit the U.S. market in a big way until the late 1980s. America's first reaction was enchantment; we loved the full flavor and body of the wines, not to mention the low cost. When the initial spell wore off, we became more critical. But now a flood of investment from Europe and California has improved both viticulture and vinification, and we're charmed once more. The quality is higher than ever—as is, alas, the price.

Wine has long been an essential part of life in Argentina, a country populated largely by the descendants of Spanish and Italian settlers. Argentina is the fifth largest wine producer in the world. Most Argentine wine is, charitably put, of rustic quality. But a number of vintners are making excellent stuff, and, happily, much of it is finding a place on the shelves of U.S. wine shops.

on the label

Argentina labels by grape variety and region. Luján de Cuyo in the upper Mendoza valley is good for Malbec. Other parts of Mendoza, especially Maipú, are known for Cabernet Sauvignon. The area around the town of Cafayate in the region of Salta is famed for Torrontés, as is the region La Rioja. Inspired, perhaps, by the fashion in California, some wineries are now adding vineyard designations to their labels to indicate higher quality.

Chile
SALTA
Cafayate
Pacific
Ocean
Argentina
LA RIOJA
Aconcagua
VALPARAISO
SANTIAGO
Casablanca
Puente Alto
Maipo
Maipú
Atlantic
Ocean
Rapel
Central Valley
Luján de Cuyo
BUENOS AIRES
San Rafael
Maule
MENDOZA
Featured
Wine-Growing
Regions

red wines

Argentina raises a lot of cattle, so it's no wonder that red wines dominate. You'll find the usual international varieties, such as Cabernet Sauvignon and Merlot, but it is Malbec (mahl-bec), an underappreciated grape from Bordeaux, that reigns supreme.

at the table

You can guess what to have with Argentina's reds: beef, whether braised short ribs, grilled steak, or roast prime rib. Simple reds are great for barbecues, especially when hamburgers or ribs are on the menu. Vegetarians should think hearty: eggplant lasagna, grilled portobello mushrooms, or a selection of sharp or smoked cheeses.

the bottom line The days of $6 reds are quickly passing, but you can still find good wines for under $10. For those who want something more luxurious, a few wineries are now providing bottles priced at about $50.

what to buy RED WINES

1996	1997	1998	1999	2000
★★★★	★★★	★★★	★★★	★★

recommended wines

1998 Alta Vista Alto, Mendoza ★★★★ $$$$
dry, full-bodied, full tannin, high acidity **drink now–10 years**
Argentina is one of the largest wine producers in the world. A few more wines like this, and it will rank among the greats in quality, too.

1999 Tikal Amorío Malbec, Altos de Mendoza ★★★★ $$$
dry, full-bodied, full tannin, medium acidity **drink now–12 years**
The first sip was thrilling. By the second, we were in love. Excellent.

1997 Catena Alta Zapata Vineyard Cabernet Sauvignon, Mendoza ★★★ $$$
dry, full-bodied, full tannin, medium acidity **drink 2–10 years**
If you drink this now, you'll find only a hint of its potential. Allow time to bring out all the fruit, herb, and mineral flavors.

1995 Famiglia Bianchi Cabernet Sauvignon, San Rafael ★★★ $$$
dry, full-bodied, medium tannin, medium acidity drink now–8 years
Simply terrific now, full of cherry and nut flavors that are in perfect balance. Find some Argentine beef and have a feast.

1997 Terrazas de Los Andes Las Compuertas Vineyard Gran Malbec, Mendoza ★★ $$$
dry, full-bodied, full tannin, high acidity drink now–5 years
Full fruit, spice, and vanilla flavors in excellent balance.

1998 Alta Vista Malbec, Mendoza ★★ $$
dry, full-bodied, medium tannin, high acidity drink now–3 years
Try this and you'll understand why Malbec is considered the best grape in Argentina.

1999 Catena Lunlunta Vineyards Malbec, Mendoza ★★ $$
dry, full-bodied, medium tannin, medium acidity drink now–3 years
Nicolas Catena needs to sell a lot of bottles to pay for his elaborate new winery. If he keeps producing wines this good, he shouldn't have trouble.

1997 Felipe Rutini Reserva Malbec, Mendoza ★★ $$
dry, full-bodied, full tannin, high acidity drink now–5 years
Rutini's Italian heritage shows in this wine, with the acidity and full flavors you expect from a Riserva Chianti.

1999 Alamos Bonarda, Mendoza ★★ $
dry, full-bodied, medium tannin, medium acidity drink now–3 years
Wines made from the Bonarda grape are rarely available. That may be a good reason to buy this wine; its great flavor is an even better one.

1997 San Huberto Cabernet Sauvignon, La Rioja ★★ $
dry, medium-bodied, medium tannin, high acidity drink now–3 years
With lovely fruit flavors and an invigorating astringency to balance them, this wine is made for food.

1999 Trapiche Oak Cask Malbec, Mendoza ★★ $
dry, full-bodied, full tannin, medium acidity drink now–6 years
A full-fruit style of Malbec, luscious from the first sniff to the last drop. The fruit flavors will really shine after the tannin mellows.

1999 Don Miguel Gascón Sangiovese, Mendoza ★ $
dry, medium-bodied, medium tannin, high acidity drink now–3 years
The style of Gascón's wines is super fruity, regardless of variety. Even tart and astringent Sangiovese gets the same treatment.

2000 Falling Star Merlot-Malbec, Mendoza ★ $
dry, light-bodied, medium tannin, high acidity **drink now**
Need a tasty wine with enough acidity to refresh the palate between bites of greasy pizza or hearty pasta? Look no further.

2000 Santa Julia Malbec-Cabernet Sauvignon, Mendoza ★ $
dry, medium-bodied, medium tannin, medium acidity **drink now–2 years**
The berry flavors with a touch of vanilla aren't all that complex, but this is just right for a barbecue.

white wines

Argentina's most interesting whites are made from Torrontés (tor-ohn-TESS) or Semillon (SEH-mee-yohn). Flowery Torrontés is light and refreshing. Heavier-bodied Semillon has hints of orange and nut flavors, with good acidity. Sauvignon Blanc offers even more acidity, plus limey flavor. Aromatic Viognier is also planted. If you can't do without your Chardonnay, you'll find a range of bottlings, a few of them quite good, made in a style that's between big, buttery California Chard and steely Chablis.

at the table

We'd be happy to sip Torrontés on its own while sitting around the pool or as an aperitif before dinner. Though dry, it has enough sugar and acidity to complement lightly spiced dishes like *pad thai,* green papaya salad, Thai beef salad, or sushi with lots of wasabi in the soy sauce. Semillon is excellent for chicken roasted with garlic, grilled vegetables with olive oil and herbs, or smoked fish. Sauvignon Blanc is a natural with fried fish. Pair Viognier with any light vegetable soup. The medium-bodied Chardonnays complement sautéed veal cutlets or pork chops with mustard sauce.

the bottom line Hardly anyone seems to know about Torrontés, so you can pick up a fine bottle for the supremely low price of $6. Sauvignon Blanc, Semillon, and Viognier sell for about $8 to $10. Most Chardonnays will be under $10, but there are some slightly better bottles for about $13, and at least one, even better, selling for $45.

recommended wines

2000 Catena Agrelo Vineyard Chardonnay, Mendoza ★★★ $$
dry, medium-bodied, high acidity, medium oak **drink now–7 years**
We're big fans of this kind of polite oak that lurks in the background but lets the complex fruit flavors speak for themselves.

2000 Santa Julia Torrontés, Mendoza ★★★ $
dry, light-bodied, high acidity, no oak **drink now**
As exuberant and refreshing as the first burst of springtime, full of honeysuckle and lavender, citrus and herbal flavors.

2000 Valentin Bianchi Sauvignon Blanc, San Rafael ★★★ $
dry, medium-bodied, high acidity, no oak **drink now–2 years**
Great acidity, perfect for pairing with butter or cream sauces. It will cut right through the richness to refresh your palate for the next bite.

1999 Alamos Chardonnay, Mendoza ★ $
dry, medium-bodied, medium acidity, light oak **drink now–1 year**
The toasty, fruity taste of this wine shows its New World influence, but rather than the usual buttery flavor from oak, it has fine minerality.

1999 Don Miguel Gascón Viognier, Mendoza ★ $
dry, medium-bodied, medium acidity, no oak **drink now–2 years**
Not the best Viognier we've ever had, but the spice, citrus, floral, and mineral flavors sure are tasty.

2000 Falling Star Sauvignon Blanc-Semillon, Mendoza ★ $
dry, light-bodied, high acidity, no oak **drink now**
Like a green apple, walnut, and mesclun salad dressed with a lime vinaigrette. Crisp and tasty.

chile

With the ample sunshine, warm climate, and abundant water from the melting snow of the Andes, grapes grow well in Chile—perhaps too well. Many producers who made a lot of money in the late 1980s from inexpensive exports to the U.S. became lax, favoring high crop yields over the quality that comes from low yields. But other vintners took the difficult path toward excellence. Due in part to investments from the Mondavis, France's Rothschilds, and Spain's Torres family, many Chilean wines are now excellent.

on the label

Chilean wine labels usually mention grape varieties, with the exception of those on Bordeaux-style blends. Regional designations are common, the most frequent being those in the 600-mile-long Central Valley, which contains the country's noteworthy Maipo (my-po), Maule, and Rapel regions, all known for their red wines. The cool coastal area of Casablanca specializes in whites.

red wines

The Bordeaux varieties Cabernet Sauvignon and Merlot are the big grapes in Chile. Carmenère (car-men-air) probably makes the most interesting, if somewhat unreliable, Chilean wines. The country is establishing its reputation for fine wine on a few gold-plated Bordeaux blends.

at the table

A lot of Chilean reds are simple and fruity, just right for basic meatloaf, beef or buffalo burgers, grilled sausages, or sweet and spicy barbecued chicken (think hot mustard and honey barbecue sauce). Save more complex wines for braised meats, such as lamb shanks or pot roast. The elite blends are made for roast beef or rack of lamb.

the bottom line For under $10, you'll find a number of Chilean Cabernet Sauvignons. Within the same range a few Carmenères can be found, but buying them is a gamble; some offer terrific value, many are best left on the shelf. Stepping up to the $15 to $20 range will get you many well-made wines. Some of the top blends are now selling for $70.

recommended wines

1998 Almavíva, Puente Alto ★★★★ $$$$

dry, medium-bodied, medium tannin, medium acidity drink now–15 years

Royalty always seems to intermarry. Here, Bordeaux's Mouton-Rothschild joins Chile's Concha y Toro to produce a regal wine.

1998 Errazuriz Don Maximiano Founder's Reserve, Aconcagua Valley ★★★ $$$$
dry, full-bodied, medium tannin, medium acidity drink now–12 years
Fruity, spicy, and smoky. We'd save this flavorful wine for a fine prime rib roast.

1997 Concha y Toro Don Melchor Puente Alto Vineyard Private Reserve Cabernet Sauvignon, Maipo Valley ★★★ $$$
dry, medium-bodied, medium tannin, medium acidity now–10 years
If you lament the trend toward Cabs that seem more like fruit bombs than wine, this dry, dry wine is for you.

1997 Cousiño-Macul Finis Terrae, Maipo Valley ★★★ $$$
dry, full-bodied, full tannin, medium acidity drink now–8 years
Chock-full of fruit and the tannin to balance it.

1997 Santa Rita Casa Real Alto Santa Rita Old Vines Vineyard Estate Bottled Cabernet Sauvignon, Maipo Valley ★★★ $$$
dry, full-bodied, full tannin, medium acidity drink now–8 years
A powerhouse vaguely reminiscent of a Napa Cab, but more acidity makes it easier to pair with food.

1999 Caliterra Arboleda Carmenère, Maipo Valley ★★★ $$
dry, full-bodied, full tannin medium acidity drink in 2–10 years
Here's a Carmenère by which to judge all others, with bold cherry and peppercorn flavors.

1998 Casa Lapostolle Cuvée Alexandre Cabernet Sauvignon, Colchagua Valley ★★★ $$
dry, full-bodied, medium tannin, medium acidity drink now–8 years
Let this breathe for an hour so the sulfur aroma dissipates; once it does, you'll be treated to a mélange of fruit flavors.

1999 Caliterra Arboleda Syrah, Colchagua Valley ★★ $$
dry, full-bodied, full tannin, medium acidity drink now–8 years
Smoky and so thick it's almost syrupy, this concentrated wine has everything a Syrah should.

1999 Santa Rita Medalla Real Special Reserve Cabernet Sauvignon, Maipo Valley ★★ $$
dry, full-bodied, medium tannin, medium acidity drink now–6 years
Bittersweet: berry flavors balanced by nice bitter-chocolate and herb notes.

1999 Baron Philippe de Rothschild Escudo Rojo, Maipo ★ $$
dry, full-bodied, full tannin, medium acidity drink in 1–8 years
This is a blend of Bordeaux varieties, including Cabernet Sauvignon and Merlot, with Chile's Carmenère. It's good.

1998 Casa Lapostolle Cabernet Sauvignon, Rapel Valley ★ $
dry, full-bodied, full tannin, medium acidity **drink now–3 years**
This reminds us of the fruity Chilean wines we loved not so many years ago, not the least for being inexpensive. This one's a lot better, though.

1999 Santa Rita Reserva Carmenère, Rapel Valley ★ $
dry, full-bodied, full tannin, medium acidity **drink now–3 years**
You can taste the soil this wine's grapes were grown on. It's full of earthy, fruity flavors and has just the right amounts of acidity and tannin.

white wines

Chile's whites are not yet peers of the world's best, but for the money, they're quite attractive. The Chardonnays are medium-bodied with a touch of oak. The Sauvignon Blancs and Rieslings refresh with good zippy acidity.

at the table

Chilean Chardonnay goes well with chicken and meaty fish like swordfish or monkfish. With lots of acidity, Sauvignon Blanc is great with salads or shellfish like steamed littleneck clams. Pair Rieslings with oysters.

the bottom line There are plenty of Chilean whites for under $10. A few Chardonnays made in the full California style sell for around $20.

recommended wines

1999 Concha y Toro Terrunyo Sauvignon Blanc, Casablanca Valley ★★★ $$
dry, full-bodied, medium acidity, no oak **drink now–2 years**
If war ever broke out between the pungent, herbal style of Sauvignon Blanc and the more fruity, citrusy version, this would be the perfect mediator.

1999 Casa Lapostolle Cuvée Alexandre Chardonnay, Casablanca Valley ★★ $$
dry, full-bodied, medium acidity, medium oak **drink now–8 years**
Loads of fruitiness, but the mineral flavors are just as full. Nice.

2000 Cousiño-Macul Doña Isidora Riesling, Maipo Valley ★★ $
dry, medium-bodied, high acidity, no oak **drink now–3 years**
The antidote to the sea of South American Chardonnays that increasingly wash upon our shores. Really appealing fruit and mineral flavors.

2000 Errazuriz Estate Chardonnay, Casablanca Valley ★★ $
dry, medium-bodied, medium acidity, no oak **drink now–1 year**
A nice wine for lovers of creamy, tropical-fruit-flavored Chardonnays. Good price, too.

2000 Veramonte Alto de Casablanca Estate Chardonnay, Casablanca Valley ★★ $
dry, full-bodied, medium acidity, light oak **drink now–2 years**
Run by California's Franciscan winery, Veramonte makes Chard that plays all the California notes. Rich tropical fruit and vanilla flavors.

south africa

Nearly two centuries ago, South African wines were among the most revered in the world. When apartheid was dismantled in the early 1990s, people inside and outside South Africa had great hopes that the country's wine industry would enjoy a revival of its former glory. That may not be recaptured for a while yet. But now, free from stifling government controls, winemakers are selecting better grapes and applying new techniques to make some excellent wines. The country is definitely a wine source to watch.

grapes & styles

Classic European grape varieties are grown throughout the country. Furthermore, unlike most of the so-called New World (the U.S., Australia, New Zealand, and South America), South Africa adheres to the European model—making wines that have more finesse than boldness. Aging in new-oak barrels, which often imparts strong oak flavors, is a novelty in the country. Instead, vinters aim for subtlety and expression of *terroir* (see page 78) in their wines, making them especially complementary to many dishes.

on the label

South Africa's Wine of Origin (WO) system is similar to France's Appellation d'Origine Contrôlée, although rules are less stringent. The most celebrated wine regions are Stellenbosch, Paarl, and Constantia. Labeling by varietal, at least among exported wines, is customary.

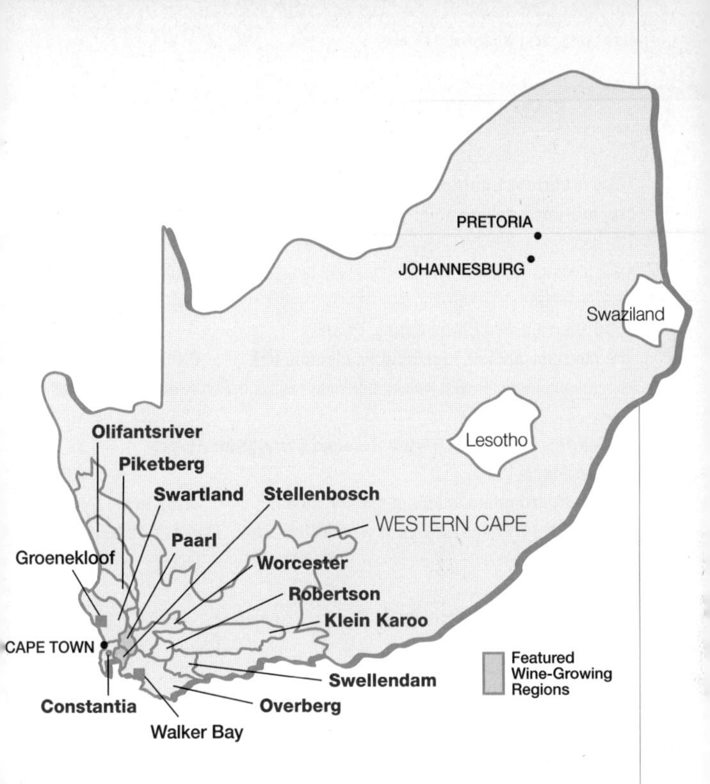

white wines

South Africa's main white is Chenin Blanc (also called Steen). Chardonnay is increasingly prominent, and Sauvignon Blanc is getting some attention.

at the table

Chenin Blanc's gentle citrus and melon flavors make it wonderful as an aperitif, but also try it with smoked fish or Southeast Asian soups, such as shrimp and lemongrass. The minerality and good acidity of South African Chardonnay are great with a range of seafood dishes, like lobster with butter, or sautéed soft-shell crabs. Assertive, lemony Sauvignon Blanc complements flavorful, oily fish like salmon or bluefish.

the bottom line Most Chardonnays cost $10 to $30; those for around $20 are great values. Sauvignon Blanc prices are $8 to about $20 or a bit higher. Chenin Blanc can be found for under $8, with the most deluxe versions selling for over $20.

recommended wines

1998 Meerlust Chardonnay, Stellenbosch ★★★★ $$
dry, full-bodied, high acidity, light oak **drink now–10 years**
The best South African Chardonnay we've ever had. Intense herbal, especially mint, flavors balanced by a background of tangy citrus and nutty notes.

2000 Glen Carlou Chardonnay, Paarl ★★★ $$
dry, medium-bodied, high acidity, medium oak **drink now–5 years**
Mineral and more mineral flavors dominate this wine. Some lemon-lime notes.

2000 Kanu Bulkamp Limited Release Sauvignon Blanc, Stellenbosch ★★★ $$
dry, medium-bodied, medium acidity, no oak **drink now–2 years**
Smoky, buttery, limey. This wine is a perfect match for fish or shellfish cooked on the grill.

2000 Mulderbosch Sauvignon Blanc, Stellenbosch ★★★ $$
dry, full-bodied, high acidity, no oak **drink now–2 years**
An unusual and refreshing Sauvignon, with lots of tart lime and kiwi flavors.

1999 Rustenberg Chardonnay, Stellenbosch ★★★ $$
dry, full-bodied, high acidity, medium oak **drink now–5 years**
Looking for Premier Cru–quality Burgundy at an affordable price? Here you go.

1999 Thelema Chardonnay, Stellenbosch ★★★ $$
dry, full-bodied, high acidity, medium oak **drink now–8 years**
This is an oaky wine, but its great minerality and light fruit flavor mean it bears no resemblance to typical Chards from Australia or California.

2000 Brampton Sauvignon Blanc, Stellenbosch ★★★ $
dry, medium-bodied, high acidity, no oak **drink now–1 year**
A wine made for oysters. Mineral laden, with lemon-lime and herb flavors, too.

1999 Kanu Chardonnay, Stellenbosch ★★ $$
dry, medium-bodied, medium acidity, medium oak **drink now–3 years**
The toasty qualities of this wine remind us of New World Chardonnay, but the light, subtle citrus flavor makes us think Old World.

1998 Mulderbosch Chenin Blanc, Stellenbosch ★★ $$
dry, full-bodied, medium acidity, medium oak **drink now–5 years**
Chenin Blanc as it's made nowhere else, with toasty oak and lots of lime flavor. It's good now, but give it a couple of years to get really interesting.

2000 Kanu Chenin Blanc, Stellenbosch ★★ $
dry, medium-bodied, medium acidity, no oak **drink now–2 years**
Nice fruity flavors make this good for casual sipping, and its smoke and mineral flavors make it great with dinner as well.

2000 Cape Indaba Sauvignon Blanc, Western Cape ★ $
dry, light-bodied, medium acidity, no oak **drink now**
If you love the jalapeño and lime flavors of some Sauvignon Blanc, you'll be moonstruck with this one.

2000 KWV Steen, Western Cape ★ $
off-dry, medium-bodied, medium acidity, no oak **drink now**
A simple sipping wine with appealing melon flavor, a bit of grassiness, and just a hint of sweetness.

red wines

South Africa's red wines are simply terrific. Generous sunshine makes the grapes ripen easily, so the wines are full-bodied and have plenty of fruit flavor. Miraculously, they are also imbued with the complexity that minerality and smokiness give. Cabernet Sauvignon, Merlot, and Syrah (called Shiraz as in Australia) are all absolutely stellar. The country's unique Pinotage (pee-no-tahj) is worth checking out for more than curiosity's sake. Simple versions of this wine resemble Beaujolais Nouveau; the best are full-bodied with velvety tannin.

at the table

Serve South African Merlots and red blends when you would the same varietals made anywhere—with red meat. Peppery South African Shiraz is great with spice-crusted meats (think steak au poivre) and chili, both vegetarian and con carne. The simple Pinotages, slightly chilled, are great with pizza and cheeseburgers. More complex bottles are especially complementary to quail, duck, goose, or roast game.

the bottom line Nearly all of the South African reds start at around $10, with the majority of them selling for between $18 and $24. You'll find a few trophy wines that are priced at $40 or even more.

recommended wines

1997 Delaire Merlot, Stellenbosch ★★★ $$$
dry, full-bodied, medium tannin, high acidity **drink now–5 years**
Sipping this is like slipping into an herb-scented bath. There are very nice fruit flavors, but the wine's eucalyptus, mint, and mineral notes really take center stage.

1998 Mont du Toit, Coastal Region ★★★ $$$
dry, full-bodied, medium tannin, medium acidity **drink now–6 years**
Proof that globalization has its advantages. Two outstanding German vintners make this excellent wine in South Africa from French grape varieties.

1998 Rustenberg Peter Barlow, Stellenbosch ★★★ $$$
dry, full-bodied, full tannin, medium acidity **drink in 2–10 years**
It isn't enough to open the bottle to let the genie out of this one; give it plenty of air so the black cherry flavor can get past the minerality and smokiness.

1999 Cloof Pinotage, Groenekloof ★★★ $$
dry, full-bodied, full tannin, high acidity **drink now–5 years**
If you're looking for a big tannic wine whose mission in life is to accompany red meat, this one is an ideal choice.

1998 Kanu Limited Release Shiraz, Stellenbosch ★★★ $$
dry, medium-bodied, medium tannin, medium acidity **drink now–5 years**
A terrific wine, as tasty as a bowl of chilled black cherries in July. And the addition of toasty oak flavors makes it absolutely luscious.

1998 Mulderbosch Faithful Hound, Stellenbosch ★★★ $$
dry, full-bodied, full tannin, high acidity **drink in 1–8 years**
The name fits for us. We're as faithful as a hound to this wine, one of our favorites from South Africa. Smoky and earthy, it's just the thing for spit-roasted meats.

1999 Wildekrans Pinotage, Walker Bay ★★★ $$
dry, full-bodied, full tannin, high acidity **drink now–5 years**
This has lusty flavor, with lots of nicely balanced cherry and spice, and tar flavors, all held together in elegant balance.

1998 Delaire Cabernet Sauvignon/Merlot, Stellenbosch 
dry, full-bodied, full tannin, high acidity **drink now–5 years**
Don't even think of drinking this on its own; the berry flavors are tasty enough, but its complex mineral and herb qualities really perk up the palate for food.

1998 Rupert & Rothschild Vignerons Baron Edmond, Coastal Region ★★ $$$
dry, full-bodied, full tannin, medium acidity **drink now–5 years**
Named in honor of Lafite-Rothschild's late owner, the grape varieties are from Bordeaux, but the smoky, herbal flavors are distinctly South African.

1998 Kanu Limited Release Merlot, Stellenbosch ★★ $$
dry, full-bodied, medium tannin, medium acidity **drink now–5 years**
The good black cherry and smoke flavors here cry out for braised meat.

1999 Mont du Toit Hawequas, Coastal Region ★★ $$
dry, medium-bodied, medium tannin, medium acidity **drink now–3 years**
An exceptionally fruity wine, nicely balanced by its tannin and acidity.

2000 Cape Indaba Merlot, Western Cape ★ $
dry, medium-bodied, light tannin, medium acidity **drink now–1 year**
The fact that sales of this wine help support a worthy scholarship fund might make you buy your first bottle. The flavor will make you come back for another.

2000 Cape Indaba Shiraz, Western Cape ★ $
dry, medium-bodied, medium tannin, medium acidity **drink now–2 years**
Not as fruity as most Australian Shiraz, this has a bit more finesse, with a nice balance between fruit and smoke flavors.

champagne & other sparkling wines

Nothing says celebration like the pop of a Champagne cork. Whether it's a simple California fizzy with a plastic stopper or one of the grand vintage wines of the Champagne region, sparklers put smiles on people's faces.

at the table

Sparkling wine ranks near the top of the list of possible aperitifs. With its relatively high acidity, it's also terrific with food. Richer styles, like many vintage Champagnes, are wonderful with fish, chicken, pork, or veal served with creamy sauces, as well as escargots. Medium-bodied sparkling wines do well with all shellfish. Off-dry versions are fantastic with brunch dishes like eggs Benedict. Off-dry wines are also great with spicy Asian cuisines.

champagne

In Europe, only wines made in the Champagne region of France using the *méthode champenoise* technique may be called Champagne. This nicety is often ignored outside Europe.

grapes & styles

Like most French wines, Champagne is normally a blend. The grapes permitted in Champagne are Chardonnay, Pinot Noir, and Pinot Meunier. Wines labeled Blanc de Blancs "white from white" (grapes), are 100 percent Chardonnay. Much less common is Blanc de Noirs "white from black," which is made from Pinot Noir or Pinot Meunier.

on the label

Most bottlings mix wines from several years in order to maintain a consistent house style; such nonvintage wines should not be regarded as inferior. Most Champagne is dry, but levels of sweetness vary according to the amount of added sugar. From driest to sweetest, the categories are: Extra Brut, Brut (the most common), Extra Dry, Sec, Demi-Sec, and Doux.

the bottom line Expect to pay from just under $25 up to $35 for regular nonvintage sparkling wines, $50 to $80 for vintage Champagnes, and well over $100 for the most exalted *prestige cuvées*.

what to buy VINTAGE CHAMPAGNE

1987	1988	1989	1990	1991	1992
nonvintage	★★★★	★★★	★★★★	★	★★

1993	1994	1995	1996	1997
★★	★★	★★★	★★★★	★★★

recommended wines

NV Krug Grande Cuvée Brut ★★★★ $$$$
dry, full-bodied, medium acidity
Here's a magnificent wine that has wonderful aromas and flavors of baked apples and peaches.

1988 Lanson Noble Cuvée Brut ★★★★ $$$$
dry, full-bodied, high acidity
Lanson was one of Champagne's great producers, and this grand wine shows they still can be.

1992 Nicolas Feuillatte Palmes d'Or
Grande Cuvée Brut ★★★★ $$$$
dry, full-bodied, high acidity
The pungent fruit flavors of this wonderful wine are almost cassislike.

1994 Taittinger Comtes de Champagne
Blanc de Blancs Brut ★★★★ $$$$
dry, full-bodied, medium acidity
Taittinger's top Champagne is graced with an unusual array of flavors that evoke citrus peel, flowers, and toasted yeast bread.

1993 Veuve Clicquot Ponsardin
La Grande Dame Brut ★★★★ $$$$
dry, full-bodied, medium acidity
Clicquot's house style is sumptuous and toasty. And here it is to the nth degree, with a cornucopia of apple and berry flavors balanced by fine acidity.

1995 Vilmart & Cie. Cuvée Création Brut ★★★★ $$$$
dry, full-bodied, high acidity
From a small estate comes a massive wine, full of fruit and spice flavors.

1992 Bollinger Grande Année ★★★ $$$$
dry, full-bodied, medium acidity
Beautiful creamy, nougat flavors in this wine.

NV Gosset Grand Rosé Brut 🍷 ★★★ $$$$
dry, medium-bodied, high acidity
Lovely to behold for its salmon color alone. The mélange of fruit and nut flavors balanced by high acidity make it wonderful to drink as well.

NV Gosset Grande Réserve Brut ★★★ $$$$
dry, full-bodied, high acidity
So creamy, yet so light; it's ethereal. Lemon and prominent mineral flavors.

1990 Jacquesson et Fils Grand Vin Signature Brut ★★★ $$$$
dry, medium-bodied, medium acidity
Rich, yeasty, and nutty qualities balanced by vibrantly fresh fruit flavors.

1993 Moët & Chandon Cuvée Dom Pérignon Brut ★★★ $$$$
dry, medium-bodied, medium acidity
Popping the cork of Dom is always a thrill. The pinpoint bubbles and citrus and toast flavors charm us even in less than exceptional years.

1995 Perrier-Jouët Fleur de Champagne
Cuvée Belle Epoque Brut ★★★ $$$$
dry, full-bodied, high acidity
This wine is full of apple flavor and a has a little Sherry-like nuttiness.

NV Ruinart "R" Rosé Brut 🍷 ★★★ $$$$
dry, medium-bodied, medium acidity
This is a serious, earthy wine with a vibrant cranberry twist.

NV Gaston Chiquet Blanc de Blancs d'Aÿ Brut ★★★ $$$
dry, medium-bodied, medium acidity
Palate-awakening citrus and apple flavors. This one is absolutely bone dry.

NV L. Aubry Fils Brut ★★★ $$$
dry, full-bodied, high acidity
Unique for its high percentage of Pinot Meunier as well as its honeylike aroma.

NV Lechère Rosé 1er Cru 🍷 ★★★ $$$
dry, medium-bodied, medium acidity
Exotic spice and rose petal aromas add a touch of glamour.

NV Moët & Chandon Rosé Brut 🍷 ★★★ $$$
dry, medium-bodied, medium acidity
Good before dinner but at the table, too; with food its mineral flavors shine.

1995 Pommery Grand Cru Brut ★★★ $$$
dry, medium-bodied, medium acidity
You taste the toastiness first; a second sip brings full fruit flavors.

NV Taittinger Prestige Rosé Brut 🍷 ★★★ $$$
dry, full-bodied, medium acidity
It's pink and has bright, berrylike flavors. Fun.

NV G. H. Mumm Cordon Rouge Brut ★★ $$$
dry, full-bodied, medium acidity
Long the standard in the U.S. for affordable sophistication.

NV Moët & Chandon Nectar Impérial ★★ $$$
medium-sweet, medium-bodied, high acidity
Somewhat sweet. Try it to see how the royals used to prefer their Champagne.

NV Nicolas Feuillatte Blanc de Blancs 1er Cru Brut ★★ $$$
dry, medium-bodied, medium acidity
Check this out. It's a good deal for a Premier Cru wine.

NV Veuve Clicquot Ponsardin Brut ★★ $$$
dry, full-bodied, medium acidity
The U.S.'s top-selling Champagne more than earns its popularity.

NV Pommery Pop Extra Dry ★ $
dry, light-bodied, high acidity
Here's a nice, citrusy sparkler in a pretty blue quarter bottle.

other regions of france

Many other sparkling wines are made by the Champagne technique and labeled *méthode traditionnelle*. Depending on regional custom, these wines are often called Crémant (creh-mahn) or Mousseux (moo-suh).

the bottom line Often overlooked in the U.S., these wines can be outstanding bargains. They run from $10 to $18.

recommended wines

NV Domaine Collin Blanquette de Limoux, Languedoc-Roussillon ★★★ $$
dry, full-bodied, medium acidity
One of the best Blanquettes we've ever had. It's as good as Champagnes that cost a lot more money. Buy it by the case.

NV Domaine du Vieux Pressoir Saumur Brut, Loire ★★ $$
dry, medium-bodied, medium acidity
A spicy sparkler, with peppery and fruity flavors and honeysuckle notes.

NV Langlois-Château Crémant de Loire ★★ $$
dry, light-bodied, medium acidity
Light as foam and refreshing as lemon sorbet. Not bad for $15.

NV Willm Crémant d'Alsace Brut ★★ $$
dry, medium-bodied, medium acidity
Floral and tart apple flavors make this even more invigorating than most Alsatian still wines. Really nice.

NV Domaine Augis Touraine Mousseux, Loire ★ $$
dry, medium-bodied, medium acidity
A creamy Mousseux with complex flavor—apple-y, floral, and nutty.

NV Trocadero Tête de Cuvée Blanc de Blancs Brut ★ $
dry, medium-bodied, high acidity
Quite tart, with some nice floral and fruit flavors.

italy

Spumante, the general name for sparkling wine in Italy, clearly adds to *la dolce vita*. The country has a great tradition of sparkling wines, many of them made using the classic Champagne method. Generally, Spumante is a little sweet, though there is a dry version, usually labeled Brut. It can be excellent. The most widely seen Italian sparklers are less serious. Moscato d'Asti (moss-CAH-toe DAH'ss-tee) is often sweet. Less serious still is Prosecco (pro-SEH-co) produced near Venice, where it is often drunk from tumblers.

the bottom line Many Italian bubblies fall in the bargain category, at or near $10 per bottle. Moscatos sell for $8 to $17. Dry Spumante wines range from $15 to $50; most are near $20. The really serious Bruts from Franciacorta cost roughly the same as Champagnes, $30 to just under $100; at the $40 to $50 range, the quality is outstanding for the price.

recommended wines

NV Bellavista Cuvée Brut, Franciacorta ★★★ $$$
dry, medium-bodied, medium acidity
This is a terrific wine that has vibrant cherrylike flavor at first and then an apple-y tang.

1995 Cavalleri Brut, Franciacorta ★★★ $$$
dry, full-bodied, high acidity
A 100 percent Chardonnay wine (unusual for Franciacorta) with the toasty, apple-like flavors and creamy texture of a fine Champagne.

NV Ca' del Bosco Brut, Franciacorta ★★ $$$
dry, medium-bodied, medium acidity
The perfect aperitif, not only to create a festive air before dinner, but because this wine's mineral flavors will whet your appetite.

NV Soldati La Scolca Brut, Gavi ★★ $$$
dry, medium-bodied, high acidity
When you're on vacation, or just decide to have a particularly civilized afternoon, enjoy a glass of this refreshing wine with peach and citrus flavors.

NV Ferrari Brut, Trentino ★★ $$
dry, full-bodied, medium acidity
Though not made by the Ferrari family of automotive fame, this nutty, full-flavored wine would be perfect for toasting the next Grand Prix champion.

2000 Saracco Moscato d'Asti, Piedmont ★★ $$
medium-sweet, light-bodied, high acidity
There's simply nothing so delightful as a glass of flowery, fruity Moscato. When the quality is as good as this, we're doubly delighted.

NV Zardetto Prosecco Spumante Brut di Conegliano, Veneto ★★ $
off-dry, light-bodied, medium acidity
Prosecco is made for pleasure, not pondering, and this is one of the best, with delicious fruit flavors and a delicate sparkle.

spain

Only a few years ago, the sparkling wine of Spain, made by the Champagne method and known generically as Cava (CAH-vah), was noteworthy more for its rock-bottom price than for anything else. Now, although they rarely achieve the complexity of Champagne, a number of Cavas can claim excellent quality.

the bottom line You'll still find the $6 bargain Cavas out there, but most of the time it's better to cross the $10 threshold and go up to $15 for really interesting wines. From there, a few dollars more will buy you the best. A small number of Cavas that are produced in very limited quantities can run you between $50 and $60.

recommended wines

1998 Agustí Torelló Mata Reserva Barrica ★★★ $$
dry, full-bodied, high acidity
Here's a Cava that's absolutely bone dry. It's an unusual, wood-aged bottling with fruit flavors and a mineral-laden earthiness.

1998 Huguet Brut Nature Reserva ★★★ $$
dry, medium-bodied, medium acidity
Compare this to Champagne, not other Cavas. A serious and completely enjoyable mélange of fruit, floral, and mineral flavors and a light toastiness.

NV Castillo Perelada Brut Reserva ★★★ $
dry, full-bodied, medium acidity
Like finding an Armani suit for under $100. A beautiful Cava, the epitome of good taste, for an amazing price.

NV Cristalino Brut ★★ $
dry, full-bodied, high acidity
Nothing fruity about this refined Cava. Indulge in its smokiness and minerality and delight in its tiny bubbles.

NV Freixenet Cordon Negro Brut ★★ $
dry, medium-bodied, medium acidity
The frosted black bottle is familiar, but it's surprising how good this Cava has gotten, with nice fruity flavors accented by an appealing flintiness.

U.S.

Sparkling wine is made all over the U.S. California dominates, but New York, Oregon, and New Mexico also make some good wines using the classic *méthode champenoise*.

the bottom line You'll find good quality American sparklers from $9 all the way up to $75. Very good quality can be found for $12 to $25.

recommended wines

1993 Iron Horse Estate Bottled Blanc de Blancs, Green Valley ★★★★ $$$
dry, full-bodied, high acidity
A wonderful wine with spiced-apple notes and a lush, Sherry-like nuttiness.

1994 Lenz Cuvée, North Fork ★★★★ $$$

dry, full-bodied, high acidity

Long Island vintners debate whether the area is better suited to Merlot or Cabernet Franc, but a taste of this superb wine might switch them all to sparkling.

1996 Mumm Cuvée Napa DVX, Napa Valley ★★★ $$$$

dry, full-bodied, high acidity

Lively apple and lemon-zest flavors. Really excellent.

1991 Beaulieu Vineyard Napa Valley Brut Reserve, Carneros ★★★ $$$

dry, full-bodied, high acidity

Made for BV's centennial year, this hearty sparkler is one of the best wines—sparkling or still—we've tasted from this producer in years. Try it if you can.

1996 Pacific Echo Brut Private Reserve, Anderson Valley ★★★ $$$

dry, full-bodied, medium acidity

Veuve Clicquot has a majority interest in Pacific Echo. Not surprising they make a great sparkler.

1998 Schramsberg Vineyards Blanc de Blancs, Napa Valley ★★★ $$$

dry, full-bodied, high acidity

With fruit notes balanced by excellent acidity, this wine again shows why Schramsberg is one of California's great winemakers.

1998 Domaine Carneros by Taittinger Brut, Carneros ★★★ $$

dry, full-bodied, medium acidity

Creamy, fruity, and floral, with velvety bubbles.

NV Gloria Ferrer Blanc de Noirs, Sonoma County ★★ $$

dry, full-bodied, high acidity

Delicious drinking for a good price. Very dry, with appealing strawberry notes.

NV Jepson Estate Select Champagne, Mendocino County ★★ $$

dry, medium-bodied, medium acidity

A really lovely wine that hits all the flavor points of good sparklers with hints of fruitiness and toastiness. Nicely priced, too.

NV Mumm Cuvée Napa Blanc de Blancs, Napa Valley ★★ $$

dry, medium-bodied, medium acidity

There's 30 percent Pinot Gris in this blend, giving it a definite fruity dimension.

NV Korbel Chardonnay Champagne, California ★ $

dry, full-bodied, medium acidity

This actually tastes like a buttery, full-bodied California Chardonnay.

OUR FAVORITE HALF-DOZEN CHAMPAGNE COCKTAILS

You needn't shell out big bucks for real Champagne here. There's lots of flavor in these drinks, and an inexpensive bottle will provide plenty of sparkle.

1. **Champagne & Lychee Cocktail** Almost fill a Champagne glass with the wine and add a large splash of lychee liqueur. Drop in a peeled lychee if you have one.

2. **Very Berry Champagne** Almost fill a Champagne glass with the wine and add a drizzle each of framboise, strawberry schnapps, and crème de cassis. Garnish with fresh berries.

3. **Citrus Ginger Mint Fizz** Crush some mint leaves and a slice of ginger in the bottom of a cocktail shaker. Add ice and the juice from a quarter of an orange. Shake and strain into a Champagne glass. Top with the wine. Garnish with a mint sprig and a slice of orange.

4. **Hot Tamale** Fill a Champagne glass with half wine and half Goldschlager Cinnamon Schnapps. Add a cinnamon stick.

5. **Lemon Drop** Fill a Champagne glass with the wine, drizzle in some sour mix, and add a lemon twist.

6. **The Big Apple** Almost fill a Champagne glass with the wine. Drizzle in Calvados or applejack brandy to taste. Drop in a small wedge of a Granny Smith apple.

fortified & dessert wines

Pre- and post-prandial wines often leave a greater impression than table wines. Whether it's dry Fino Sherry before dinner or sweet Sauternes with or after dessert, fortified and dessert wines frame a meal. And, depending on the wine, many can be enjoyed throughout dinner as well.

fortified wines

As the name implies, fortified wine has been strengthened from its natural state by the addition of alcohol.

madeira & port

on the label

The great majority of Madeiras are blends from various years. The labels of quality wines indicate approximate age: five, ten, fifteen years. Four grapes make the best Madeiras, and each is made into wine of a specific level of sweetness. Sercial is dry, Malmsey is sweet, and Verdelho (vair-DAY-l'yo) and Bual are in between. Simpler Madeiras are often labeled *Rainwater.*

Ports are categorized as follows: **White Port** is simple Port made from white grapes. **Ruby Port** is the most common, usually a simple blend of wines aged for two or three years. **Vintage Character Port** is a blend of premium Ruby Ports aged up to five years. **Late-Bottled Vintage (LBV) Port** is Ruby Port made from a single, but not great, vintage. It's aged four to six years in barrels. **Vintage Port** is made entirely with grapes from an exceptional year and is aged in casks for two to three years. The ultimate Port, it requires years, often thirty or more, of aging in the bottle. **Single-Quinta Vintage Port** is made from a single vineyard (quinta) that has produced great fruit in a generally unexceptional year. It's aged in casks for two or three years. **Aged Tawny Port** is kept in barrels significantly longer than other Ports. The age on the label (ten to over forty years) indicates the average or approximate age of the wines in the blend.

at the table

Sercial and Verdelho Madeiras make good aperitifs, perfect with salty hors d'oeuvres. They're also excellent with salt-cod dishes. Buals and Malmseys are great with crème brûlée, pecan pie, or anything with caramel or almond paste. Chilled White Port makes a nice aperitif, whether alone or with a splash of tonic. Simple Ruby Port is a good accompaniment to uncomplicated cherry or berry desserts, like compotes or cobblers. More complex Tawny Ports are best enjoyed with desserts containing dried fruits and nuts, caramel, or both. Vintage Ports are classically paired with Stilton.

the bottom line Simple Rainwater Madeiras sell for $12 to $16. Five-year varietal Madeiras cost $17 to $25. Ten-year varietals cost $25 to $35; fifteen-year varietals cost $45. Spectacular Madeiras aged for many decades will be well over $100. The simplest White, Ruby, and Tawny Ports sell for $10 to $20. Late-Bottled Vintage Ports cost $15 to $30. Vintage Ports from recent years range between $40 and $85. Single-Quinta Vintage Ports are an excellent value, selling for about half the price of regular vintage wines. Considering their quality, Tawny Ports with age designations represent good value, especially at the twenty-year level. Ten-Year Tawnies sell for $18 to $28; Twenty-Year Tawnies for $27 to $40. Thirty- and Forty-Year Tawnies can cost from $75 to $100 or more.

recommended madeiras

1958 Cossart Gordon Bual ★★★ $$$$
medium sweet, medium-bodied, high acidity
Rich burnt sugar, herb, and dried fruit flavors and powerful acidity.

Blandy's 15 Year Malmsey ★★★ $$$
sweet, full-bodied, high acidity
Orange and spice aromas. Baked pear and nut flavors. Wonderful.

Broadbent 10 Year Malmsey ★★★ $$$
medium sweet, full-bodied, high acidity
Luscious orange peel, herb, and roasted hazelnut flavors. Great Madeira.

Cossart Gordon 5 Year Bual ★★★ $$
medium sweet, medium-bodied, high acidity
Full of burnt orange, nut, and fennel flavors against a mineral background.

Blandy's 5 Year Verdelho ★★ $$
medium sweet, full-bodied, high acidity
Beautiful apricot, herb, and mineral flavors with peppery notes on the finish.

Broadbent Rainwater ★★ $$
medium sweet, medium-bodied, high acidity
Most Rainwater is a pallid affair, but this has nut, orange, and spice flavors.

Leacock's 5 Year Dry Sercial ★★ $$
dry, medium-bodied, medium acidity
Unusual, with mineral, herb, and orange flavors. Try it with tapas.

recommended ports

1995 Taylor Fladgate Quinta de Vargellas ★★★★ $$$
medium sweet, full-bodied, medium acidity
This Single Quinta offers more flavor than most 1995s, for less money.

1997 Cockburn's Vintage ★★★ $$$$
sweet, full-bodied, high acidity
Vintage Port usually takes years and years of aging; give this just three more.

1998 Quinta do Noval Silval Vintage ★★★ $$$
sweet, medium-bodied, medium acidity
Full cherry flavor, but tannin is noticeable on the finish, indicating a long life.

1994 Osborne LBV ★★★ $$
medium sweet, full-bodied, medium acidity
Cherry and cedarlike flavors with a bit of spiciness on the finish. Good value.

Cockburn's Director's Reserve 20 Year Tawny ★★ $$$
medium sweet, medium-bodied, medium acidity
Very luscious for Twenty-Year Tawny. Light cherry and orange peel flavors.

1982 Dow's Reserve Tawny ★★ $$$
sweet, medium-bodied, high acidity
From a single year—unusual for aged Tawnies. The result is great character.

1990 Smith Woodhouse Late Bottled Vintage ★★ $$$
sweet, full-bodied, medium acidity
Enjoyable now, but if you can wait, it will get even better.

Fonseca 10 Year Tawny ★★ $$
sweet, full-bodied, high acidity
Burnt orange and almond flavors with a kick of spice on the finish.

NV Graham's Six Grapes ★ $$
sweet, full-bodied, medium acidity
A proprietary blend with more oomph than most. Grapey and spicy.

Taylor Fladgate Chip Dry White Port ★ $$
dry, light-bodied, medium acidity
A refreshing aperitif that tastes like a just-cut apple with a squeeze of lemon.

Cockburn's Fine Ruby ★ $
sweet, full-bodied, high acidity
A good, basic Port, with cherry flavor, a bit of spice, and medium tannin.

sherry

From the southern tip of Spain come some of the finest—though in the U.S., least appreciated—wines in the world.

on the label

There are two basic types of Sherry, Fino and Oloroso, each with its subcategories: **Fino** has flavors of yeast, flowers, and minerals that develop due to *flor,* an oxygen-stifling yeast that grows on the wine's surface during maturation. **Manzanilla** is Fino aged in the Sanlúcar de Barrameda area, which is on the sea. It has an almost salty, sea-breeze quality. **Amontillado** is Fino that continues aging after the oxygen-blocking flor dies, which happens when temperatures rise. It develops a nutty flavor due to oxidation and is usually dry. **Pale Cream** is Fino that has been sweetened with grape-juice concentrate and sweet wine. **Oloroso** is aged without flor and therefore exposed to oxygen, which results in a nutty flavor. It's usually sweet. **Cream** is Oloroso further sweetened with wines made from Pedro Ximénez or Moscatel grapes. **Palo Cortado** is Oloroso that has happened to develop a bit of flor. It's rare and revered. **Pedro Ximénez** is made from the grape of the same name in the Montilla-Morilés region, and therefore technically not Sherry, but very similar. It's motor oil thick, with treacly sweetness balanced by exceptionally high acidity.

at the table

Try dry Fino Sherries with olives or antipasto. Pair dry Oloroso Sherries with cream-based soups or pâtés; sweeter versions can stand up to chocolaty desserts like brownies, flourless cakes, and profiteroles with chocolate sauce.

the bottom line If any wine is underpriced, it's Sherry. Many bottles cost under $12. Those from top producers sell for $10 to $18. Older wines or special blends are $20 to $25. Exceptional bottles cost over $100.

recommended wines

Pedro Domecq Venerable Very Rare Pedro Ximénez ★★★★ $$$$
sweet, full-bodied, high acidity
Really thick. Fig, molasses, orange, cedar, and spice flavors, perfectly balanced by acidity.

Romate Very Rare Amontillado ★★★★ $$$
dry, full-bodied, medium acidity
A great, rare Amontillado, full of coconut cream, vanilla, and caramel flavors that seem like they should be sweet, but are quite dry.

1972 Don PX Gran Reserva ★★★ $$$
sweet, full-bodied, high acidity
More than twenty-five years of aging go into this dense wine, with fig, caramel, and tangerine flavors.

Lustau Pasada de Sanlucar Manzanilla ★★★ $$$
dry, medium-bodied, high acidity
Extra aging yields a paradox: rich and nutty, but also light and smoky.

Sandeman Limited Release Rare Fino ★★★ $$$
dry, medium-bodied, high acidity
Lots of flavors here: salty, nutty, spicy, lemony, and a bit of orange peel as well.

Gonzalez Byass Apostoles Muy Viejo Palo Cortado ★★★ $$
medium sweet, medium-bodied, medium acidity
Smooth as *dulce de leche,* with an orange tang at the end.

Hidalgo La Gitana Manzanilla ★★★ $$
dry, light-bodied, high acidity
One of the best Manzanillas at any price, with a briny, sea-breeze freshness and almond and apple flavors. This is a bone-dry wine and an amazing bargain.

Hidalgo Napoleón Amontillado ★★★ $$
dry, medium-bodied, medium acidity
Here's a connoisseur's Amontillado: almond and toffee flavors in a relatively light wine.

Hidalgo Napoleón Cream ★★★ $$
sweet, medium-bodied, medium acidity
A luxurious wine that tastes like pecan praline and roasted coffee.

Lustau Los Arcos Dry Amontillado ★★★ $$
dry, medium-bodied, medium acidity
Full of caramel, orange, and toasted almond flavors balanced by minerality.

Williams & Humbert Dry Sack Solera Especial Fifteen-Year Finest Old Oloroso ★★★ $
medium sweet, medium-bodied, medium acidity
Candied citrus, date, nut, molasses, and rum flavors. Perfect with fruitcake.

Gonzalez Byass Tio Pepe Muy Seco Fino ★★ $$
dry, light-bodied, high acidity
Fruit and nut flavors meet a touch of saltiness in this fine fino.

Lustau East India Solera ★★ $$
sweet, medium-bodied, high acidity
A well-balanced cream sherry, with plum, orange, and nut flavors.

Lustau Península Palo Cortado ★★ $$
off-dry, medium-bodied, medium acidity
Tasty baked-fruit, herb, and nut flavors.

Osborne Premium Osborne Cream ★★ $$
sweet, medium-bodied, medium acidity
As far as Cream Sherry goes, this one's fairly light and still has lots of flavor.

Osborne Premium 10 RF Medium Oloroso ★ $$
dry, medium-bodied, medium acidity
Osborne's style puts minerality front and center.

vin doux naturel

Long a specialty of the south of France, Vin Doux Naturel (van doo nah-too-rel), or naturally sweet wine, is dosed with brandy while it is fermenting, making Port-like reds and remarkably light, aromatic sweet whites.

on the label

The appellations Banyuls and Maury in the Roussillon region and Rasteau in the Rhône produce the best red Vins Doux Naturels. The Rhône's Muscat de Beaumes-de-Venise and Roussillon's Muscat de Rivesaltes are famous whites.

at the table

Banyuls and Maury are perhaps the only grape wines that truly complement chocolate. They're also wonderful with nuts, blue cheeses like Roquefort, and cakes made with dried fruit. Muscat-based wine is a natural with fruit desserts, soufflés, and light custards. Try a white with *panna cotta,* or for the perfect pairing, with pears poached in the same wine.

the bottom line Given their quality, Vins Doux Naturels are an amazing bargain. Excellent Muscat-based wines can be found for $12, and Banyuls, Maury, and Rasteau for under $20. You'll pay $50 or more for special aged bottles, but these, too, are good value. The prices are for 375-milliliter bottles.

recommended wines

1998 Domaine de la Coume de Roy, Maury, Roussillon 🍷 ★★★★ $$$
medium sweet, medium-bodied, high acidity
Simply great, with strawberry, tamarind, and burnt orange flavors and lots of minerality.

2000 Domaine de Durban Muscat de Beaumes-de-Venise, Rhône 🍷 ★★★ $$
sweet, medium-bodied, medium acidity
Gorgeous honeysuckle, peach, apricot, and pear aromas and flavors.

Mas Amiel 10 Ans d'Age Cuvée Speciale, Maury, Roussillon 🍷 ★★★ $$
off-dry, medium-bodied, medium acidity
A wine redolent of dried plums, figs, and orange peel, with a touch of smokiness. Try it with chocolate.

1999 Bouquet des Dentelles, Muscat de Beaumes-de-Venise, Rhône 🍷 ★★★ $
sweet, medium-bodied, high acidity
One of the best Beaumes-de-Venise we've had, with spice, citrus, pepper, and floral notes.

2000 Domaine Sarda-Malet, Muscat de Rivesaltes, Roussillon 🍷 ★★★ $
medium sweet, medium-bodied, high acidity
This sweet wine is very refreshing due to its high acidity. It has lovely honeysuckle, lemon, and herb flavors.

1998 Domaine du Mas Blanc Rimage, Banyuls, Roussillon 🍷 ★★ $$$
medium sweet, medium-bodied, medium acidity
A delightful Banyuls that seems flowery at first sip, but then becomes intensely plummy.

1993 Domaine du Mas Blanc "Rimage Mise Tardive," Banyuls, Roussillon 🍷 ★★ $$
sweet, full-bodied, medium acidity
Here's a thick Banyuls with lots of burnt-orange, spice, and smoke flavors. It's a real treat.

2000 Paul Jaboulet Aîné, Muscat de Beaumes-de-Venise, Rhône 🍷 ★★ $$
sweet, medium-bodied, medium acidity
We're glad this is easy to find. Lovely apple blossom, vanilla, and citrus aromas.

dessert wines

Dessert wines, usually sold in half bottles, can be quite expensive, but their luscious concentration of sweet, complex flavors often makes them worth the price.

at the table

Sweet wines are normally enjoyed with, after, or in lieu of dessert. They complement fruit desserts beautifully: poached or baked fruit, gratins, or tarts. In addition, there are some savory dishes that sweet wines seem made for, such as prosciutto and melon, foie gras, and blue cheeses like Stilton, Roquefort, and Gorgonzola.

france

Bordeaux's legendary Sauternes (so-tairn) is France's best-known dessert wine. Five communes within Bordeaux's Graves district—Sauternes, Barsac, Bommes, Preignac, and Fargues—fall under the appellation Sauternes. Barsac may also label wines with its own name. Sauternes' neighboring appellations, Cadillac, Loupiac, and Ste-Croix-du-Mont, produce similar, if simpler, sweet wines. The dessert wines of the Loire Valley and Alsace also deserve recognition. From the Anjou area of the Loire come the ambrosiae of Savennières, Bonnezeaux, and Quarts de Chaume. Anjou is also home to the pleasant wines of Coteaux du Layon. Alsace produces two types of dessert wine, Vendange Tardive (late harvest) and Sélection de Grains Nobles (selection of noble berries). The latter is made from grapes that are harvested late and have been affected by botrytis (noble rot, see page 287).

the bottom line Sauternes is expensive, period. It starts at over $30 and goes to more than $200 for the most revered of all, Château d'Yquem. Wines from the lesser neighboring appellations are $12 to $25. These are generally good value. The Loire's sweet wines are inexplicably overlooked and, therefore, can be bargains—between $12 and $25. The best Savennières can be more than $50. The top wines, especially those from Bonnezeaux and Vouvray, can hit $100. Quarts de Chaume can be had for between $40 and $75, and Coteaux du Layon ranges from $12 to $75. Montlouis runs $12 to $25. From Alsace, Vendange Tardive prices range from $35 to $100 or more. Sélection de Grains Nobles begin around $50 and can go to more than $200. Keep in mind that all of these prices are for 375-milliliter bottles.

what to buy SAUTERNES

1990	1991	1992	1993	1994
★★★★	★	★	★	★★

1995	1996	1997	1998	1999
★★★	★★★	★★★	★★★	★★★

recommended wines

1995 Château d'Yquem, Sauternes, Bordeaux ★★★★ $$$$
sweet, medium-bodied, high acidity
There's nothing better than Yquem, as luxurious as silk. Haunting citrus peel, mineral, and earthy flavors.

1997 Domaine Patrick Baudouin María Juby Sélection de Grains Nobles, Coteaux du Layon, Loire ★★★★ $$$$
sweet, full-bodied, high acidity
The nobility that inhabited the Loire's many castles must have sipped some great dessert wines. This nectar would have fit right in.

1998 Domaine Weinbach Furstentum Sélection de Grains Nobles Gewurztraminer, Alsace ★★★★ $$$$
sweet, full-bodied, high acidity
Glorious. All the stony, floral qualities of great Gewurz, plus luscious fruit and spice flavors. Worth hunting down.

1997 Foreau Domaine du Clos Naudin Moelleux, Vouvray, Loire ★★★★ $$$
medium sweet, medium-bodied, medium acidity
A very flexible wine: Lovely apple and citrus flavors and good acidity make this perfect for foie gras; the honey flavor means it's superb for dessert.

1998 Domaine des Baumard, Quarts de Chaume, Loire ★★★★ $$
medium sweet, medium-bodied, high acidity
One of France's great sweet wines, with spice, herb, and truffle notes against a background of lemon cream.

1995 Cru Barréjats, Sauternes, Bordeaux ★★★ $$$$
sweet, full-bodied, high acidity
Smooth and luscious, with orange, spice, and coconut flavors.

1998 Château de Fesles, Bonnezeaux, Loire ★★★ $$$
medium sweet, medium-bodied, medium acidity
A favorite, with unique citrus zest flavors plus a big dose of fresh herbs.

1997 Château de la Guimonière Les Julines, Coteaux du Layon Chaume, Loire ★★★ $$$
sweet, full-bodied, high acidity
Sumptuous, with rich fruit flavors and earthy mineral notes. An excellent wine.

1995 Hugel & Fils Vendange Tardive "Hugel" Riesling, Alsace ★★★ $$$
sweet, full-bodied, high acidity
We haven't come across many Rieslings we'd call buttery, but here's one. It also boasts pineapple flavor along with the typical petrol notes.

1998 Château de Chamboureau Roche aux Moines Cuvée d'Avant, Savennières, Loire ★★★ $$
medium sweet, medium-bodied, high acidity
Luscious ripe grapes offer orange and peach flavors, botrytis adds earthy truffle and sweet pea flavors, and oak aging gives just a bit of spice.

1995 Château Doisy-Védrines, Barsac, Sauternes, Bordeaux ★★★ $$
medium sweet, medium-bodied, high acidity
Lovely apricot and tropical fruit flavors, but also earthy notes. Great with foie gras.

1996 Yves Soulez Château de la Genaiserie Les Simonnelles Sélection de Grains Nobles, Coteaux du Layon St-Aubin, Loire ★★★ $$
sweet, full-bodied, high acidity
The peach, papaya, and orange flavors are easy to love, but it's the peppery and earthy notes that stir us to passion.

1999 Yves et François Chidaine Tuffeaux, Montlouis, Loire ★★★ $
medium sweet, medium-bodied, high acidity
Though identified as a demi-sec, this delicious wine is actually sweeter.

1998 Château de Cosse, Sauternes, Bordeaux ★★ $$
sweet, medium-bodied, high acidity
A second-label Sauternes from Château Rieussec at half the price of their first.

1997 Château du Cros, Loupiac, Bordeaux ★★ $$
sweet, full-bodied, high acidity
This is not so complex as most Sauternes, but then again, it's not nearly so expensive either.

1995 Château Pascaud-Villefranche, Sauternes, Bordeaux ★★ $$
off-dry, medium-bodied, medium acidity
Drier than most Sauternes, but still full of lovely fruit flavors.

germany & austria

Every year, nearly all of Germany's finest wine producers hope that some of their grapes will ripen enough to make dessert wines. Auslese (OUSE-lay-zuh), or select harvest, wines are usually medium sweet. Beerenauslese (BEAR-en-OUSE-lay-zuh) is made from grapes that have been been picked even later, often after having been partially affected by botrytis (see page 287). Trockenbeerenauslese (TRAW-ken-BEAR-en-OUSE-lay-zuh) is made from grapes left on vines so late that they've been shriveled to raisins by botrytis. Eiswein (ice-vine) is made from grapes unaffected by botrytis that are picked and pressed only after they have frozen on the vine. The terms Auslese, Beerenauslese, Trockenbeerenauslese, and Eiswein all apply in Austria as well.

the bottom line For good sweet German Auslese, count on paying $40 (although you can spend as much as $160). Beerenauslese is $30 to $260. Trockenbeerenauslese costs between $140 and $400, and Eiswein starts at $55 and can top $300. Austrian wines are not inexpensive either; however, a better climate allows producers to charge a little less for wines that are no lower in quality. Still, expect to spend $35 to $80 or more. All prices are for 375-milliliter bottles.

recommended wines

1996 Dr. Heger Ihringer Winklerberg Muskateller Trockenbeerenauslese, Baden, Germany ★★★★ $$$$
sweet, full-bodied, high acidity
A thick, incredible wine with a mélange of flavors, like apricot, date, orange, and honeysuckle, all balanced by searing acidity.

2000 Fritz Haag Brauneberger Juffer-Sonnenuhr Riesling Beerenauslese, Mosel, Germany ★★★★ $$$$
sweet, full-bodied, high acidity
Intense peach and apricot flavors and lots of herb and flower notes. Very fine.

1998 Heidi Schröck Ruster Ausbruch Gelber Muskateller, Neusiedlersee-Hügelland, Austria ★★★★ $$$$
sweet, full-bodied, high acidity
Floral and pine aromas; lime, honey, and nutmeg flavors. Just great.

2000 Josef Leitz Rüdesheimer Drachenstein Riesling Eiswein, Rheingau, Germany ★★★★ $$$$
sweet, medium-bodied, high acidity
Powerful peach flavor. A magnificent Eiswein.

1998 Kracher "Zwischen den Seen" Scheurebe Trockenbeerenauslese No. 12, Neusiedlersee, Austria ★★★★ $$$$
sweet, full-bodied, high acidity
Extremely thick, sweet, and flavorful—with the necessary high acidity.

1998 Nigl Riesling Beerenauslese, Kremstal, Austria ★★★★ $$$$
sweet, medium-bodied, high acidity
Martin Nigl makes some of the best sweet wines in Austria.

1999 Reichsrat von Buhl Forster Ungeheuer Riesling Trockenbeerenauslese, Pfalz, Germany ★★★★ $$$$
sweet, full-bodied, high acidity
Like apricot nectar, with the added vigor of herbs. Superb.

1999 Schloss Gobelsburg Grüner Veltliner Eiswein, Kamptal, Austria ★★★★ $$$
sweet, medium-bodied, high acidity
Outstanding, with sweet, savory, and spicy flavors. Outstanding value, too.

2000 Selbach-Oster Zeltinger Sonnenuhr Riesling Auslese, Mosel, Germany ★★★★ $$$
medium sweet, full-bodied, high acidity
One of the Mosel's best producers offers another great, reasonably priced wine.

1996 Vineyards of Pannonia Pannonia Serendipity "Divitiae Aureolae" Eiswein, Lake Neusiedl, Austria ★★★ $$$$
medium sweet, full-bodied, high acidity
An unusual Eiswein, smoky at first, followed by fruity and earthy notes.

1998 Weingut Erich Bender Bissersheimer Steig Huxelrebe Beerenauslese, Pfalz, Germany ★★★ $$
sweet, full-bodied, high acidity
Lovely tropical fruit flavors balanced by a tea-like earthiness.

1999 Kracher Cuvée Beerenauslese, Neusiedlersee, Austria ★★ $$$
medium sweet, light-bodied, high acidity
Kracher is Austria's king of sweet wine. This is his most affordable.

hungary

Tokaji (often referred to as Tokay but not to be confused with the Tokay grape) has been a fabled elixir for centuries. Tokaji Aszú (toh-KYE ah-SOO), the most commonly available Tokaji in the U.S., is made with regular white wine and a mash of botrytis-affected grapes. It's graded according to the quantity of crushed grapes used, from three to six *puttonyos,* each *puttonyo* equaling a bin's worth of crushed grapes. Four or five *puttonyos* result in the best flavor and acid balance.

the bottom line Nearly all Tokaji Aszús available in the U.S. are four- and five-puttonyo wines that sell for $30 to $35. The prices are for 500-milliliter bottles.

recommended wines

1994 Oremus 5 Puttonyos, Tokaji Aszú ★★★★ $$$
sweet, full-bodied, high acidity
All the lusciousness that is Tokaji finds its way into this wine, with orange and apricot flavors joined by the musky, floral notes of botrytis. Great.

1993 Chateau Pajzos 5 Puttonyos, Tokaji Aszú ★★★ $$$$
sweet, full-bodied, high acidity
A rich blend of apricot, peach, orange, and honey flavors from one of the best Tokaji vintages in the last decade.

1996 The Royal Tokaji Wine Company Royal Tokaji 5 Puttonyos, Tokaji Aszú ★★★ $$$
sweet, full-bodied, high acidity
Amazingly vibrant orange and apricot flavors, balanced by spice and mushroom notes.

1998 Oremus Late Harvest Furmint, Tokaji ★★ $$
off-dry, light-bodied, high acidity
It's rare to see this in the U.S.—a non-Aszú Tokaji made from late-harvest, botrytized grapes.

italy

The best-known Italian dessert wine is Tuscany's Vin Santo (veen SAHN-toe). Like most Italian sweet wine, it is made using the *passito* method: Late-harvest grapes are picked and then allowed to dry partially before crushing. Soave is home to a *passito* known as Recioto (reh-t'CHO-toe). The small island of Pantelleria off the tip of Sicily produces a sweet wine from Muscat grapes.

the bottom line Italy's dessert wines can be found for as little as $10 a bottle. However, most cost between $20 and $35. Prices are for 375-milliliter bottles.

recommended wines

1999 Maculan Torcolato, Breganze, Veneto 🍷 ★★★★ $$$
sweet, full-bodied, high acidity
One of Italy's finest dessert wines, with the complexity of flavor that comes from partially dried grapes and oak barrel aging.

1997 Leonildo Pieropan Le Colombare Recioto di Soave, Veneto ★★★ $$$
medium sweet, medium-bodied, medium acidity
Pear, lemon, and light spice flavors make this ideal with a pear and almond tart.

1996 Tre Monti Passito, Albana di Romagna, Emilia-Romagna ★★ $$$
medium sweet, medium-bodied, medium acidity
A uniquely Italian wine, with flavors reminiscent of pine nuts, pears, and spice.

1999 Ferrandes, Passito di Pantelleria, Sicily ★★ $$
sweet, medium-bodied, high acidity
Exotic: flavors of orange peel, honey, cloves, and black pepper.

1995 Lamole di Lamole, Vinsanto del Chianti Classico, Tuscany ★★ $$
sweet, medium-bodied, high acidity
The aroma of chestnuts followed by subtle apricot and orange flavors.

2000 Santa Lucia, Aleatico Dolce de Puglia, Apulia ★★ $$
medium sweet, medium-bodied, high acidity
A unique red dessert wine. Delicious.

u.s. & canada

California and the Pacific Northwest make some good dessert wines, and, depending on the year, New York produces some excellent examples. Not surprisingly, the Niagara Peninsula in Ontario, bordering New York, also produces outstanding dessert wines.

the bottom line Quite unlike the prices of many California wines these days, nice sweet ones can be found in a relatively low range. Look for late-harvest wines starting at around $15. Some excellent botrytis-affected wines start at $25 and go up to $70. There are superb late-harvest New York wines that sell for $15. Ice wines sell for up to $80. Canadian ice wines are expensive as well, but a favorable exchange rate lowers the prices to about $60. All prices are for 375-milliliter bottles.

recommended wines

1998 Dolce Late Harvest Wine, Napa Valley, California ★★★★ $$$$
sweet, full-bodied, high acidity
No need to go to France for remarkable Sauternes-style wines. Nectarous is the best way to describe this, with musk, honey, and tropical fruit flavors.

1998 Inniskillin Oak Aged Vidal Icewine, Niagara Peninsula, Canada ★★★★ $$$$
sweet, medium-bodied, high acidity
A unique ice wine featuring the spiciness that comes from oak aging and the orange and apple flavors that come from Vidal grapes.

2000 Long Vineyards Estate Grown Botrytis Johannisberg Riesling, Napa Valley, California ★★★★ $$
sweet, full-bodied, high acidity
World-class? Let's put it this way: This is the only California Riesling exported to Germany.

1999 Navarro Vineyards Vineyard Select Late Harvest White Riesling, Anderson Valley, California ★★★★ $$
sweet, full-bodied, high acidity
An amazing tropical-fruit-, floral-, and honey-scented wine.

1999 Freemark Abbey Edelwein Gold Late Harvest Johannisberg Riesling, Napa Valley, California ★★★ $$$
sweet, medium-bodied, high acidity
From one of the few California wineries that still take Riesling seriously comes a wonderful wine with luscious tropical fruit flavors balanced by excellent acidity.

1999 Henry of Pelham Riesling Icewine, Niagara Peninsula, Canada ★★★ $$$
sweet, medium-bodied, high acidity
Lovely, clear pineapple and apricot flavors. Sweet but not syrupy.

2000 Kiona Chenin Blanc Ice Wine, Yakima Valley, Washington State ★★★ $$
sweet, full-bodied, high acidity
Yakima is apple country, and apple (and pear) flavors characterize this wine.

1995 Grgich Hills Late Harvest Violetta, Napa Valley, California ★★ $$$
medium sweet, medium-bodied, medium acidity
Nice orange and spice flavors.

1998 Hunt Country Vineyards Vidal Ice Wine, Finger Lakes, New York ★★ $$$
sweet, full-bodied, high acidity
From one of New York's ice wine experts comes lovely sipping, with orange and butterscotch flavors.

1998 Mendelson Pinot Gris Dessert Wine, Napa Valley, California ★★ $$$
medium sweet, full-bodied, medium acidity
Pinot Gris is rarely made into sweet wine in the U.S. Different.

2000 Paumanok Estate Bottled Late Harvest Riesling, North Fork of Long Island, New York ★★ $$
sweet, medium-bodied, high acidity
Half of the family behind Paumanok is of German winemaking stock; it shows.

1998 Shenandoah Vineyards Daphne Late Harvest Sauvignon Blanc, Amador County, California ★★ $$
sweet, medium-bodied, medium acidity
Well-balanced peach, honey, and floral flavors. Nice.

2000 Andrew Quady Essensia Orange Muscat, California ★ $
medium sweet, medium-bodied, medium acidity
Made from Orange Muscat grapes. A zingy, very orangey wine.

NOBLE ROT

A fungus, *Botrytis cinerea* (known oxymoronically as noble rot), leads to some of the most exquisite dessert wines. It essentially sucks the water from the fruit, leaving behind shriveled grapes that are extremely concentrated in flavor and high in sugar. Winegrowers who want to make botrytis-affected wines take a big risk. They must leave the grapes on the vine past the usual harvest time and hope that the fungus will attack. While they wait, autumn rains might demolish the whole crop. Wild animals, lured by the scent of ripe grapes, have been known to make a feast of the precious fruit. If the grapes survive and attract the botrytis, harvesting must be done by hand, grape by grape. Understandably, the prices of these wines are high.

vintage chart

You've ordered a wine that's supposed to be great—but isn't? Maybe it's the vintage. This chart, which covers the wines that are commonly aged, will aid you not only in ordering wine but in

	1984	1985	1986	1987	1988	1989	1990
Bordeaux							
Right Bank	★	★★★★	☆☆☆	★	★★★	☆☆☆☆	☆☆☆☆
Médoc	★	★★★★	☆☆☆☆	★★	☆☆☆	☆☆☆☆	☆☆☆☆
Red Graves	★★	★★★★	☆☆☆☆	★★	☆☆☆	☆☆☆☆	☆☆☆☆
Burgundy							
Côte d'Or Reds	☆	☆☆☆☆	☆☆☆	☆☆	★★★	★★★	☆☆☆☆
Chablis	o	☆☆	★★★	★★	★★	★★★	★★★
Loire							
Chenin Blanc	★	★★	☆☆☆	★	★★★	☆☆☆☆	★★★★
Cabernet Franc	o	★★★	☆☆	★	★★★	★★★★	★★★★
Rhône							
Northern Red	☆	★★★★	★★★	☆☆	☆☆☆☆	☆☆☆☆	★★★★
Southern Red	☆☆	★★★★	★★	★★	★★★★	☆☆☆☆	☆☆☆☆
Italy							
Barolo & Barbaresco	☆	★★★★	★★	☆	★★★★	☆☆☆☆	☆☆☆☆
Chianti	o	★★★★	★★★	☆☆	★★★	★★	★★★★
Spain							
Rioja	o	★★★★	★★	★★★	☆	★★★	☆☆☆
Ribera del Duero	★	★★★	o	★★★	☆☆	★★	★★★
Germany							
Mosel-Saar-Ruwer	★	★★★	☆☆	☆☆	★★★	★★★	☆☆☆☆
Rhine Regions	★	☆☆☆	☆☆	☆☆	★★★	☆☆☆	☆☆☆☆
California							
Cabernet Sauvignon	★★★★	★★★★	★★★★	★★★★	☆☆	★★★	★★★★

o = Very bad vintage; a disaster
★ = Poor to average vintage; only the best wines are good quality
★★ = Good to very good vintage
★★★ = Excellent vintage
★★★★ = Outstanding vintage

evaluating those you already have and in choosing recent wines to purchase. The quality of the wine is indicated by the number of stars, just as in the "What to Buy" sections of this book. The color of the stars tells where the wine is most likely to be in its progress, from "not ready" through "well past peak." For example, ★★ indicates a good wine at peak, and ☆☆☆ an excellent wine whose time has almost passed.

1991	1992	1993	1994	1995	1996	1997	1998	1999	2000
O	☆	☆☆	☆☆☆	☆☆☆	★★★★	☆☆	★★★★	★★★	★★★★
★	★	☆☆	★★★	★★★★	★★★★	☆☆	★★★	★★★	★★★★
★	★	☆☆☆	☆☆☆	★★★	★★★	☆☆☆	★★	★★	★★★★
☆☆	☆☆	☆☆☆	★★	☆☆☆☆	★★★	☆☆☆	★★★	★★★	★
☆☆	★★★	★★	★★★	☆☆☆☆	★★★★	☆☆☆	☆☆☆	☆☆☆	★★
O	★★	☆☆☆☆	☆☆☆	★★★★	★★★★	☆☆☆	★★★	★★	★★
O	O	☆☆☆☆	★★	☆☆☆☆	★★★★	☆☆☆	☆☆☆	☆☆	★★
☆☆☆☆	O	★★	☆☆☆	★★★★	☆☆☆	☆☆☆	★★★	★★★	★★★
☆	☆	★★	★★	☆☆☆☆	☆☆	☆☆☆	★★★★	★★★	★★★★
★★★	★★	☆☆☆	☆☆	★★★★	★★★★	★★★★	☆☆☆	★★★	na
☆☆☆	☆☆	★★★	★★★	★★★★	★★★	★★★★	☆☆☆	★★★	na
★★★	★★	★★	★★★★	★★★★	★★★	★★★	☆☆☆	★★	na
★★★★	★	☆☆	★★★★	★★★★	★★★★	★★★	★★★	★★★	na
☆☆	★★	☆☆☆	☆☆☆☆	☆☆☆☆	★★★★	☆☆☆	☆☆☆	☆☆☆☆	☆☆
★★	★★	★★★	☆☆☆	☆☆	★★★	☆☆☆	☆☆☆	☆☆☆☆	☆☆
★	★★★★	☆☆☆	☆☆☆☆	☆☆☆	★★★	★★★	★★★	★★	★★★

★ = Not ready; needs more time
☆ = Can be drunk or held
★ = At peak; perfect for drinking now
☆ = Past peak but still enjoyable
★ = Well past peak
na = Not yet available

food & wine pairing chart

= white wine
= red wine
= rosé wine

	barolo/ barbaresco	beaujolais	bordeaux, red	bordeaux, white	burgundy, red	burgundy, white	cabernet franc	cabernet sauvignon	chardonnay
cheese, mild		red		white		white			
cheese, strong	red		red				red	red	
creamy sauces & soups				white		white			white
fish, lean				white		white			white
fish, rich		red		white	red	white	red		white
game	red		red		red		red	red	
meat, red	red	red	red		red		red	red	
pork	red	red	red		red		red	red	white
poultry, chicken & other light		red		white	red	white			white
poultry, duck & other dark	red	red	red		red	white	red		white
shellfish				white		white			white
spicy dishes									
veal		red	red		red		red		

You'll find many uses for this handy chart—at home, in wine shops, and in restaurants. For example, it's helpful when everyone at the table has ordered something different; you can see at a glance what goes with salmon, steak, *and* duck. For a more detailed reference, turn to the "Food & Wine Pairing Index," page 293.

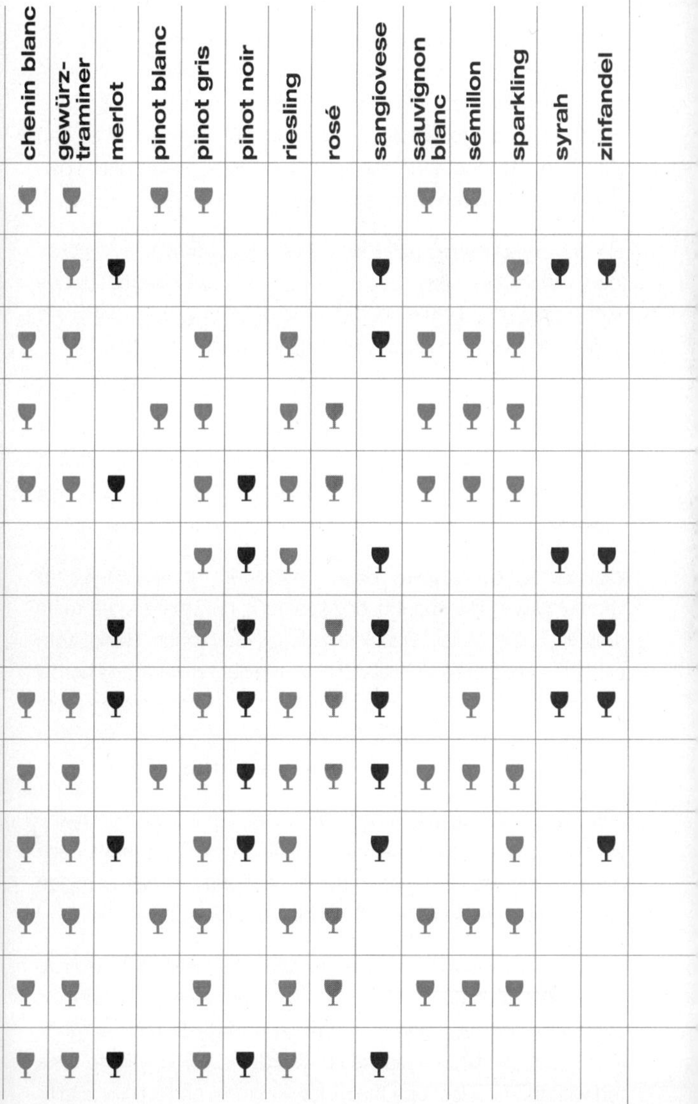

chenin blanc	**gewürz-traminer**	**merlot**	**pinot blanc**	**pinot gris**	**pinot noir**	**riesling**	**rosé**	**sangiovese**	**sauvignon blanc**	**sémillon**	**sparkling**	**syrah**	**zinfandel**
▽	▽		▽	▽					▽	▽			
	▽	▼						▼			▽	▼	▼
▽	▽			▽		▽		▼	▽	▽	▽		
▽			▽	▽		▽	▽		▽	▽	▽		
▽	▽	▼		▽	▼	▽	▽		▽	▽	▽		
				▽	▼	▽		▼				▼	▼
		▼		▽	▼		▽	▼				▼	▼
▽	▽	▼		▽	▼	▽	▽	▼		▽		▼	▼
▽	▽		▽	▽	▼	▽	▽	▼	▽	▽	▽		
▽	▽	▼		▽	▼	▽		▼			▽		▼
▽	▽		▽	▽		▽	▽		▽	▽	▽		
▽	▽			▽		▽	▽		▽	▽	▽		
▽	▽	▼		▽	▼	▽		▼					

pairing wine with food

We used to hear, white wine with fish and red with meat. The modern adage seems to be, drink whatever you like with whatever you want. Both approaches have advantages, but you're bound to encounter pitfalls by adhering too closely to either. The trick is to pair food and wine so that neither overwhelms or distorts the other. Some suggestions to help you on your way:

Be body-conscious Pair light-bodied, delicately flavored food with similar wine and heavy-bodied, full-flavored dishes with matching wine. The subtle flavors of sole meunière are going to get lost if washed down with a hearty Napa Cabernet.

Balance extremes If a dish is rich and creamy, you need a tart wine as a counterpoint—and to cleanse your palate. A bit of sweetness in wine balances salty or spicy foods. If you can't wait to drink those young, astringent Bordeaux, Barolo, or California Cabernets, the protein and fat of meat will moderate their tannin.

Dance to the same beat Foods with unusual herbal or vegetal flavors like cilantro or asparagus can make wine taste metallic. Loire Valley Chenin Blanc or Sauvignon Blanc from either the Loire or New Zealand have the right mineral and herbal nuances to create a flavorful tango on the palate. Peppery meat dishes work well with spicy Rhône Valley reds. Dishes with fruit sauces are great with richly fruity wines from southern Italy.

Do as the Romans People have been pairing food and wine for centuries, eating dishes and drinking wines that have been made locally. More often than not, wines from a particular region are just the thing to drink with foods from the same place.

Mix and match Though the red with meat, white with fish rule is too sweeping (Pinot Noir is perfect with salmon; Riesling is great with pork and game), tannic reds do taste metallic when drunk with oily fish like mackerel or sardines. If you want to drink red with them, select one that is low in tannin and high in acidity.

food & wine pairing index

There's no single perfect wine match for any given dish. In fact, the possibilities are virtually infinite. This index will lead you to all the many food and wine pairings that we've suggested in the "At the Table" features.

names you can trust

Some importers consistently distribute excellent wines. If the name of one of these importers is on the label, you can bet that the wine is good for its type and price range.

Australian Premium Wine Collection Wines from small Australian producers.

Cape Classics Wines from excellent South African estates.

Cellars International Elite-estate wines from Germany.

Chartrand Imports Organic wines.

Classical Wines Fine wines of Spain and Germany. Some stunning bargains.

Marc de Grazia Modern-style wines from Piedmont, Tuscany, and southern Italy.

Robert Kacher French wines, especially Burgundies.

Leonardo LoCascio Selections Italian wines, true to their regions and at good prices.

Louis / Dressner Selections Complex French wines at bargain-basement prices.

Kermit Lynch Gem-like traditional wines from France.

Jorge Ordonez Excellent values from Spain.

Eric Solomon European Cellars Wines from traditional regions of France, Italy, and Spain. Good prices.

Terry Theise Champagnes and Austrian and German wines from small but first-rate growers.

P. J. Valckenberg Great German values and top-estate wines.

Vin Divino Outstanding Austrian and classic Italian wines.

Vineyard Expressions Terrific wines, mostly organic and biodynamic, from France.

index to wines & producers

Names of producers are in **bold.**

d

g

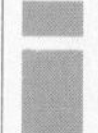

l

m

q

r

u

v

W

Y

Z

talk to us

Comments or Questions

about *FOOD & WINE Magazine's Wine Guide 2002*?

e-mail them to
wineguide@foodandwine.com